Hitchcock Blonde

A Cinematic Memoir

Sharon
Dolin

Also by Sharon Dolin

Poetry

Manual for Living
Whirlwind
Serious Pink
Burn and Dodge
Realm of the Possible
Heart Work

Translation

Book of Minutes by Gemma Gorga

Hitchcock Blonde

A Cinematic Memoir

Sharon
Dolin

Terra Nova Press
NEWARK   CALLICOON   MATSALU

2020

© 2020 by Sharon Dolin
ISBN 978-1-949597-08-0
Library of Congress Control Number: 2020932921

Published by:

Terra Nova Press
NEWARK   CALLICOON   MATSALU

Publisher: David Rothenberg
Editor-in-Chief: Evan Eisenberg
Designer: Martin Pedanik
Proofreader: Tyran Grillo

Set in Caslon and Gotham

Printed by Tallinn Book Printers, Tallinn Estonia

1 2 3 4 5 6 7 8 9 10

www.terranovapress.com

Distributed by the MIT Press, Cambridge, Massachusetts and London, England

I have a feeling that inside you somewhere, there's somebody nobody knows about.

–Alfred Hitchcock

What once was the future is now the past, but the past comes back as a present memory, is here and now in the time of writing.

–Siri Hustvedt

What we miss—what we lose and what we mourn—isn't it this that makes us who, deep down, we truly are.

–Sigrid Nunez

Contents

Preview: At the Movies

A glimpse into the world proves that horror is nothing other than reality.

–Alfred Hitchcock

My sister marla has taken me to see *A Thousand Clowns* at a local movie theater in Brooklyn—either the Marine Theatre on Flatbush Avenue or the Brook Theatre around the corner on Flatlands Avenue, these being the two movie theaters we used to frequent after getting a slice of pizza and a soda for lunch. It is 1965 and I am eight years old: a skinny girl with dirty-blonde hair and bangs, wearing a candy-striped blouse over powder-blue shorts. Marla is thirteen, on the cusp of puberty, with reddish-brown hair parted on the side and a light sprinkling of freckles on her face. She is wearing a paisley button-down shirt over culottes. I cling to her and follow her whenever she will let me.

We are in the middle of watching the movie when my mother enters the darkened theater and leans over to speak to us from the aisle. "Come on. We have to go," she tells us in a loud whisper. My sister and I both hesitate. *What is she doing following us into the movies?*

"Don't you wanna see where I work?"

I have no memory of my mother holding down a job. Under pressure from my dad, she would find a clerical job for a week or two, then collapse under the strain of it and have to quit. Perhaps this is one of those rare weeks.

Maybe there is something manic in her voice. Or maybe it is just her peculiar behavior, coming after us like this in a movie theater. My sister and I both sense something is off, but really, what can we do? She is our mom, after all. We nod our heads and creep out of the theater along with her.

We have our Chrysler convertible then—a big, pale-green car with a white top, stainless steel, gleaming trim, and whitewall tires. Of all the used cars my dad has bought over the years, this is our favorite. It is summertime and Mom has the car's top down.

What does Mom look like this afternoon? I picture her wearing one of her sleeveless, loud, flowered tent dresses with a two-stranded choker of iridescent white glass beads at her neck. She is already beginning to get plump. She has just had her hair done at the beauty parlor, so it swoops up, away from her broad forehead into a raised confection over her head, a bouffant made popular by Lady Bird Johnson. The hairdo always reminds me of the spun cotton candy I get at Coney Island. Mom always wears lipstick, hot pink or orange. And *rouge*, as she calls it, which I like to watch her apply by first touching her lips and then rubbing some of the lipstick into her high cheekbones. Her face always has a greasy shine to it (she never applies face powder), which makes her large nose stand out between her small blue eyes.

We jump in the back seat and she begins driving us down Flatbush Avenue, then all the way into Manhattan. After a while, it becomes clear that she has no idea where she is going or why. "Ma, where is the office already?" my sister calls out.

"Soon. Don't you like driving around with me?"

Neither of us replies. The longer she drives, the more we understand there is no office to show us. My sister and I are silent. Our mom is having one of her breakdowns, we both realize, as we give each other a knowing look. We are in danger. It has happened before. Mom is out of control. Who knows where she is taking us, what she will do. We need help. Fast.

Mom stops the car at a red light and my sister jumps out, telling me, "Wait here." I jump out and run after her, afraid to be left alone with Mom. I see Marla has spotted a cop and is running up to him, crying out, "Help! Help! Please help us! Our mother is running away with us. She's having a nervous breakdown. Please, please call our dad!"

Surely my mother comes running up at this point. Is she yelling? Is she telling the cop to take his hands off her kids? How does he know to trust me and my sister and not my mother? Is my mom so obviously crazy-looking?

All I know is that the cop, tall and handsome, looking like an Irish version of my dad, grasps each of us by the hand and says, "Mrs. Dolin, I'm going to have to ask you to wait here until your husband shows up to sort things out." He has already radioed the station and someone there miraculously locates my dad, who arrives in about twenty minutes. How lucky we are he was in the office and not out of town on one of his sales trips.

"Daddy, Daddy." I run to embrace him, knowing we are safe, and get caught up in a queasy, familiar feeling of relief mingled with guilt: I am betraying my mom, showing my dad how relieved I am to be rescued from her. I know she will be taken away—hospitalized—for who knows how long. I will lose her and she will lose me.

PART ONE

Hitchcock in Brooklyn

*Give them pleasure—the same pleasure they have
when they wake up from a nightmare.*

–Alfred Hitchcock

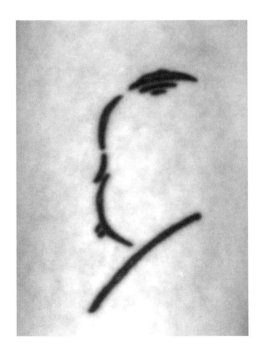

A SUMMER NIGHT in Brooklyn. It is 1963. My father stands outside in the backyard, tending the barbecue near the rose of Sharon that grows along the fence separating our backyard from our neighbor's. Next to him is a collie: what I called a "Lassie dog" as a child. Like the one that fanged my upper lip and cheek when I was in the first grade, so I needed stitches.

A disembodied voice beckons me. "Look over there—at the man in the window." I glance over to see a shadowy profile in the ground-floor window of my parents' bedroom.

It's Alfred Hitchcock! His bald head and round belly. The same figure I see at the start of his TV show. In the semi-dark, lit up by street lamps that flicker burnt orange, all I can see is the head and upper torso of this darkened figure at the window.

"That man," the voice whispers. "You see *that man* . . . He has no bottom half."

At which point I wake myself up. In those first moments, in the dark, I don't know where I am. Then I become aware of my sister asleep beside me. I sit up in bed until my breathing slows, and I look over to make sure there is no one at the window.

♦

My Hitchcock dream is the only recurring nightmare I had as a child. Or the only one I remember having had. And don't dreams rely on our remembering them?

"All the things one has forgotten scream for help in dreams," wrote Elias Canetti. What things have I forgotten that this dream—Hitchcock's truncated profile—wants me to remember?

Perhaps something about the absence of limbs or body parts, which always terrified me as a child. Or else it is a stand-in for other kinds of forgotten absences—amputations of memory. Memory itself being always partial and therefore, in a sense, amputated.

Or is Hitchcock, for me, the embodiment of fear itself?

Sometimes, dreamwork can take a very long time to begin. For me it has taken fifty years.

◆

Now I see before me the wizened mother of our next-door neighbor in Brooklyn, where I grew up. I lived with my mother, my father, and my older sister on Glenwood Road in Flatlands from the time I was ten. A place where there was no glen, no wood, only roads and numbered streets with attached, two-family brick houses like the one we lived in, a cluster of apartment buildings nearby that we called the Projects, and a few faded green- or yellow-shingled homes like my neighbor's, whose frail, elderly mother scarcely ventured outside. I saw her only a few times. She was tiny, with a fragile head like a bobble-head doll's that might wobble and break.

She stands outside by the gate in front of her son's house, as though that is all she has the energy for, always holding up a flowered handkerchief to cover her neck and chin. Each time I study her carefully without appearing to, and each time I wonder why she holds up that handkerchief.

Until the one time she does not.

What I see just once—and what I keep on seeing—is the absence of the bottom part of her face. She has no lower jaw. No chin.

I probably ran into the house. I am sure I never spoke to her; I am not sure she *could* speak. But the memory of her, or the memory of what I thought I saw, is indelible.

◆

From Hitchcock I learned early on that nightmares could be made real. That we cover up an absence to suggest a presence. That a normal suburban family may have a serial killer for an uncle. Or that a neighbor across the way may kill his wife and dispose of the body in plain sight. Hitchcock understood absence. He understood the power of the partial view: that a profile, more than a full face, could haunt.

My childhood was filled with absence, haunted by partial views.

As a child, I watched Hitchcock's movies with my parents, lying prone on their bed. My mother Selma was so drugged up with antipsychotics that I picture her mostly lying in bed. My father Irving was a traveling salesman who often acted like a kid to entertain us, telling jokes and dancing around the kitchen table. As a teenager I watched those movies with my older sister Marla in the bedroom we shared. As an adult, I watched them yet again. Hitchcock, whose TV program *Alfred Hitchcock Presents* entered my neighborhood through dreams.

Now I am returning to Hitchcock in order to make sense of the painful episodes in my life, which often feel as distant and oneiric as a movie. As though I were not only the creator of my story but also its nocturnal spectator in the darkened theater of memory. I have chosen Hitchcock as both lens and shield to help me face trauma: to touch the wounds that have, to reverse Shakespeare's Romeo, never felt a scar.

Yet I know that no memory is fixed. That our memories are not static pictures we summon up from some mental filing cabinet. Memories, as we now understand, are creations we construct in the moment, influenced by context and motivation.

I am the director behind the camera each time I conjure up and reconstruct a scene from my past. Braiding together my reading of Hitchcock with my reading of my life, I hope the context of each scene will enrich and inform the other. Like Hitchcock, who stepped inside the frames of his movies, I am stepping inside the frame for more than a walk-on role in mine.

The Man Who Knew Too Much and The Girl Who Knew Too Little

*Say nothing of what
you found or you will
never see your child again.*

–Kidnappers' note

HER BOBBED BLONDE HEAD in profile, Jill Lawrence (Edna Best) reads the note her husband has just handed her. Only a few minutes before, at their hotel in the Swiss Alps, she had been dancing with their French friend Louis (Pierre Fresnay), the champion skier, when a sniper shot him in the chest. Dying, he slips her his room key and tells her to send her husband Bob (Leslie Banks) to take his shaving brush to the British consul.

"Don't breathe . . . Don't breathe a word to anyone," Louis whispers.

I am watching Hitchcock's first version of *The Man Who Knew Too Much* (1934). It opens with an adolescent girl at its center, wreaking havoc. First, Betty (Nova Pilbeam) runs out after her dachshund on the ski course while Louis is performing a ski jump. Louis veers away, tumbling into the crowd, to avoid crashing into her. Betty then distracts her mother Jill, causing her to lose a clay pigeon shooting match.

"Trouble," her father calls her. "A little wretch," says her mother affectionately.

When Bob, having retrieved the secret message rolled inside the handle of Louis's shaving brush, demands to speak to the British consul, he is handed the note threatening his child Betty, the troublemaker.

After Betty's mother reads the note, nearly half a minute of exquisite silence follows. She turns her face toward the ceiling, her eyes rolling upward with a look of numbed shock, before her head slowly veers to the side.

Cut to a silent, blurry, dizzying pan around the room that captures her failing vision.

Cut to an objective shot that shows her collapsing in a faint on the floor of the local inspector's office with a thump, which ends these long seconds of silence. She has just understood that their daughter Betty has been kidnapped.

Cut to a close-up of an animal-faced skier on the tiny brooch pinned to the girl's lapel—her mother's gift to her that afternoon. In the background, the furious insistence of sleigh bells.

Pan out to a large gloved hand slowly lifting to unmuzzle the girl's open mouth as she gasps for air in a state of silent terror. The bells of the horse-drawn sleigh in which Betty and her kidnapper are riding continue their incessant jangling as she is whisked away into the snowy mountains of St. Moritz. Kidnapped.

♦

My mother was my kidnapper. Not a stranger. But when she turned strange. When she went *off*. Broke down. And a frenzied woman came to inhabit her body. When one of her paranoid episodes erupted, I was often the one she wanted to run away with. I was her baby, and no one was going to take me away from her. Not the police. Not the psych wardens. Especially not my father, who always initiated the process of her hospitalizations.

Summertime in the Catskills with my family at one of the Borscht Belt hotels. I think it must have been The Pines. One of the few times my maternal grandparents have paid for us to come visit them for a few days. I am quite young, no more than four or five, alone in the day camp arts and crafts hut. How can this have happened? I am looping a potholder onto its frame, so intent on weaving together the red, blue, and yellow bands that I do not notice at first when my mother comes in to retrieve me.

Instead of taking me back to the hotel, where my father and sister are waiting to meet us, Mommy pulls me by the hand and we run into the woods in back of the hotel property. Farther and farther we fly, though the woods, past the occasional house. *Where is she taking me?*

It may seem strange to write that my mother used to kidnap me, but that is what it felt like.

I can summon up only these few rushes: My hands busily looping the colored bands over the skinny teeth that edged the metal loom. My mother's swirling, short peach coat. Running through the woods with her. A flurry of trees overhead as we flee. A feeling of panic inside.

How long were we gone? How far had we gotten before my father found us and rescued me from my mother? Somehow, we did not get lost in the woods forever. We were probably missing for no more than an hour.

Remembering early incidents like this one makes me wonder if that is why I sometimes feel so lost and anxious inside my life. Like I am running away with myself. Or that my feelings are. But somewhere inside me, I always find my father to bring myself back home.

No matter that, all through my childhood, my father was in and out of work as a traveling salesman, childlike in his hobbies (he flew kites into his early eighties and collected geodes) and in his actions (he told jokes and danced around the kitchen table), and was often away on the road for a month or more at a time. My father was the one I counted on to protect me. He was all I had.

♦

In *The Man Who Knew Too Much*, Betty's captors have been plotting to assassinate a foreign diplomat. They allow the girl a brief reunion with her father before they plan on killing them both. When Betty is led into the room, she cries out, "Daddy!" and dashes over to him, burying her face in his chest to bawl inconsolably for several long moments. Finally, she asks where her Mummy is.

Mummy is at the Albert Hall. There, in the lobby before the performance, the hired assassin surreptitiously hands Jill her daughter's small brooch as a silent warning. Jill knows she should keep quiet if she wants to see her daughter alive. Loyal British subject that she is, once she figures out the location of the marksman and his intent, she cannot stop herself from standing up and screaming, a split second before the marksman shoots during the clash of the cymbals, thus throwing off his shot.

In the final, protracted shoot-out between the police and the assassins, Betty is in the most danger, freed by her father from the locked room, then lifted up by him to flee over the rooftops before he is shot in the wrist. Seconds later, the marksman inches toward Betty, who is as terrified as a cornered animal. Down below, her mother, the sharpshooter, spies them on the rooftop and dares to take the shot to kill the marksman—a shot that the policeman "daren't," because it "might hit the kiddie."

I watch as Betty, traumatized, sobbing in her striped pajamas, is being lowered by the police through the roof's escape hatch into the arms of her heroic mother and wounded father.

The girl's sobbing. Her ordeal. That's what grips me. Did I sob when my daddy finally rescued me?

◆

I was sure God had marked my baby by making her pitifully "different" and I know why, so I didn't dare let anyone on our tiny island even see her. For over a year no one knew she was there in our home until that terrible day I had to reveal my shameful secret or perish with her on the island where **I Hid My Baby.**
—*Intimate Story*, November, 1959

This is the teaser for "I Hid My Baby," a sexually lurid tale in a trashy, modern romance magazine I imagine housewives flipped through, whiling away their afternoons at the hairdresser. Most of the stories are about illicit sex and its accompanying shame. "Too Hungry for Love" and "Picket-Line Pickup" bookend this story.

A full-page black-and-white photograph accompanies the tale. A handsome, dark-haired young couple and their blonde-haired child are caught in a storm. The brunette, with windswept hair and bangs, half clings to, half hides behind her man while he looks up at the sky.

A pixie blonde girl of three is in the young man's arms. He is holding her clumsily, so the folds of her plaid dress are crumpled and pushed up around her legs. They are in a hurry.

The girl, her face in profile, is crying and scared and very unhappy. What is happening to her?

I know she is scared because I am the girl in the photograph.

"Some man came up to us on the beach and asked, 'Is that your little girl?' Then he handed me a card and asked me to call him up. So I did. And that's how you started modeling. But you didn't seem to like it very much, the modeling, so I stopped it after a few months." So my mother explained when, years later, I found a copy of the magazine in her bottom dresser drawer.

My mother was right. I hated modeling. She had not bothered to tell me what was going to happen to me. Or at least I have no memory of her or anyone else telling me. And what would I have understood at such a young age? Things were just done to me, without warning or explanation. As she did so often—even when she was well—my mother just picked me up and whisked me places without telling me where we were going.

Early on, I must have had trouble telling when my mother was fine and when she was beginning to have what we called a *nervous breakdown*. As though my mother were a car that was being taken away for repairs. When could I trust her and when could I not? When I was very young, I do not think I always knew the difference.

Gradually I learned to pick up on the smallest cues: her trembling hand, her glittering eye, a mania in her voice and movements. This was how I survived.

♦

I am standing beside a Lassie dog and some strangers—big men in jumpsuits—are throwing water at me and there are big bright lights on me and I'm screaming. Why are they doing this? Why am I standing here soaking wet with this Lassie dog? I want my Mommy!

I have a visceral memory of having modeled for this photo shoot. I feel myself standing there with the dog. Feel the bright lights and the shocking splash of water from a pail. Again and again. I am crying and crying. Everything feels so strange. Except for the familiar feeling of being lost and scared.

Until recently, I had never been able to read through "I Hid My Baby" in its tawdry, formulaic entirety. The narrator has to hide her baby because she is illegitimate and "different." How is she different? The woman's shame has marked the child as "Mongolian," the term used then for a child with Down's Syndrome. "She was a child of sin, and anyone who looked at her would know." As though the woman's illicit affair caused the baby's difference.

I imagine the vicarious pleasure that prurient readers derived from reading of another woman's sexual escapades. A crass, titillating story, not unlike those in *True Confessions*, a magazine my friends and I would sneak a peek at as we neared puberty.

What strikes me now about the photograph is how genuine my expression looks. I am traumatized. Not acting at all. Crying into the turned-up white collar of my dress. *Who are these people? Why am I with them? What are they gonna do to me? Are they gonna run away with me?*

It could be a roughened-up version of a scene from my own young life. There is a stormy wind, probably manufactured in the studio with the help of some large standing fans. Some strange man has hurriedly grabbed a hold of me, hoisted me up and locked me in his arms so my plaid dress is mussed up and hiked up around my still-babyish legs. I want to get down and away. *What's going on?* The swirl of fright and sheer unhappiness must have surfaced inside me with all its attendant terror.

Is my mother in the room watching as they do the photo shoot? Or does she have to wait outside?

I always thought I started modeling at age five. When I check the date on the magazine, I realize I was no more than three, just barely out of toddlerhood, when my brief career as a model made its stark entrance into my life, erupting like the studio's storm. Or like my mother's paranoid abductions of me.

♦

I enter a dance studio with Mommy. I am no older than five. I am crying even as we enter. Mommy leads me over to a lady. *Is she gonna give me away to this stranger?* I cry and cry. That is all I know how to do. Until the lady reaches into a dressing table drawer and pulls out a red lollipop, which she hands me. Then Mommy takes me home.

In this way I learn that crying, long and hard and without pause, can get me somewhere. Or at least take me home. That the only power I have as a child is through my tears.

♦

My sister Marla, who is five years older than me, used to taunt me for being a crybaby. I never saw her cry. When I was young, we sometimes took showers together and she liked to lift me in the air. I was so skinny, it was easy for her to do. One time, when I was about six, and she had hoisted me up, just to see how high she could raise me, I slipped out of her arms (or did she drop me on purpose?) and fell, cutting open my chin on the bathtub rim. As the blood ran from my chin, I ran out of the shower crying, "Mommy . . . Mommy!" I can touch my chin now and still feel the scar.

Once, just once, can't I make her cry? I wondered.

I had a hobby of collecting rocks that I found on the street and I would crack them open on the sidewalk with a hammer to see if there were any gems, any crystals that sparkled inside. I kept my rock collection in a large rectangular tin box that shut with a metal clasp. On its lid I had written "Sharon's Rock Collection" and I stored it in the basement closet

on one of the dank shelves where we kept all of our board games. On summer afternoons, I would take the box outside with a hammer and crouch on the sidewalk with a dozen dull gray and brown rocks I had scavenged from the neighborhood. One by one, I cracked them open: I raised the hammer and struck it down hard on the center of each rock, sometimes several times, careful not to hit one of the fingers on my left hand that held the rock in place.

I was looking for some mystery. Some treasure. Some radiant shine. Something I could discover and collect. Even in Brooklyn, where the traffic whined by on Kings Highway, where we lived until I was ten, and few trees grew, aside from the rose of Sharon that opened its large lavender blooms each summer in our small concrete yard, at the back fence separating our house from our neighbor's, where another Sharon, my friend Ruby's big sister, lived.

Sometimes I found what I was searching for: milky-white crystals gleaming inside. Veins of pink or blue or purple. I loved the contrast between the rocks' dull exteriors and the interior glitter I longed to discover and keep as my own. These were the secret gifts of the neighborhood, overlooked by everyone but me.

The summer I turned nine and my sister Marla was thirteen, she stepped outside to see what I was doing. "Are you still cracking open rocks?" I stood up, still holding the hammer. "Yeah. It's for my rock collection." She started laughing at me. I swung the hammer back and belted her in the stomach. Hard. She bent over screaming. I saw tears spilling down her face as she went running into the house to tell Mom. I stood there, gloating. For once, *I* had made *her* cry.

I knew I had done something awful, and when my dad got home from work that evening, my mom told him. He turned around and with his booming voice said, "No TV! No TV for you tonight and fuh the rest of the week!" I began crying. Wailing. I had the stamina to go on for hours. In the past, my crying would make my dad give in.

"If you don't stop crying, I'm gonna pick up this phone and have you taken away!" I watched him walk over to the phone, pick up the receiver, and begin dialing. *Is he serious?* In my household, this was a real threat, one that had been acted on many times before.

Am I going to be taken away, just like Mom? I blanched and quieted myself down. He put the receiver back in its place.

That threat hung over me through my teens and into my early twenties. If I cried too much, someone might pick up the phone and have me taken away.

Was I destined to become like my mother? Would I need to be hospitalized? My dad planted that fear inside me. After that incident, it was as though every time I cried, the tears themselves watered that fear and made it grow. Would I cross over some invisible line this time and become like her?

Sometimes I used to visualize my shifting emotional states as though I were running toward a cartoon cliff. If I cried too much or if I became too depressed, then I would edge out onto and over that cliff. Unlike Bugs Bunny or Road Runner, I feared I would not survive—that I would fall down, down, down into the whirlpool of madness that rose up periodically and swallowed up my mother.

♦

British psychoanalyst D. W. Winnicott coined the phrase "the good-enough mother," now in common parlance: "The good-enough mother," he wrote, "starts off with an almost complete adaptation to her infant's needs, and as time proceeds she adapts less and less completely, gradually, according to the infant's growing ability to deal with her failure." He also wrote about the importance of the "holding environment" of the mother, where the infant transitions to further autonomy.

Was my mother good enough? I have photograph after photograph of my mother holding me as an infant in her arms and then as a toddler sitting in her lap. I look safe and bonded to her. I knew she loved me, yet I fantasized I might have a different mother entirely. Like my Aunt Fran, my mom's younger sister, who was talkative, loud, and flamboyant. She played mahjong with her friends just like my friends' moms did. Maybe she could become my mom.

◆

As a child, when I first watched on television Doris Day playing Jo McKenna in Hitchcock's American Technicolor remake of *The Man Who Knew Too Much* (1956), she struck me as the ideal mother. Beautiful and vivacious, she is suspicious, some might say paranoid—but, unlike my mother, with good reason. She recognizes that the Frenchman Louis Bernard (Daniel Gelin), whom the family has just met on the bus on their way to their hotel in Marrakesh, has asked lots of prying questions, particularly of her husband, while revealing almost nothing about himself. "You don't know anything about this man, and he knows everything there is to know about you," Jo tells her ingenuous, Midwestern doctor husband Ben (James Stewart).

When, upon entering their hotel, Jo and Ben pass a British couple, she catches and registers the woman's sinister gaze. "We're being watched," she tells her incredulous husband. That evening, Jo is stunning in her white chiffon A-line dress covered in delicate, flowery green sprays. Each time I watch, I catch my breath at her glamour—a mom, no less, who sings "Whatever Will Be, Will Be" in duet with her son Hank (Christopher Olsen), a boy of ten, as she waltzes him off to bed. At the traditional Moroccan restaurant, Jo tells Ben, "Those people are staring at us . . . right in back of us." "Jo, will you please stop imagining things," says Ben, exasperated.

But as the Sixties slogan has it, "Just because you're paranoid doesn't mean they aren't out to get you." At this exact moment, the same British couple, Lucy Drayton (Brenda de Banzie) and her husband Edward (Bernard Miles), who have indeed been staring, introduce themselves. "You *are* Jo Conway, *the* Jo Conway." Ben corrects them, "We're Doctor and Mrs. McKenna." Jo, a singing star, has given up an international career as a soloist (as well as her surname) to become a doctor's wife in Indianapolis—not an unusual thing for a woman to do in the Fifties. Later on in the movie, when Jo and Ben have gone to London in search of their kidnapped son, Jo's friends from her days as a singing star burst into their hotel room and, in a lovely feminist twist, assume Jo's husband must be Mr. Conway, having taken on Jo's surname and not vice-versa.

The next day, Louis Bernard, unrecognizable in Moroccan garb and with a darkened face, is pursued by a Moroccan man and the police in the outdoor market until the man catches up to him and stabs him in the back. As Bernard stumbles forward, he chooses to reveal his identity to Ben and to whisper to him his dying words.

In this moment of crisis—as Jo and Ben are about to be taken to the Marrakesh police station for questioning—this ideal mother lets down her guard. "You don't want your little boy to go, do you?" asks Mrs. Drayton, clasping Hank firmly with her right hand. "I think it's better if I take him back to the hotel." And when Jo agrees, "Would you, please?" Mrs. Drayton returns Jo's large sun hat in exchange for the boy. The Draytons, we will learn, end up kidnapping Hank and flying out of the country with him on a private plane to London, where he will be held hostage to keep his father from telling the Moroccan police or Scotland Yard that he knows of Louis Bernard's dying words: namely, that a foreign statesman is to be assassinated and that Ambrose Chappell (Chapel) is the clue.

In this American version, we never see the kidnapping itself. No terror-stricken face. No smothered cries. After Mrs. Drayton calmly leads Hank away through the outdoor market, we next see him playing checkers in a back room inside Ambrose Chapel in London with a bored, somewhat nasty underling of the Draytons. The kidnapped boy looks somewhat bored, too, not scared—something I never quite understand, even upon repeated viewings.

♦

I watched this later version of *The Man Who Knew Too Much* on television with my parents, lying on their bed, sprawled on my stomach, leaning on my elbows, while they leaned back against their mahogany headboard. I identified with the boy Hank and felt scared for him. How frightening to be stolen away from one's parents.

I never thought consciously about the fact that in my own life, either parent could be taken from me: My dad could leave on a month-long sales trip or my mom could be taken away to the hospital. Or, what was still worse—and surely I must have tried to think about it as little as possible—my own mother, during one of her paranoid episodes, could force me to run away with her.

♦

As I watch this movie yet again, I linger over a scene I never paid much attention to before. Ben and Jo return to the hotel room after the Marrakesh police have finished questioning them. Ben already knows the Draytons have kidnapped and fled with Hank. He has read the note but has withheld this information from Jo. He pulls rank as a doctor and gets Jo to swallow a sedative. "I make my living knowing when and how to administer medicine. . . . Now Jo, you know what happens when you get excited and nervous. . . . You've been excited. You've been talking a blue streak. You've been walking around in circles." She has been doing none of these things, but he induces her to take the tranquilizers by tantalizing her with the withheld information about Louis Bernard's murder. Once she has taken them he tells her everything, including that the Draytons have kidnapped their son.

Before the sedative has taken effect, Jo has the kind of reaction any mother would have if she discovered that her child had been kidnapped. She becomes enraged and nearly violent with grief, partly because she realizes Ben had deliberately withheld this information from her. "How *dare* you! You gave me sedatives!" she bawls, struggling against him and punching his arms as he grips her upper arms tightly.

Ben physically restrains her, compels her to sit on the bed, and forces her to lie down as he pins back her arms, all the while soothing her and apologizing as she continues to sob, until the powerful sedative knocks her out.

It is the hardest scene for me to watch. Perhaps it triggers scenes I never saw—or have forgotten I saw, even repressed—but can imagine must have happened to my mother. How many times did doctors take my mother away against her will? How many times did I see her struggling with the police or ambulance attendants in the house or on the street? How many times did they do things to her *for her own good*: give her medication, strap her down, administer electroshock treatment—what is now called ECT, or electroconvulsive therapy. "Therapy." A word that still makes me wince. Did my mother ever have a say in any of it?

Of course my mother's paranoid, schizophrenic episodes were much more serious than Jo's tearful outburst, but neither of these two women had a choice. Men, doctors mostly, made decisions for them for their own good. Did my mother *feel better* after they gave her electroshock? I know that, because of it, she was terrified of being hospitalized.

Did my mother feel better after psychiatrists prescribed so many pills for her that she went through life as a sleepwalker? Once she was on all those pills, I could never tell what she was feeling, or how much she felt at all. Which may have been the doctors' goal: to stop my mother from feeling. To contain her at any cost.

♦

"You wanna do drugs?" my dad once asked me and my sister while we were both still teenagers. He flung open the hall closet, whose door held racks and racks of my mom's prescription pill bottles. "Here! We got lotsa pills. Right here."

Is he serious? I shrunk away in shock. *Who wants to turn into a zombie?* I used to wonder, as I discovered more and more teens in my high school were taking Quaaludes, a strong sedative. *Who wants to be like my mom?*

♦

One memory rises to the surface. It was my first year at South Shore High School—a brand new public high school. I was in the tenth grade, working in the Program Office along with my friends, which gave us the privilege of special hall passes so we were free to run around the school building. "What are you on?" students would ask as I flew by—this being 1970, when many teenagers were on drugs. "Raisins!" I held up my daily snack of Sun-Maid raisins in a bright red box with a picture on it that did look a bit psychedelic: a smiling girl in a tomato-red bonnet holds a cornucopia of green grapes, with a huge, atomic sunburst behind her. They stared at me, a bit stunned, as I shook the box and raced on.

♦

Knowing too much and knowing too little. As with so many Hitchcock movies, the plot turns on knowledge, acquired too late or just in the nick of time. In London, where the couple knows the Draytons have taken Hank, Ben goes off on a "wild goose chase," as he calls it afterwards, to find Ambrose Chappell, who turns out to be a taxidermist. After his own hysterical outburst, Ben ends up in a physical struggle to get out of there. In an instance of Hitchcockian drollery, with half-stuffed wild cats all around him, Ben momentarily gets his hand trapped between the fangs of a stuffed tiger, itself trapped in a silent roar.

Meanwhile, Jo, the smart, beautiful, talented, blonde mom, ends up figuring out the mystery of Ambrose Chapel: "It's not a man, it's a place!" And it's not the man (the doctor), it's the woman (the wife and mom and former stage singer) who deciphers all the clues and rushes to Albert Hall, where she figures out who the assassin is, anticipates his actions, and—moved to tears by the internal struggle of wanting to protect her son yet unable able to stand by—prevents the assassination.

♦

Knowing too much and knowing too little. I remember so little about the kidnapping episodes of my childhood, as though I needed to forget them once I had survived them. One episode stands out, but even those details need filling in and I know that, as I write this version, the details I select will solidify in my memory, convincing me that I remember them more vividly than I do.

One weekend, the summer I turned ten, my parents took me and my sister for a drive upstate. I have no memory of packing a suitcase; perhaps my mom did it for me. After several hours, my dad stopped the car in front of a wooden building in the woods, handed me over with the family's small powder-blue suitcase to a woman I had never seen before, said goodbye, and quickly drove away with everyone but me. *What am I doing here?* I found myself in a large cabin with about two dozen beds lining the walls. I soon realized I was the only white girl. The black girls were kind to me, but I was too frightened, felt too different, to make friends.

This was 1966. I attended a public elementary school in Brooklyn, P.S. 119, with a mixture of Jewish, Italian, and African-American children. I had Jewish and Italian friends, and an occasional Irish friend from the neighborhood who went to parochial school, but no black friends. My school was "integrated," but still racially segregated when it came to friendships.

Each evening, I would watch, with horror and fascination, the black girls in the bunk ironing their hair. It must have been right before Afros were in style. I strain to picture this nightly ritual: One girl would lean her head forward (or else backward) over the ironing board and another would slowly run an iron over her draped hair, which looked like raw black cotton, flattening it out as much as she could. I had never seen such a thing, nor did I entirely understand it, being white and having long, thin straight hair that I always wished was thick and curly.

I spent each night face up on my cot, looking at the ceiling and crying, as I counted the wooden planks that ran across the width of the roof and met at the middle beam: *One plank. Two planks. Three planks. Four.* Crying. *Keep going. Five. Six. Seven. Eight.* Again and again. Crying. Crying. Until I fell asleep.

Crying during the day as well. There was a lake I never swam in. I spent my days sitting in the nurse's office. The staff probably had no idea what to do with me. *Why have my parents left me here?*

These are the images I have been able to conjure from my memory: The girls ironing their hair. A lake seen through the trees. The planks in the ceiling that I counted each night in bed. My crying, which I did for long bouts. Crying was the only weather I knew.

After one week, my mom and dad showed up. They brought along a popular novelty toy that they knew I had wanted and they gave it to me as soon as we got back in the car. It was called *Bupkis*: a greasy, rubbery, plump figure, the size of my hot-chocolate mug, whose sallow yellow body was all face with a huge painted-on, cartoonish toothy smile, jiggly arms where its ears should have been, and skinny legs dangling from each side of its chin.

In Yiddish, *bupkis* means nothing, zilch, nada. Bupkis: that was all I wanted from my parents. To be with them. They tried to give me a sleepaway camp experience, when all I wanted was to be riding in the back seat of our car, going home.

Years later, I realized my parents had dropped me off at a Fresh Air Camp. My failed sleepaway camp experience felt, as time passed, as real and unreal to me as a nightmare. My parents never mentioned it and I bracketed it off from my life. Now, when anyone asks, "Did you ever go to sleepaway camp?" I usually say no, because I have always found it too shameful to talk about, perhaps until now. How could my friends understand? I felt like I had been given away, against my will, a kind of abduction in which my parents were complicit. At the time, I thought I might not survive.

The Lady Vanishes
and My Absent Mother

You'll excuse me if I run away?

–Miss Froy

SOMETIMES I FIND IT EASIER to remember things by not thinking about them directly. I call this method *peripheral memory*. Just as I can see a star in the sky better by letting my gaze veer to the side of it, I can often recall a name only when I turn my mind to something else.

Perhaps that is why I find myself drawn to Alfred Hitchcock's *The Lady Vanishes* (1938): because of what it might trigger in my peripheral memory about absence, which I lived with throughout my childhood, when my mother would periodically disappear from my life. When I attempt to remember these scenes too directly, they stay hidden in the cloudy night sky of childhood memories. So I let my gaze drift, intermittently, over to Hitchcock in order to allow certain early childhood scenes to come into focus.

♦

The enigmatic Miss Froy: Who is she? She writes her name with her finger on the steamy club car window and shortly afterwards she vanishes. I ponder her name, mouth the sound of it. *Froy.* What's in a name? Sometimes everything and nothing. "Did you say *Freud*?" her young companion asks her.

Froy does sound like *Freud*, only missing the final consonant—an amputated name, like the amputated Hitchcock of my Brooklyn nightmare. No wonder, since Hitchcock produced a body of work obsessed with sexuality, unconscious drives, and dreams—all of Freud's major preoccupations. Add to the list Hitchcock's obsession with voyeurism. We *are* speaking about the movies, after all.

Even Hitchcock's own name (and there *is* something in a name) confirms his preoccupation with the male gaze and male desire, with what psychoanalysts and film theorists refer to as the *scopic drive*. He liked to be called Hitch. In the recent biopic called *Hitchcock* (2012), he corrects someone, "It's Hitch. Hold the 'cock.'" It hardly matters whether he uttered those exact words. The effect of the nickname, which he did prefer, is the same. It is almost too easy to interpret his choice of nickname as his self-castration: the ugly obese man who then *hitches* himself to handsome, sexually alluring male actors—Cary Grant, James Stewart, Sean Connery, Rod Taylor. And develops an obsession with certain blonde actresses—Kim Novak, Ingrid Bergman, Grace Kelly, and, most destructively, Tippi Hedren.

In *The Lady Vanishes,* Iris Henderson (Margaret Lockwood), the pretty young brunette—a rare exception to Hitchcock's blondes—becomes frantic when she realizes that Miss Froy (Dame May Whitty), who has become a guardian to her on the train, has disappeared. Everyone in her compartment denies having seen her. As Iris goes running through the cars searching for Miss Froy, she bumps into Gilbert (Michael Redgrave), a young ethnomusicologist she scuffled with the night before in the inn. Now smitten with Iris, he still does not believe there *is* a missing Miss Froy, since the other passengers are in on the cover-up and insist Miss Froy never existed.

Nothing Iris says to Gilbert convinces him she is not hallucinating. She *was* hit over the head, after all. No matter that she can recount in excruciating detail what Miss Froy was wearing ("tweeds, oatmeal flecked with brown, a three-quarter coat with patch pockets, a scarf, felt hat, brown shoes . . ."), their walking together to the club car, Miss Froy ordering a pot of her special tea, even Miss Froy asking one of a pair of cricket fans to pass the sugar.

Gilbert only believes there *is* a missing Miss Froy when, by sheer chance, he sees the torn carton of her special tea flung out with the trash, sticking to the window in a momentary backdraft before it, too, vanishes. He sees the carton long enough for him to read the label: "Harriman's Herbal Tea."

A fleeting physical trace. Ocular proof (how Shakespearean!) that leads instead of misleads.

Hitchcock once said: "If it's a good movie, the sound could go off and the audience would still have a perfectly clear idea of what was going on." Hitchcock started out by making at least a dozen silent movies between 1920 and 1929, where the visuals had to do the storytelling. *The Lady Vanishes*, like so much in Hitchcock's oeuvre, continues to hinge more on images than dialogue.

Just prior to Gilbert's discovery, Iris has begun to doubt her own sanity—until she sees the trace of the letters FROY that Miss Froy had written with her finger on the steamy glass of the club car window. That peculiar name. But before she can show it to Gilbert, the train enters the tunnel and the lady's name, too, vanishes.

◆

A summer day in Brooklyn in the late 1940s. A young woman in her twenties boldly leans back against the boardwalk railing, flaunting her body in a provocative two-piece outfit: high-waisted flowered shorts that reveal most of her upper thigh and a matching, flowered cap-sleeved top that shows off her midriff and ties between her voluptuous breasts. Her light-brown hair, parted on the right above her high forehead, is gathered in a rush of waves to the side, highlighting her prominent Polish cheekbones. She has planted her sandaled left foot on the ground and bent the other leg back at the knee to rest on the bottom crossbar of the railing. Joyfully at ease and squinting up into the bright sun of Manhattan Beach, a few blocks from where she grew up on Dover Street, Selma gives Irving a full, toothy smile as he snaps the picture.

Selma snaps the companion photograph of Irving wearing a navy cap, in a pair of loose-fitting khaki shorts that highlight his slender thighs. He is bare-chested with a slim torso he enjoys showing off. Like her, he stands posed, back to the railing, one foot resting on the lower bar as he squints into the sun, grinning at her.

Wintertime. Selma, self-possessed, is beaming with Irving on the front lawn of her parents' home on Dover Street. She wears an ankle-length lambswool coat, strap-on heels with a peephole at the toe, and a sheer scarf thrown over the back of her hat, tied gracefully under the chin. Irving has a winter coat on over a suit and tie and he wears a hat whose large brim shades his face from the sun. He is smiling broadly as he grips her around the waist with his right arm.

Early spring, 1949. Now they are on their honeymoon, skiing in the Laurentian Mountains in Canada. Wearing a ski sweater, Selma chuckles as she makes a show of rubbing snow into Irving's bare chest as he leans in toward her, both of them hamming it up for the camera. Selma, so at ease in touching her new husband, and equally at ease in being touched by him.

I study these photographs as though they are movie stills because that is what remains of my mother's past before I was born. Looking at these snapshots reminds me that my mother was not always as I knew her. By the time I came into the world, and throughout my childhood in the 1960s and early '70s, she was a woman who frequently disappeared, who stopped being Mommy every time she had to enter the psychiatric ward at Kings County Hospital. The label she wore for life was *paranoid schizophrenic*. She would receive electroshock treatments and high doses of antipsychotics before she came back home to be Mommy.

She is *my* lady who vanished.

♦

I must be around seven years old the one time my father takes me and my sister to visit my mother in Kings County Hospital's psychiatric unit, where she often remained for three or four weeks. My father leads us into a large visiting room with gray-green walls. I quickly glance around to see other seated families visiting patients. *Oh. So I am not the only one with a mommy they have to take away.* He takes us over to a seated woman who looks like Mommy the way a wax figure resembles a live figure, and I sit down opposite her.

Her thin, light-brown hair is brushed and parted to the side. She is wearing her hot-pink lipstick and her small blue eyes fix me with a maniacal, moist stare before she comes to life—this usually quiet, slow-moving woman—the words tumbling out of her faster than I have ever heard her speak. "Sharon honey I missed yuh so much, yuh know what they did to me tuhday, they stuck something in my tushy so I could go to the bathroom and yestuhday they put electric wires in my head and oh it was *terrrrible*. You can't buhlieve what goes on here."

I sit there frozen, not knowing what to do or say. Mommy still sounds like my mommy, but speeded up, like a 45 rpm record played at 78.

She leans in towards me, fishing something out of the pocket of the apron she wears over a green hospital gown. She holds out her right hand, which curves in, as though her fingers have tight webbing between them and are stuck together. "Here, Sharon, I made something for yuh. I wan'cha to have it."

She puts something in my hand. Cool to the touch, the size of a Benjamin Franklin half dollar but much thinner. I am too frightened to speak, so I look down. A circular copper pendant with a muddy enamel swirl of greens and pinks fired into it sits in my palm.

"I made it special for you. Yuh know, I wanna get outta here and go home with you." My daddy steps between us. "All right. That's enough, Sel. We all came to visit you. How yuh doin'? Say hello to Marla." He prods my big sister in the back to get her to move forward. "How's the food? What're they feeding ya here?"

I get up from the chair and step back, and spend the rest of the time a bit dazed, half-listening and looking at her, as I finger the gift she has just given me. *Is this now my mommy?* I feel dizzy and nauseated as I turn the pendant over in my hand. *Why is she making this kid stuff?*

Soon Daddy tells us it is time to leave. On the car ride back home, no one says a thing, as the radio wails: *Don't let the sun catch you cryin'. . .*

He never takes us to visit her in the hospital again.

♦

For fifty years, I have held on to this fired copper medallion, never able to wear it, never able to throw it away. It traveled with me across country when I moved to California, sat in storage in my grandmother's basement in Brooklyn, and still hides inside one of my jewelry boxes until I fish it out. As I rub my thumb over it, this stilled kaleidoscope with a bumpy shine on its enameled side, roughly tarnished on its back, feels like a maternal reliquary. My ocular proof.

As an artifact from that time, it tells me that at least once, I saw my mother at her most helpless and childlike and I understood, however vaguely, that I could never go back to being the child again. Like the end of "Toyland," a song my mother liked to play on the piano: *Once you pass its borders you can ne'er return again.*

I vaguely understood that things with electricity were done to her there. Though no one told me, I knew I had to hide from my friends what had happened to my mother and where she was. That there was shame in it. When the Rolling Stones came on AM radio—*Here comes your nineteenth nervous breakdown*—I belted it out along with my friends.

My friends lived in single-family homes their parents owned in Mill Basin and Bergen Beach, middle-class neighborhoods a bus ride away from my working-class one that had no particular name other than being near Canarsie. My parents rented the downstairs apartment of a modest two-family brick home, where my sister and I shared a cramped bedroom. Each night we pulled out the high-riser bed, each morning we tucked it away.

♦

While Iris and Gilbert are searching for Miss Froy in the luggage car, they discover Miss Froy's broken spectacles. One more visual trace and piece of ocular proof of her existence. The magician appears and fights for possession of the spectacles, vanishing with them through a trap door in the wooden chest they had managed to stuff him inside.

The scene is pure slapstick, but packed with self-referential irony: the appearance/disappearance of Miss Froy's spectacles as I sit here watching the spectacle of it all on screen. The clear-eyed one in search of Miss Froy from the start is called Iris, whose name refers to the part of the eye that regulates how much light gets in, much the way a camera lens aperture does. When Iris recognizes and then loses Miss Froy's spectacles, the scene seems to be communicating something about the importance of vision. Perhaps how easy it is to gain or lose it.

What does a magician do but make things and people vanish and then reappear? The chief act of this magician, Signor Doppo, is "The Vanishing Lady," as Gilbert discovers from a rolled-up poster. And what does Hitchcock the magician do in all of his films but distract us with a MacGuffin: a plot device that motivates the characters to act but in itself may prove beside the point. "There's a lot to look for in Hitchcock films," writes Donald Spoto in *The Art of Alfred Hitchcock*, "but watch out for the MacGuffin. It will lead you nowhere."

In *The Lady Vanishes*, the MacGuffin is the message encoded in a song that Miss Froy is carrying, which then motivates the rest of the action: her disappearance and Iris's search for her. It is the answer to the questions: Why did Miss Froy vanish? Why are there some who want to kill her or erase having seen her?

But though we might not care about the specific meaning of the encoded song that Miss Froy must deliver to the Foreign Office in London, the fact that this matronly looking governess is actually a British spy does seem significant to the movie as political allegory. Produced right on the cusp of World War II, the movie implies that everyone, even an older Englishwoman, can—and should—help out in the war effort. Miss Froy also plays a pivotal role in the romance, a subplot threading its way through most of Hitch's thrillers.

◆

What was wrong with my mother? Was this the hidden code that I was ashamed of and sought to cover up? But my mother's condition was never an arbitrary plot device. Like the pink and green swirls in the copper medallion she gave me, it was the secret around which so much of my childhood roiled.

After disappearing into the hospital for several weeks, my mother would return home and turn back into being Mommy. She nurtured me through my childhood hurts (being bitten by my friend's collie when I was in first grade) and when I was sick (as I often was) with a fever, swollen glands, and a sore throat. When I stayed home from school, Mommy would pick up a Venus Paradise color-by-number set and heat up a Swanson Chicken TV Dinner, and I would spend the day propped up on pillows on her side of my parents' bed, with the TV on, watching *The Hollywood Squares* and coloring tropical birds or African wild animals with shiny colored pencils. I can still hear the scritch of the sharpener making thin wooden fans of shavings as I turned the pencils around inside it.

Mommy was the one I would cling to, the one who would comfort me when I cried. I was a shy, sensitive child with straight blonde hair in a pixie cut and short bangs, a snub nose, and prominent brows above almond-shaped blue-green eyes. Up until I was four or five, I often hid myself inside the generous folds of Mommy's long, brown mouton coat or her gray lambswool one, one hand clutching a cloth diaper as I sucked my thumb, the other holding on to one of her legs. In several family photographs, the only sign of my presence is a bit of white cloth sticking out from the side of my mother's ankle-length coat.

◆

Sitting at breakfast one particular morning, when I was seven and my sister was almost twelve, I suddenly knew that the woman putting away the dishes, who bore an exact resemblance to my mommy, had turned into someone else. Once again, Mommy had disappeared.

There had been an argument the night before. "Why can't yuh getta job!" Daddy roared at her, one of the few times he ever raised his voice. "Why can't yuh go out to work like everybody else? You *see* how I'm struggling!" Mommy just stood there, saying nothing, a tremor starting in her hand, letting his frustrated rant rain down on her until it was over. Then my parents got into bed and watched TV as usual.

Even I knew my mother was incapable of working outside the home. But my father was a traveling salesman, in and out of work. First he sold clip-on shoe ornaments. By the 1970s, he was selling "woven woods": slatted wooden window shades with pieces of colored yarn woven through them, which were popular then. He struggled to support us, and most of the time, no one—not even my mother's own well-off parents in Manhattan Beach—would help him. When I was in my thirties my dad told me, "I was worried I wouldn't have enough money to put food on the table. So I rented a freezuh because it came with a two-week supply of meat."

The morning after his outburst, Mommy was reaching up inside the kitchen cabinets, putting away the clean dishes with their usually comforting clatter. I was sitting with my sister having our breakfast of orange juice and cold cereal, and I could feel something was wrong. Something had taken possession of her. Something had made the Mommy I knew and loved vanish from our Brooklyn kitchen, replaced by a woman who might do anything.

It was a subtle transformation: something awkward, even robotic, in her movements that I could sense, even with her back turned. An extra tremor in her hand as she raised a dish. Some manic glitter in her eyes when she looked at me, and I knew. So did my sister.

On that morning, my sister and I are accomplices. As the older one, Marla speaks first. "Hey. This orange juice tastes funny. You sure you didn't poison it, Ma?" Then she pokes me in the ribs while Mommy's back is turned. I go along with her this time. "Yeah, it does taste funny." We both know our mom would never do such a thing. She ignores us or pretends not to hear us and continues putting away the dishes.

Is this our way of getting back at her for having a nervous breakdown? Soon, in accordance with the pattern my sister and I know so well, my dad will make a phone call and the police or emergency van paramedics will show up to take her away—before, I hope, she loses control and does something frightening.

Once, I remember my mother running out into the street with a suitcase, screaming, "Someone, help! He's tryin' to take them away from me! You gotta stop him!"

In a way, my mother was right. When she was having a breakdown, she went on a paranoid rampage, attacking my father for taking her children away from her. My father would have her hospitalized, and so her children *were* taken away from her. Or, rather, *she* was taken away from her children, but it amounted to the same thing.

My mother's breakdowns happened so many times—at least once every two years—that I developed a hair-trigger sensitivity to her subtle changes in mood. I knew that when one of her episodes was beginning, the change in her would be sudden and possibly dangerous to me. Would she pull me out into the street and try running away with me, her baby, as she had done in the past? I knew she never meant me any harm. But she was both my mommy and someone else—someone fleeing frantically, at any cost.

Here's one more scene that keeps coming up in my memory: Before I turned ten, while we were still living on Kings Highway in a two-family home, Mommy cut the phone cord and went running out into the street with the receiver and the dangling pig's tail of a wire, dragging me with her. "He's trying to take them away from me again!" she screamed into the dead phone, to anyone who might listen. "Somebody help me!"

After making a call from our other phone, Daddy rushed into the green-shingled house of our next-door neighbors, the ones who had two dark-gray poodles—a mother and son called Mimi and Pepe—I liked to visit and play with. My sister and I stayed over their house that night while Daddy rode in the emergency van with Mommy.

♦

The Lady Vanishes. Why do I feel compelled to rewatch it? Each time I am doing my own dreamwork of a woman in search of her mother, identifying with Iris and casting off my childhood role of being in on the cover-up.

Why is Iris so desperate to find Miss Froy? I cannot help but see Miss Froy as Iris's adoptive mother. Right before boarding the train, Iris is mysteriously hit on the head by a planter falling from a high window as she attempts to return to Miss Froy her dropped spectacles. From the outset of the train journey, Miss Froy assumes the maternal role, reassuring Iris's two friends, "Don't worry. I'll look after her." Struck by the planter, Iris briefly loses consciousness and, when she awakens, finds Miss Froy sitting opposite her in the train compartment. Miss Froy soothes her, offering her a handkerchief daubed with eau de cologne to put to her forehead. Steadying Iris, who is still quite woozy, Miss Froy leads her by the arm to the club car for a cup of her special tea—the same tea she proudly declares her own parents still drink, and which she is now offering to her adopted daughter. When they return to their compartment, Miss Froy urges Iris to rest, and the concussed, dizzy Iris dozes off.

When Iris awakens to find Miss Froy has vanished, she becomes frantic. No one in the compartment will admit to having seen her—neither the sinister-looking woman in a black headdress by the window nor the magician. When Iris returns to the club car, the steward is adamant that she took her tea alone. Iris *must* find Miss Froy. Because Miss Froy acted like a mother to her before she disappeared, Iris is determined to act like her daughter. There is a desperate edge to Iris's search, which is what I find so arresting.

Didn't I spend my entire childhood covering up my mother's condition? And haven't I spent my adulthood searching for her?

◆

Who was she? Where was the lively, playful, glamorous woman I saw in the photographs from before I was born? The woman who, before she met my father, posed in several shots with different boyfriends. Who also hammed it up in a bathing suit with her girlfriends. Who sat right in the center of a circle of teens, the popular girl laughing into the camera.

Selma, the nineteen-year-old who stood in Washington Square Park, smartly dressed in a black woolen skirt and a blouse with a bow at the neck, a self-possessed young coed at New York University before her first schizophrenic episode forced her to drop out. The young married woman who (I discover only after her death, when my dad hands me a small black notebook and a sheaf of typed pages) kept a diary and made lists of the books she wanted to read, including *Finnegans Wake*, and wrote essays such as "The Value of Socialized Medicine to the American Public." The woman who wrote poems in English and in Spanish under a pseudonym before I was born. Who sent a poem called "Patience" to *Redbook Magazine* and received a typed, one-page rejection letter. Where had she gone?

◆

One evening stands out. I must have been around ten. I am sitting at our Formica kitchen table with its familiar marbled white, gray, and pink design. My sister Marla is sitting beside me, and my dad opposite her. Mom is serving us dinner: I can still see her at the electric broiler, her left hand inside a worn potholder mitt, taking out the lamb chops to place beside boiled Birds Eye mixed vegetables on our plates.

In the living room, on the other side of the wall, in two forest-green, plush velvet armchairs, sit two police officers. They arrived shortly after my dad made a phone call. We all know why they are there, waiting until my mom finishes dinner, at which point they will take her away to the hospital.

See, her movements seem to say, her hands shaking as she serves us our plates. *I can do it. I'm fine. I don't need to be taken away.*

Mom sits down opposite me in her usual seat. She squints at me with her small blue-gray eyes in a face grown rounder and plumper over the years. Her shock of wavy brown hair is thinner than it is in her photo album, and her lipsticked mouth is pursed and twisted slightly, biting her inner cheek. Her pleading look is always aimed at me, the younger one, the sensitive one. Sarah Bernhardt, as my dad calls me because I cry so much and only Mom knows how to comfort me. Now her look sears into me a swirling, queasy mixture of guilt and shame and complicity, like a darker swirl of the colors fired into the copper medallion she once gave me.

How can I let them take her away? Why didn't I say something before my dad made that call? How could I stand there and watch him open the side door to lead the two officers through the kitchen into the living room, where they are waiting calmly, out of sight but a foreboding presence? They are Mom's prison guards, the ones who will rob her once more of her children and thus extinguish the role that matters to her most: that of being our mother.

I feel so jumbled up inside. I know why Dad has called the police. Mom is having one of her breakdowns. We all know the signs by now. Her eyes get that wild look to them and she sheds her meek nature, as if tearing off a mask to reveal a woman on a paranoid rampage. How could I blame Dad when I know he is protecting us?

And yet: I have to quell an onrush of sadness and guilt. I can still save Mom from the men in uniform—or so her gaze pleads with me from across the kitchen table. But I sit there, chewing my lamb chop in numbed silence, and let her be taken from us once more.

♦

Sometime after that episode, my dad, who must have worried that my mom would have a breakdown while he was away on one of his sales trips, sought the advice of a psychiatrist. From then on, my mother took pills daily and her breakdowns ceased.

Now I lived with a mother who was no longer taken from us and hospitalized. Instead she became a zombie. She slept until 11:30 each morning. Afternoons, she would buy some groceries and do a bit of dusting. Sometimes she would pick me up from school in the car, bringing me a hot cocoa. When we got home, she would recline in bed the rest of the afternoon, flip through the *New York Post*, then rest, her right arm bent at the elbow to cover her face.

This was a different kind of vanishing act.

Throughout my teens, I sought to hide who my mother was, just as she had become hidden from me. Mom moved slowly through the house like a sleepwalker. She gained a lot of weight, though she continued to wear her bright pink lipstick. When she undressed in my parents' bedroom after dinner, I watched her deflated breasts slump out of her brassiere before she slipped into one of her pastel cotton nightgowns and into bed once more to watch TV with my dad. Many times I would join them.

My mother still loved me, but she moved in slow motion, as though she were walking through water. In her drugged haze she spoke little and held her hands stiffly at her side with her thumbs lying like spatulate spoons, limp and useless, in the palms of her hands. Her hands always unnerved me, reminding me she was not normal. I was afraid it must be obvious to my friends.

◆

My mother took Thorazine (chlorpromazine) for years. Until now, I have resisted reading up on the drug. It always felt too painful to learn more. Now I discover that Thorazine was (and still is) routinely given to schizophrenics, starting in 1954. French researchers discovered the drug and thought it would be a good "sedative" for surgery. It was commonly referred to as a "chemical lobotomy" because the doctors were pleased to find it controlled and sedated patients, producing "detachment, relaxation, and indifference," according to clinical trials. Chlorpromazine (Thorazine) is still the first drug mentioned in a list of antipsychotic medications on the National Institute of Mental Health's website.

From the patient's point of view, Thorazine's frequent effects include sedation, drowsiness, lethargy, difficulty thinking, poor concentration, nightmares, emotional dullness, depression, and despair.

I recall my mother taking Stelazine (trifluoperazine hydrochloride), another strong antipsychotic, at the same time. When I read the list of side effects, they characterize my mother perfectly. She was sedated, drowsy, lethargic, emotionally dull, and didn't have much to say, probably because she had difficulty thinking.

The mother I lived with for the latter half of my childhood was really just a set of side effects.

Why did no one monitor my mother's dosage? She visited a psychiatrist every three months in order to renew her medication. My dad would accompany her and he was in the consulting room during these visits.

When they came home, he sometimes acted out the five-minute session verbatim as my mother stood by, listening silently.

"How are you feeling, Mrs. Dolin?"

"Fine."

"How are relations with your husband?"

"Fine."

"And how are your children, Mrs. Dolin?"

"They're fine."

"Any problems taking the medication?"

"No."

"All right, Mrs. Dolin. Here are your new prescriptions. I'll see you in three months."

Even as a child, I understood the consultation was a charade. Surely the psychiatrist noticed my mother's *marked sedation*, the phrase used in the pharmaceutical literature. In the Sixties and Seventies, this cursory approach was standard psychiatric practice, especially with working-class patients. Better to keep my mother sedated than risk a schizophrenic episode, the doctor must have decided. As if these two extremes were the only ones possible. My dad deferred to the doctor because he worried that my mom's breakdowns were too difficult and dangerous for everyone. But that did not stop him from mocking the whole process in front of us.

According to the psychiatric literature, these drugs were never supposed to replace psychotherapy. I doubt the psychiatrist ever suggested my mom see a psychotherapist. If he had, my dad could not have afforded it.

No matter that my mother slogged through life a somnambulist, barely speaking or showing much emotion, gaining weight, and sleeping most of the time. After all, she belonged to a working-class family, and psychotherapists have always preferred treating the middle and upper class.

Despite her drugged state, my mother continued to drive my father to the airport for his sales trips and pick him up when he returned. She continued to run special errands with me, like driving me to fabric shops down Flatbush Avenue, when I was in junior high, to pick out fabric for making a midi skirt in my sewing class.

The year I turned ten I had twenty-one cavities, all at the same time. My mom was in the kitchen, frying up fishcakes for lunch, as I began running around the house crying from the pain. The more the pain grew, the faster I ran around the apartment, and the louder I began to wail. My mom took me for an emergency visit. The dentist lowered a black rubber mask over my face, and I slept while he filled all the cavities.

For at least a year afterwards, my mother drove me all the way into Manhattan, to the Upper East Side, to see a special dentist who gave me laughing gas. I wonder how my parents afforded it. Perhaps this was one of the few times my grandfather was willing to help out.

At home, my mom allowed me to pile up toys, school projects, all kinds of tchotchkes on the green-padded mahogany dining-room table that we hardly ever used for dining. At one point, the table held the racetrack my sister and I shared, zooming our electric slot cars around it.

"That's Sharon's stuff. Don't touch it," Mom announced to Dad. This may have been the only time she stood up to him, in order to defend me. One evening he put his arm straight out, like a giant windshield wiper, and swept everything from the table onto the floor. "Clean it all up," his voice boomed at me. I put everything away. Over time, my things would accumulate on the table once more.

As I sit here writing these lines at my dining room table, littered with extraneous books and papers, a cordless phone, tall sea salt cylinder, silicon eyeglass case, I have to smile. This is the license my mother gave me: to be messy. It ticked off my neat-freak, former husband, but it remains the way I feel at home enough to write. William Carlos Williams has a line near the beginning of his long poem *Paterson* where he warns that "[m]inds like beds always made up" will only produce "stale poems."

♦

I used to wonder how it was possible for my mom to pass as normal. To me, it seemed so obvious she was drugged up. When I was around twelve, I went shopping with her in downtown Brooklyn at A&S, one of our favorite department stores. On the main floor, my mom went over to the Elizabeth Arden cosmetics counter. Perhaps the salesgirl was particularly persuasive and succeeded in luring her over. Or perhaps my mom was inspired, this once, to fix herself up. The salesgirl pressed her to buy a set of skin-care products: cleanser, astringent, lotions. "You're going to have real problems in the future if you don't take care of those enlarged pores now."

What is she talking about? Real problems? My mom's real problems have nothing to do with her skin. Doesn't she see that? I stared at the salesgirl with her flawless skin. Was my mom's drugged state that invisible? We walked away with her purchase—a small case that held four small bottles. Once we got home, I saw Mom tuck them away in her dresser drawer, where they were forgotten.

◆

As a teenager, I was ashamed of my mother in her semi-embalmed state, and sought to cover up her condition. Would my friends still be my friends if they found out? Would any boy still like me and want to go out with me?

I grew up in the Sixties and early Seventies, an era when we started calling our parents by their first names. A false chumminess. An ironic bravado. As a teenager, I took to calling my mom Sellie and my dad Irv. As much as feminism was the air we breathed, there was still a thick miasma of Ozzie and Harriet that I could wrap my mother's drugged state inside of. This is what housewives did: they lounged around and watched TV, read the afternoon paper in bed. That is what my mother was doing. And no one—neither my closest friends nor my boyfriends— ever suspected otherwise.

"Oh, you know Sellie. She just likes to lie in bed and watch TV," my friends teased me. I laughed along with them, anxious to draw attention away from my mom. I distracted them with Irv, *the funky father*, as my friends referred to him, and the trick worked, distracting even me. Irv would crack jokes and drive us out to Coney Island or to Buddy's Amusement Park nearby on Flatbush Avenue, and treat us to rides and ice cream and cotton candy. In the Seventies, my dad grew a mustache, but otherwise looked and acted like Johnny Carson, a dapper wisecracker. I was so proud of how handsome and lively he was. In the middle of dinner, he would *have* to get up from the kitchen table to show us some dance step or act out a joke.

◆

Once, after returning from an out-of-town trade show, my dad told us this story over dinner. "All the people at the trade show went to the hotel's nightclub and a comedian got on stage doin' his bit. At one point, he said, 'Imagine I'm an open-heart surgeon with a beating heart in my hand.' He opened and closed his fist like this. Then he threw the heart out to different people in the audience and said, 'Here, catch.' And someone pretended to catch it and throw it back to him. He threw it out again. The same thing happened. Well, I was waitin' for him to throw it to me. When he finally did, I pretended I *almost* caught it . . . Whah? I looked down between my legs, oh-my-god I dropped it. 'Wait,' I held up one finger and stooped down to pick it up. 'I got it!' My hand opened and closed like I had picked up the heart, then I threw it back to the comedian. You shoulda seen—the whole nightclub went wild." I loved it when he told us this kind of story. My dad had stolen the show.

◆

Another time, we were visiting Boston on a family trip, when I was about eleven and my sister sixteen. My dad took us out for dinner at Anthony's Pier 4, a famous seafood restaurant on the water, known for its fresh seafood and for the celebrities who would dine there. That night, just as we were seated, we spotted a familiar figure at a large table not too far away.

"Look! Look!" my dad said: "It's Alfred Hitchcock!"

After we ordered our food, he rose and walked up to Hitch's table. I watched him get Hitch's attention, bending forward to say something to him, but they were too far away for me to hear the exchange. "What did you say? What did you say to him?" my sister and I clamored before my dad had a chance to sit down. Even my mom's face, always subdued, brightened with curiosity as she listened. "I went up to him and said 'Goot ee-ven-ing,' and he laughed. The guy has a real sense of humor."

My mom, my sister, and I beamed at my dad's daring. How funny he was. He knew just what to say and when to walk away. Like all of us, he enjoyed mimicking Hitch's thickly accented greeting at his TV show's opening.

Anything to divert attention away from Sellie. Irv would regale us with dirty limericks ("There once was a man from Nantucket . . .") He would tease us that someday he would light up the joint that he kept for years in his top dresser drawer. He played hide-and-seek in the house with our dog. He would hide in a closet and squeak, "Here I am!" and MacDuff, the Bedlington terrier he'd gotten for free from a friend who owned a pet shop, would have to find him. A jocular kind of disappearance. Like a more grown-up game of Fort-Da. And we were all in on the act.

◆

In my poetry journal from college, I find a draft of a poem I wrote as a junior that feels like a thinly disguised portrait of my mother. I was nineteen—the age she was when she had her first breakdown and had to leave NYU, where she was studying Romance languages. My mother was forty-nine.

learning to talk, at 40

her lips are stuck
together with too many
unsaid words
floundering through dinners
the effort of chewing

so many forkfuls
the conversation slips by—
she raises her head to the
sound of a train pulled
out of the station
where did the first
toast begin
someone is on to the tactics
of betting, a smooth joke,
some slow gin
she is still digesting the cherry—
chewing it for the third time
jokes get lost in
all those stomachs
if she opens her mouth now
the 60's will pour out—
and what SHE
thought of Millhouse
My Lai
Kennedy's death—
the way the radio froze
her hands to the steering wheel
all those shoes slamming
the sidewalk
if she opens now her husband
would close
his eyes then
open them
and they're on to birth control
a new movie, the last vacation
she remembers her first child's fingernails
a size 12 dress
her cut thumb holding the napkin
she must stop eating
they are on to dessert and are not even
looking at her

she will eat her pie though
they are on to second coffees
teaspoons whirring in cups—
she has missed another train
and they are not even
looking

Under the influence of Seventies feminism, I had written a fantasy about my mother gaining a voice. Perhaps it was my way of giving her a subterranean internal life I had no access to. I never knew my mother, I realized more and more the older I grew, but I needed to believe there was someone there to know.

Years later, I asked my father why he stayed in the marriage for so long, over thirty years. "Because I'm a good Jewish fathuh and I loved you and your sistuh," he replied. "And I loved your mothuh and I kept hoping she'd get bettuh."

♦

Near the end of *The Lady Vanishes*, Gilbert first replaces Miss Froy (finally revealed to be a British secret agent) as the carrier of the coded folk song and then displaces Iris's fiancé, who has been waiting for her at London's Victoria Station. Just after Gilbert becomes Iris's lover (and has his first onscreen kiss with her in a London cab), he forgets the tune that he's been humming incessantly, the encoded message he must deliver to the Foreign Office. In place of the folk song he remembers Mendelssohn's "Wedding March." Why? The power of Eros. He can be the spy and carry the tune or he can be the lover and carry off the woman. Not both.

Miss Froy, the maternal figure, reappears at the movie's end, having vanished in the woods during the shootout when the train was rerouted and ambushed. The door to the Foreign Office opens to reveal her, seated at the piano, no longer pretending to be a governess, but dressed up as a fine lady, playing the vital tune. In the movie's final moments, she grabs Iris's and Gilbert's hands in an effusive greeting, as though reaffirming her maternal role for Iris. With her gesture Miss Froy appears to be sanctioning the young couple's bond—whose initiating cause was her very disappearance.

♦

Here the comparison between Hitchcock's movie and my life falls apart (*breaks down*, that infelicitous phrase, is what I wanted to write). I can picture my mother toward the end of her life, frail and emaciated in a pink-lavender chiffon dress, at my first wedding to a man so ill-suited for me (paranoid, a pathological liar I discovered later) that I feel certain she would not have approved of him, if I had bothered to ask. Had I inadvertently sought out an unstable, damaged man because of her? If I could not save my mother directly from disappearing inside her illness, perhaps, unconsciously, I tried to save her by loving a man equally damaged whom I imagined my love could heal.

I return to Selma in her photo album from before I was born: the woman in a white turtleneck who rode a bicycle. The one who went fishing with Irving on the *Dorothy B.* from Sheepshead Bay. The woman who occasionally wore her hair up in a turban like a Hollywood starlet. The one who played show tunes like "Some Enchanted Evening" on the piano. A lively, curvaceous woman with a broad smile who (she once told me) had several boyfriends propose to her.

That Selma had vanished. I would never catch a glimpse of her again.

Psycho: Brassieres, Breasts, and Female Pleasure

You can do anything you've a mind to ... and bein' a woman you will!

–Used car dealer to Marion

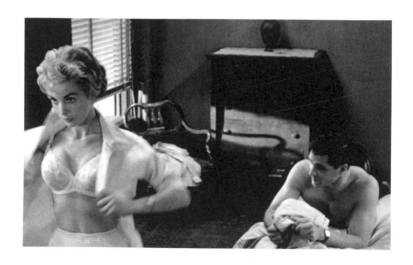

IT IS TRUE one can be too young to watch sex and violence.

The first time I saw *Psycho* (1960), I was eleven or twelve, reclining on my high-riser bed, with my older sister Marla reclining on hers beside me.

I fell asleep during the shower scene.

For that matter, the nearly fifty-minute prelude to the shower scene left no traces in my memory that I can detect. Yet I now find it more gripping than the murders of Marion and Detective Arbogast and the police procedural that take up the final hour of the movie.

Who can relate to being stabbed in the shower by a psychopath? Or to being stabbed so you fall backwards down a flight of stairs, dead? Who *cannot* relate to a clandestine afternoon tryst? The frustrations of a long-distance romance? The temptation to get even with someone by stealing?

I return to the masterful, opening scene of *Psycho*: the camera's overhead pan of Phoenix before zooming inside the open window to catch the end of Marion's lunch-hour tryst with her lover Sam. Almost the first thing I would have seen as a twelve-year-old is the huge white brassiere with its several straps that Marion (Janet Leigh) is wearing as she reclines on the bed while Sam (John Gavin) stands over her in trousers, bare-torsoed, getting dressed.

As a preteen, I must have felt overwhelmed, watching the intimation of sex and seeing those big breasts in their white cups. So, gradually, I fell asleep.

Even now the scene disturbs me. The camera's overt voyeurism compels my complicity, so that I feel myself spying on the couple at a stolen moment. I still feel uncomfortable watching Marion in her big white bra that holds so much in.

Hitchcock had wanted to film Janet Leigh without a brassiere, which he thought a younger audience would have found closer to their own experience, but he knew the censors would not have allowed it. "The scene would have been more interesting if the girl's bare breasts had been rubbing against the man's chest," Hitchcock tells the French New Wave film director François Truffaut in the most extensive series of interviews conducted with Hitch about his film career. So Hitch did the next best thing and showed the couple in various stages of post-coital disarray: Sam pulling on his undershirt, Marion putting on her blouse.

After Marion absconds with the bulging envelope of cash she jams into her purse, she changes out of her white bra and slip into a black bra and slip in her bedroom while packing to flee town. *Psycho* buffs love to discuss the symbolism of this color change as a blatant mark of her change from angelic to evil. I continue to be struck by how large-cupped the bras are. How terrifying, I used to think as a girl, it was going to be to grow breasts that needed such a contraption.

Surely I had seen my mother undress. I had seen her in her *brassieres*, as she referred to them. My mother's breasts were not as large as Marion's. They sagged, half-deflated. Less scary than sad to look at, because they looked so old.

◆

I keep replaying the parlor scene, where Norman Bates (Anthony Perkins) confides in Marion in an intimate tête-à-tête.

Norman: You know what I think? We're all in our private traps. Clamped in them. And none of us can ever get out. We scratch and claw but . . . only at the air, only at each other. And for all of it, we never budge an inch.
Marion: Sometimes we deliberately step into those traps.

Marion does not realize how prescient her words are. She is referring to the trap she fell into back in Phoenix by stealing the money. She does not realize she has stepped into yet another, deadlier trap by staying at the Bates Motel.

♦

Private traps. As a young teen I had no breasts, no need for a bra, and I felt trapped in my shame and isolation by the boys who chose to single me out. To tease me for having too little. *We fix flats!* One of the many notes they left on my desk at school to taunt me.

Why did the boys choose to pick on me? Even then I knew it had something to do with my best friend Donna, the dark-haired Italian beauty who played "Blowin' in the Wind" on her acoustic guitar. How all the boys wanted her, yet I got to spend time with her. How uninterested she was in them. She had dark-brown, almond-shaped eyes, olive skin, and the serene Etruscan smile of someone unfazed by how attractive she was.

I was her opposite: her blonde, skinny, Jewish best friend. The outspoken one. The one who had not yet gone through puberty. The one who did not feel attractive at all.

> 8/27/69 All I am saying is give me a chance.
> I wish someone liked me for what I am, not what I could be because I can't be what I'm not.
> Donna is like a cane in the old age of my youth.
> ....
> I'm all mixed up! I want to be a part of the click that won't accept me and I don't want to be a part of the one that does!!
> 10:48 P.M. I have a terrible urge to make out.

I wrote this diary entry when I was thirteen. Though I had no name for it, I sensed that the boys' collective rage at my beautiful Italian girlfriend had gotten displaced onto me, her best friend, the flat-chested girl with long, dirty-blonde hair and granny glasses.

I was one of the very few in my junior high who refused to stand for the Pledge of Allegiance during school assembly. And I was the smartest gr in the two-year SP, the Special Progress class, in which we all skipped from seventh to ninth grade. Here is another diary entry:

4/9/70

Dear Elly,

I'm scared!!! Why? Because Donna has just been giving me a prediction of hers. She hasn't been wrong in 3 weeks!!!! You see, David is giving a party and a lot of kids are invited. Donna feels there is going to be a fight (with words). I have a feeling that I know about what. Donna agrees. Politics. Let me explain. I don't pledge. Not because I hate the U.S. but because I don't believe in a lot of America's policys and this is the only way I can show my opposition. I happen to love America, probably much more than a lot of other people that do pledge. Robin and Tobi don't pledge either. Michael feels this is communistic. But it really isn't. I just pray that the subject doesn't come up at the party and if it does

H E L P . . . . . .

I was nearly fourteen. All through seventh and ninth grades, the boys had shunned me or teased me. Not one boy had invited me to his bar mitzvah, the main social event of those years. Aside from my small circle of girlfriends, I was a social outcast. A party invitation near the end of ninth grade was the first one I had received in nearly two years.

When I thought about going to a grownup for help over the relentless shaming I was subject to, I ruled everyone out. I could hardly turn to my mother, who lay in bed until almost noon, her bent arm covering her eyes as she slept, too sedated to question or even notice how often I stayed home from school for one- and two-week stretches with a sore throat or a bad cold in order to avoid the endless taunts and notes left on my desk. *No Parking — Flat Tire Zone.* Notes I'd tear up, but they still stung.

Nor could I tell my father or my homeroom teacher, Mr. Balsam, because the teasing was sexual and I felt too ashamed. Nor my sister, because I feared she might just laugh at my plight. Apart from a few girlfriends who knew and tried to comfort me, I lived in isolation. As in Thomas Hardy's poem "The Wound":

> Like that wound of mine
> Of which none knew,
> For I'd given no sign
> That it pierced me through.

All I could do was hide the teasing, hide the wound, and hide myself from it. Yet a wound that is hidden has no chance to heal.

I hid my chest for years. All through high school and college, I wore T-shirts beneath baggy plaid work shirts and overalls. I knew I was flat, and therefore sexually unattractive. The boys' view of me had won.

During my freshman year at Cornell, when I was seventeen, I met a girl in the dorms with wild, kinky hair, who was flatter than I was. (Breast size was one of the first things I noticed about every young woman.) I was incredulous when I saw that several guys liked her. That it might even be possible to have a boyfriend, no matter how flat-chested I was.

Here is a poem from a notebook from my college years:

for 20 years I've been staring into the mirror

and today a lion
leaped out

but she told me (the other day)
I was finite
as a coat on a peg
with my small breasts
and my nervous fingers

that would always be
small and nervous
but today I did not have
breasts or fingers
only buttons down to my knees
and sleeve ends

That vision of myself hidden beneath some garment was one I lived by for a very long time.

♦

The thing about the movies is that we keep hoping the story will turn out differently. As I rewatch *Psycho*, I linger over the awkward yet intimate conversation between Norman and Marion in the motel parlor. As though it might have a different outcome.

How could she not see what the camera shows the viewer—a loner with the somewhat macabre hobby of taxidermy who admits he has no friends? "A boy's best friend is his mother," he tells her. Who would have trusted a stranger—no matter that he ran a small motel—so far as to go into a back room with him? Why does she stay so long?

How stupid we women can sometimes be. How trusting.

♦

At twenty-one, after graduating from college, I spent the summer studying at the University of Edinburgh. When the program ended, I decided to hitchhike south to visit a graduate student I had met who studied at Oxford. I caught a ride with a lorry driver who dropped me off at the London rotary, from where I needed to hitch a ride northwest to Oxford. A car stopped and I quickly—too quickly—got inside. The driver was a man in his late twenties. Out of the corner of my eye, I thought I glimpsed that he was not *wearing* his slacks—the slacks were lying *on top of his bare legs*. Reflexively, I opened the door and put my foot out as though I were breaking a bicycle. A crazy gesture to do while inside a moving car, but I was not thinking, just reacting and determined to escape. The man stopped the car without saying a word, as if he understood why I wanted to get out, and I fled.

Shaking, standing by the side of the road as the traffic whizzed by, not thinking clearly, I could not imagine there was any public transportation nearby. I was in the middle of a major rotary, feeling lost and vulnerable. What else could I do but put my thumb out once more.

◆

Marion looks far older than a woman in her early twenties. Janet Leigh was thirty-three at the time of the filming. Marion should have known better. Where are *her* street smarts? She appeared to have them earlier.

"Hot as fresh milk!" Mr. Cassidy (Frank Albertson) exclaims, when he enters the un-air-conditioned office where Marion works. She has just returned from her lunchtime tryst and is feigning a headache. We watch her expertly fending off the flirtations of rich man Cassidy, who waggles a huge wad of cash at her, $40,000, which her boss asks her to deposit in the bank immediately. In this scene, Marion seems savvy about the way men can take advantage of women and she is having none of it. She just stares back up at Cassidy with her large, dark, mascaraed eyes, a close-lipped smile on her face that makes it seem to him as though she is playing along. But we know better. The scene feels as though it is shot from her point of view. What a fool this rich man is making of himself, sitting on the edge of Marion's desk, leaning in close to her face and trying to chat her up. We gloat—at least I do—over her getting the better of him by stealing his cash.

We next see Marion at home, now in black bra, black slip. This time, in place of a lover on the bed, there is the loosely rubber-banded envelope with its bulging wad of cash: the visual suggestion of the erotics of money, which she stuffs but can't quite fit into her black handbag.

The bulging cash, her unbridled sexuality, her brimming breasts, her eyes bright with fear and guilt as she flees out of town.

The psychiatrist at the end of the movie focuses on Norman's sexual attraction to Marion as his twisted reason for having to kill her. It strikes me that Marion is also attracted to Norman and, as an older woman, acts seductively with him. She hears, coming from the main house, what appears to be Norman's mother scolding him for thinking of bringing a strange *girl* to dinner (an invitation Marion has readily accepted). When Norman sheepishly returns with a tray bearing food and a big pitcher of milk, she says, "As long as you've fixed a supper, we may as well eat it." She steps back to lean against the open doorway to her motel room, takes a sideward glance inside, then looks back at Norman and smiles, as though inviting him into her room—a small room dominated by a double bed. She is waiting for him to make a move toward her, which he does—then hesitates, edges back, and suggests they go to the office, and from there into the parlor.

♦

I must have been about twenty-two when I traveled to London and checked into a bed-and-breakfast. I had caught a cold and was running a fever, but I decided to go out and stroll up and down the busy street. When I stepped out of a grocery market, a young American couple stopped me to say hello. They recognized me as another American, traveling alone and feeling lonely. They urged me to come back to their flat so we could keep each other company, and I could save some money by staying with them for the night.

They let me in through the basement, which was where they lived. The woman, as it turned out, worked as a nanny for the owners, the family who lived upstairs, while her boyfriend worked as their handyman.

"Hey, it's getting late. I think it makes sense for you to sleep downstairs and Peggy will sleep upstairs with the children," said Chris. "The owners wouldn't want a stranger sleeping upstairs with them." He made it all sound so reasonable.

Before long, I found myself lying in bed beside a strange man. As soon as he turned out the light, I felt his hands searching in the dark for me.

I pushed him away. My head was aching from the fever, I was sweating, and I moaned in pain. *What am I doing here?* He tried again, and again I pushed him away. I spent much of the night wordlessly fighting off his advances. At some point, after repeated rebuffs, he gave up and let us both sleep.

◆

Why did I have a tendency to trust almost anyone, at least initially? Was this my mother's legacy? From a young age I never knew when I could trust her and when she was having a paranoid episode. Perhaps I unconsciously put myself in situations of danger because they felt uncannily familiar. There have been many moments in my life, and this was just one of them, when I have felt helpless and lost, and here was someone who seemed willing to help me. That was often how I felt with my mother when she was having a schizophrenic break: helpless and lost. And yet I clung to her.

Perhaps, too, I thought myself unlikely to be sexually preyed upon, since I was convinced no one could find me sexually attractive. I still had small breasts, and the wound to my self-image still lived inside me.

Now let me stop here to remind myself of what I looked like, not what I *felt* I looked like—though I realize objectivity, especially about one's own appearance, is impossible.

I pull out a favorite snapshot of myself, taken in August after I turned eighteen. I am sitting by the Seine in Paris, where I have traveled with my best friend Barbara after my freshman year of college. I have fine, dirty-blonde hair parted down the center and reaching to my waist. I am wearing a navy cardigan over a gray T-shirt, with CORNELL printed in bold red letters across the front, and khaki-colored pants. In the photo I am wearing contacts that accentuate my large blue-green eyes. Squinting slightly in the bright sun, I am grinning up at Barbara who snaps the shot.

Looking at myself in the photo today, I see a cute American teenage girl, a hippie chick. She is about to get a ride with her friend to Amsterdam from two guys driving a Volkswagen bus.

Diagnostic criteria for 300.7 Body Dysmorphic Disorder
A. Preoccupation with an imagined defect in appearance. If a slight physical anomaly is present, the person's concern is markedly excessive.
B. The preoccupation causes clinically significant distress or impairment in social, occupational, or other important areas of functioning.

Imagined ugliness. Body dysmorphic disorder (BDD). It entered the *Diagnostic and Statistical Manual of Mental Disorders* (DSM) in 1994, more than twenty years too late for me.

Up until this writing, I never even thought of finding a label for my bodily shame, my excruciating self-consciousness. It externalizes the condition and makes it feel less constitutive of who I am to be able to say: I suffered from a disorder, BDD, brought on by teasing that began when I was at the susceptible age of twelve. Now that I know there is a name for my condition, I feel more compassion for my own suffering. What if I had understood then it was a disorder? What if my friend Barbara had understood? She knew I felt too ashamed to share a dressing room with her when we went shopping for clothes. I like to believe she would have urged me to seek help. I like to believe I might have listened.

♦

Marion's shower scene:

She is in the shower for less than a minute before the curtain parts and Norman, dressed as his mother, murders her with a series of jagged, jump-cutting stabs until her hand slides down the white tile. Cut to a shot of her face down to her collarbone as her dying body slowly slides

onto the tub floor. Cut to her right hand grasping and pulling down the shower curtain as her body falls forward, her head on the tile floor. Cut to the image of her blood swirling into the drain. Cut to her dead eye with a bit of blood in the white, watching him, watching us, accusing him, accusing us of some shared culpability.

As I write this description of her brutal murder, I see the way it practically erases from my mind (probably from every viewer's mind) the memory of Marion's sensual pleasure before her horror, her shrieks, the stabs of violins in Bernard Herrmann's score, her futile attempts to cover and protect her body, the camera cutting seventy-eight times as her body is cut over and over again. This is, after all, the iconic murder, the most famous in film history. Yet the stabbing itself lasts for only about ten seconds.

I want to dwell, as the camera does, on the fifty seconds Marion has in the shower *before* she is murdered. For 1960 and for Hitchcock, these shots remain shocking and groundbreaking.

The foreboding music stops as soon as Marion enters the bathroom. Mostly, we hear the ambient sound of water: as she flushes down the toilet the evidence of her monetary calculations, then locks the door and turns on the shower and steps in. Now there is only the soothing sound of the shower as she opens herself up to the spray.

Naked and touching herself, feeling the spray of water all over her body, Marion is in a state of bliss. I watch her face crane up into the shower spray, her mouth open, as though she wants to drink in these few moments of ecstasy that reveal how easily and fully she can give herself over to sheer bodily pleasure. And this is where I want to stop, rewind— or at least slow down—time.

In these crucial fifty seconds, which almost feel leisurely compared to the quickness of her murder, Hitch uses only eight jump cuts, which means the camera lingers over each shot for several seconds.

In those first moments in the shower, as she lifts up her face and throws her head back, her mouth slightly ajar in a state of rapture, I imagine Marion conjuring up her afternoon tryst with her lover Sam. Or else fantasizing about their next lovemaking session. Or simply pleasuring herself. There she is, soaping up her body with a look of such abandon on her face. She dwells on her neck and arms, caressing them under the water's stream, frequently closing her eyes.

Marion might be on the verge of having—or beginning to have—a spontaneous orgasm before she is stabbed to death.

Is this Hitch's cruel joke: so much erotic pleasure is quite literally going to kill her? Or is Marion a dangerous renegade outside the sexual order imposed by men, who are the only ones who ought to do the looking and have (or give) the pleasure?

I know one thing: Marion has the most sensual pleasure on screen of any Hitchcock woman.

The repeated, yet varied, shots of Marion's unbridled pleasure remind me of William Carlos Williams's poem "To a Poor Old Woman"—a woman Williams watches eating a plum—where the phrase "They taste good to her" is repeated three times in a row, each with a different emphasis because of where the line breaks. That is what Marion's sensual pleasure in the shower looks like to me. It feels good to *her*. It feels *good* to her. It *feels* good to her.

Marion is reveling in the sensuous pleasure her own body affords her. Repetition, through camera shot and angle, is sometimes the most effective way of conveying the intensity of pleasure or pain. In *Psycho*, each shot of Marion showering, each montaged moment as she gets herself wet, raises her face to the shower spray, opens her mouth in utter surrender, then begins to soap up her body, conveys a steady buildup of sheer erotic pleasure.

These private moments we are privy to reveal a female sensuality that is taboo. The more I watch *Psycho*, the more I think the movie uses violence to convey this message. A woman such as Marion, who lusts and fulfills herself—first with her lover Sam and now luxuriating naked under the shower spray—will have to pay with her life for the sensual pleasure she has experienced.

Marion is a thief in more senses than one, and the money is the least of it. She has stolen time and pleasure for herself in the overly long lunches that she admits give her boss "excess acid." Was he, too, in love with her? Now she is caught stealing a few more moments of auto-erotic bliss (unaided by a man and therefore even more reprehensible). She is supposed to be the object of male pleasure, not the subject, which is too threatening and disruptive of the prevailing sexual order. Before she gets away with it any longer, she must be killed.

♦

Sexual pleasure was not something I expected to have. Growing up in the Sixties and reaching puberty in the early Seventies, I knew it was possible to have sex while quite young. My friend Lynda had done so when she was thirteen. But guys seemed to have most of the pleasure. This was the dirty secret of what we called at the time the *Sexual Liberation Movement.*

"If sexual pleasure is ten parts, then nine parts belong to women," claimed Tiresias, who experienced being a man, then a woman, then a man again. That angered Hera, who had bet against herself with Zeus. Despite reading Greek mythology, I never felt I experienced more sexual pleasure than men.

◆

I am fifteen when I have my first real make-out sessions in the back seat of my boyfriend's car. Michael and I remain clothed while we kiss and he gropes my small breasts. I put my hand down his pants and, with his guidance, soon figure out how to please him. But when he tries to do the same for me, I stop him. I feel unready for someone to fumble down my pants. Maybe it is a way to hang on to my power with someone five years older than me. Michael is already in college, impatient to have sex. He breaks off the relationship with me after a few months because of my refusal. I am too young for him.

Which is not to say I had no erotic pleasure. In my poetry journal, I wrote about this first boyfriend from high school:

> 24 april a.m. [1975]

> and i remember the 15 yr-old
> loves
> the strange fleshiness of tongues
> slapping
> and the tickling of small wings in
> my crotch
> as my young hands swooped
> through other grasping fingers . . .

When, nearly eighteen and in college, I felt old enough to have sex, the pleasuring seemed to go mostly one way. Looking back, I see that little had changed between my parents' generation and my own. The assumption remained, at least in my experience: the man's orgasmic pleasure was the goal and the woman took whatever pleasure she could manage along the way. When it was over for him, it was over for her.

During college, having sex with my boyfriend Brad felt like he was putting a record on the turntable and lowering the needle onto it, the way he lowered his body onto mine. There was never any question of his trying to figure out how to please me, in a way separate from what pleased him. I was complicit in thinking that was normal. Real orgasmic pleasure, I knew, would happen reliably when I was alone, masturbating.

Here is a poem from my poetry journal that I wrote more than a year later:

5 may a.m. [1976]

> the girl in the blue bath-
> robe is taking it
> off
> the man in the red
> room is taking it
>
> the hands on the blue
> cloth are eager
> for the man
> who takes
> it and leaves

Now, as a middle-aged woman, I see the poem shows both the woman's desire (at least her desire for *his* desire) and her focus on pleasing the man. Though the poem's starkness and its harsh ending are critical of the man's behavior, the man and woman have become gender archetypes.

It would take years—until I turned twenty-six—before I learned that full erotic pleasure was possible with a man—that I, too, could make sexual requests, even demands, could *take pleasure* too, as I like to imagine Marion had done with her lover Sam in *Psycho*'s opening scene.

♦

I decided to leave California in 1982, partly because I felt like a heterosexual pariah in a gay man's paradise. *Here I am, twenty-five years old, in my prime, and I am going to waste,* I used to say to myself, as I stood on the BART platform, returning to San Francisco from UC Berkeley, where I was a graduate student.

While I lived in San Francisco, I was invited to participate in a study for a new type of birth control from England, a cervical cap. When I tried it on, it fit me perfectly. I liked the idea of something less messy than a diaphragm. The cervical cap looks like a large, flesh-colored, thick rubber thimble with a lip and a thin groove inside. After putting a dollop of spermicidal jelly inside the bottom of the cap, I would insert it into my vagina and dial it around my cervix like a rotary phone until I could feel that the suction created a tight seal around my cervix.

Every month, I would report to the nurse who took down my answers for the study:
"Hi, Hun. Have you had sex this month?"
"No."
"Have you had a chance to use the cervical cap?"
"No."
"Oh you poor thing. I hope you get the chance to try it out next month." The nurse would pat me on the back and I would leave, knowing I was headed for another sex-parched month.

Now I was leaving San Francisco, traveling cross-country with my friend Gabe, a straight man. Why could I never picture him as my lover? He was tall, with a shock of wavy brown hair falling over his right eye. I knew that he was handsome. "If I married Gabe, I'd cheat on him," I told my friend Barbara. Something was always missing: some erotic friction that would have ignited me. He was too blandly nice, he lacked mystery. When he smiled or laughed, I looked at his large yellow teeth, and I could not imagine kissing him. What if I had felt more of his desire for me, instead of feeling like we were buddies?

"To be desired was at the heart of women's desiring," wrote Daniel Bergner in *What Do Women Want?* "Being desired is the orgasm.'. . . it was at once the thing craved and the spark of craving."

It is that magnetic pull of desire that draws me: *the desire to be desired* that fuels women—that fuels this woman—in the erotic dance with men. But in this dynamic, how little agency I actually have. Unlike Marion, who seems in control of magnetizing a man's desire wherever she goes.

Gabe and I left San Francisco on our three-week road trip in early July. We intended to camp out the whole time, sleeping side-by-side in our sleeping bags in my small green Kelty tent. Our cross-country trip would take us through Oregon, Washington, Montana, Wyoming, and into Denver to visit his family, at which point I would catch a Greyhound bus back east.

On one of the first nights, I am lying beside Gabe in the tent, each of us in our own sleeping bag. I feel my body lighting up, responding to Gabe, to some light touch, to some extra hint of his desire for me. Or perhaps in the quiet of the wilderness, I can finally tune in to him. I lean over and begin kissing him.

Gabe coaxes me on top of him and whispers, "Do whatever you want." And so, shyly, slowly, I move the way it pleases me with him inside of me, to the rhythm and pressure I need. I think this is the first time I am not in the missionary position with a man, though by now I have had sex with about a dozen men. I reach orgasm before he does.

For the first time, a man has asked me what I want and given it to me. Or, rather, allowed me to take it, with his help. I feel fully pleasured during sex. *So it is possible.*

I sketched this fragment of a poem into my journal:

> now in so short a time by this fire
> with the moths happy in their final
> dance—I could desire someone so
> that my body jumps with live embers
> inside all day.

We continued on to see Crater Lake, then the Cascades, hiking through canyons and forests, spotting bighorn sheep in Glacier National Park as we backpacked into the wilderness, not seeing (but fearing we would see) a grizzly. Thirty-five years later, it is the sex that remains a revelation to me. I, too, can do more than feel mildly turned on during sex. With the right man, I can feel as much pleasure as he does. As much pleasure as I imagine Marion in *Psycho* did during her lunch-time tryst with Sam.

◆

My shower scene:

I am twelve years old, taking a shower one evening, after dinner, in the sole bathroom in my family's small, rented Brooklyn apartment. The bathroom walls are covered by dull Pepto-Bismol pink tiles that come up to about chin height, rimmed by a row of black tiles. I have already pushed in the tiny button beside the doorknob to lock the bathroom door. I like my privacy.

I enter the stall shower, with its translucent, bevel-glassed door. I love the way it clicks shut and I'm sealed in a dank, slightly mildewed space. Sealed in with the Ivory soap and Breck Gold shampoo, free to touch myself all over. Free to sing with the reverberant echoes so it feels like I'm miked.

Now the spray begins and I wash my hair first. Rinse it out. Then wash it again. This is my weekly routine. Then I am soaping myself up. The year is 1968 and I am singing, *Come on baby light my fire.* Not the Jim Morrison version, but José Feliciano's much smoother version—*mellower*, as my friends and I like to say. *Mellow Yellow*, like Donovan.

I have a skinny-skinny body and like it that way. After washing my hair, I soap up my neck and arms. Then my breasts, the non-existent little nubbins they are—only this time I feel something strange. Something that is not supposed to be there. Inside each breast, beneath the nipple, I touch a hard, flat stone. *This is it. I'm dying. I'm 12 and I have breast cancer and I'm going to die.* I start to cry and cannot stop. I am sure I never felt these flat, immovable lumps before. I check again. *Yup. They're there.* Like small, flat, chipped pieces of sidewalk slate. *Are they new? How can I have missed them before?*

I get out of the shower, dry off quickly, wrap the towel under my arms and around my middle, covering my chest and front (my mom's name for the pubic area). Unlock the door, poke my head out and scream, "Mommy! Mommmm-my! Come in here!"

"What is it, Sharon?" I can hear her coming down the short hallway and I wave her into the bathroom. Lock the door. Then pull back the towel and show her what I have found.

"What are these? I'm going to die, right? I've got cancer, don't I?" Sobbing, I look up at my mother, who is grinning at me.

"You're not dying, honey. You're *de-ve-loping.*" She emphasizes that last word, her voice rising on the second syllable in a sing-song so that, if it were not my mom, I would think she was teasing me. And I can tell she is happy, smiling, even half-hiding a chuckle.

"You're becoming a *wo-man.*" She hugs me and strokes my wet hair, as I stand there in my towel. Then she leaves me alone to cope with this awful realization.

I know immediately what she means. *Developing.* Her way of saying that I am beginning to go through puberty, another word I hate. *Maturing*, as she also says. Beginning to grow breasts and pubic hair and underarm hair. Eventually, getting my period. Which is still two years away.

What is happening to me? It feels like a catastrophe: my body is undergoing an irreversible metamorphosis. Some internal violence is being done to the body I have always lived with and counted on. It has begun a relentless change that feels like a betrayal. *I am being betrayed by my own body.* And I can do nothing to stop it. I am powerless.

I stand stock still on the bathroom mat, trying to take it in, this first drop into awareness that I am not in control of my body. It has its own clock. Its own wants. Its own direction. And my will can do nothing to alter its course. My girl's body is slowly going to be replaced by a woman's body. And I will have to adjust to this disturbing transformation—even, somehow, learn to find pleasure in my new form.

Unlike the radio, my body has no dial to turn it back to its former station. Now I hear it playing: *Light my fire, light my fire, light my fire, yeah, yeah, yeah-eah.*

The Birds: Teen Phobias, the Power of the Mother, and Female Rage

After all, the picture isn't just about the birds; it's about the bees, too.

–Alfred Hitchcock, 1963 press conference

BEGINNING IN MY EARLY TEENS, I was afraid of birds. Of any creatures with wings flitting around my head. Afraid of them flying into my hair, pecking at my face. Ornithophobia, it turns out, is quite common, and is usually triggered by an unpleasant incident with a bird. A gull stealing a child's sandwich, a swallow flying into the house.

Watching *The Birds* (1963) triggered my bird phobia.

I was fourteen years old. Barely a teenager. Barely had breasts. But I had a boyfriend named Jay who went to my high school. He had chestnut-brown hair swept to the side that often fell over one of his brown eyes. He had a large smile and he used to make me laugh by stretching his mouth wide with his fingers, as though his skin were made of rubber, and pulling funny faces. He liked my sarcasm. We talked on the phone a lot, and when we were together, we had tickling battles. On weekends, my dad drove me over to Jay's house and Jay and I hung out in his parents' basement. Nothing else happened. No kissing. No make-out sessions.

When are we going to kiss? I was much too shy to make the first move. What would I do, anyway?

It was 1970. My dad brought home a bunch of buttons and spilled them out on the dining room table. As a traveling salesman, he was always picking up sidelines in addition to what he had been hired to sell. On the table were dozens of buttons in different sizes: peace-sign buttons. Woodstock buttons with the logo of the dove sitting on the guitar. Yellow and Day-Glo smiley-face buttons. "Here. Pick any ones you want." I took several, then picked up one with two sets of feet, one pair going up and, in between them, the other pair going down. My dad quickly pulled the button out of my hand and said, "You can't have that one." I chose another one, pale blue, with the number 69 composed of the swirling figures of a man and a woman. He grabbed that one away from me, too.

♦

One night, Jay and I are reclining in his family's paneled basement in Mill Basin, Brooklyn, a Jewish and Italian enclave of one-family homes where many of my friends from junior high school live. We are lying on the couch together, watching *The Birds* on TV, Jay's skinny body scrunched behind mine.

In the middle of the movie, as a murder of crows descends upon the fleeing school children, attacking them as they go shrieking down the hill, I feel Jay's hands coming around to the front of my T-shirt, where my small breasts, a source of continual shame for me, are hidden inside my stretch bra. He begins rubbing them. Harder and harder. I freeze. I can feel his whole body begin to stiffen and push against mine as I continue watching one girl fall, her glasses smashed, her face bloodied, crying for help as the crows peck at her back. Jay is breathing hard. *What is he doing?* I am too scared to ask him, so I stay completely still, trying to keep my attention on the movie, watching the birds continue their attack and hoping he will stop soon. I never turn around. Just pretend to focus on the movie and act as though nothing is happening as I feel his body moving against mine in increasing agitation. Now he is breathing hard, his movements alternating between jerky and rhythmic. *What is he doing?* He just keeps pushing against me and feeling me up through my bra. *Please, let it end.*

Eventually, he stops.

When the movie is over, I stand up as though nothing unusual has happened and call my dad to pick me up and drive me home. After that night, I refuse to speak to Jay or spend time with him again.

The next day, I visit my friend Kathy who lives nearby me. Her mom is home, vacuuming in the living room, as Kathy and I go to her bedroom to talk. I have to tell somebody, to try and make sense of what happened. But Kathy looks blank. "Let's go ask my mom." Kathy and I return to the living room. "Hey Mom? Sharon has something she wants to ask you."

Kathy's mom turns off the vacuum cleaner and stands there in her apron.

"Um, my boyfriend Jay and I were watching TV last night in his basement when he suddenly started pushing against my back and touching my bra and breathing hard. I was so scared, I didn't know what was happening. Is that normal?"

Kathy's mom smiles. "Oh, honey. That's called *humping*. All boys do that. Of course it's normal."

"Really?"

"Yes. When you're a little bit older, you'll see. That's what teenagers do. It's completely normal."

I look over at my dark-haired friend Kathy, who is standing there getting a quick course in teenage sexual behavior along with me.

How could Jay have continued without my responding? I thought at the time. *Shouldn't he have coaxed me to turn around? Shouldn't we have at least kissed first?* Now I have to wonder: Why was I so passive? Why didn't I tell him to stop? And how was it possible for me to have understood so little about sex?

My mom, comatose from all the psychiatric medications she was on since I was ten, never had the clarity of mind to talk to me about sex. The most she did was give me a dog-eared pamphlet called *You're a Young Lady Now* that she kept in the bottom drawer of her nightstand. The pamphlet talked about a girl getting her period and using Kotex sanitary napkins.

As far back as I can remember, I had always touched myself, but I did not understand that I was doing something sexual. I called it *rocking*, because I rocked back and forth, rubbing myself up against something soft. I had once tried showing my sister Marla, who was four-and-a-half years older than me, how to rub herself against a blanket because it felt good. She didn't get it.

One summer, my sister was reading *Summerhill*, a book about a progressive boarding school in England, when she came up to me, first pointing at a word on the page and then pointing her finger at me. "Masturbation! That's what *you* do, Sharon!" I said nothing and she walked away, victorious. She had succeeded in shaming me. I had not known that what I did had a name.

Later, I took a peek at the pages of her book under the bold letters **Masturbation**:

> Most children are masturbators. Yet youth has been told that masturbation is evil, that it prevents growth that it leads to disease or what not. If a wise mother paid no attention to her child's first exploration of his lower body, masturbation would be less compulsive. It is the prohibition that fixes the interest of the child.
> –A. S. Neill, *Summerhill*

Okay. So I can keep doing what I'm doing. Only now I understood I had to do it in secret.

◆

Though I no longer have a bird phobia, it has taken me forty years before I am ready to watch *The Birds* again. Now the movie strikes me as an allegory of sexual desire, almost Greek in its framing disaster. A plague descends upon the land in the form of attacking birds—not unlike what happens at the beginning of *Oedipus Rex*, when Oedipus must find the source of the plague in Thebes.

In *The Birds*, Melanie Daniels (Tippi Hedren), the arresting, sexy, platinum blonde, as perfect as a Barbie doll (created just several years before the movie), brings the plague with her, and it escalates as the movie progresses. She has traveled north from San Francisco to Bodega Bay with two lovebirds in her sports car, ostensibly to give as a birthday present to the kid sister of Mitch Brenner (Rod Taylor).

Here is no deep metaphor for her desire, and both Mitch's former lover, the schoolteacher Annie Hayworth (Suzanne Pleshette), and Mitch's possessive mother Lydia (Jessica Tandy) understand fully, even as Melanie acts oblivious to the motivation behind her actions. Why, after all, has she driven fifty miles up the coast to deliver lovebirds to the kid sister of a man she quarreled with in a pet shop?

In one shot, the camera captures the sexual threat Melanie poses when she arrives for dinner at Mitch's invitation on the first night she is in town. While his mother is making a phone call, he offers Melanie a drink. Lydia is standing in the foreground while her son and this striking blonde intruder, the head-turner who gets whistled at in the first few seconds of the movie, are clinking glasses, intimately, almost conspiratorially, in the background.

Lydia will brook no rivals for her son's affection and she has her ammunition ready in the kitchen while she is washing up after dinner. She unloads on her son the gossip she read in the paper about Melanie, the reckless socialite, diving naked into a fountain in Rome the previous summer. This provocative scene is exactly what excites Mitch. No matter that he brings up the incident disdainfully while giving Melanie the third degree as she is leaving in her car that night. Just as Melanie herself, when Mitch muses that she must like him to have driven so far to deliver the birds, says, "I loathe you."

I loathe you. I love you. They are identical, interchangeable, in passion. At least in this movie.

Melanie's chief crime is that she has intruded upon the mother's domain when she drives up the coast, motors a skiff across the bay to surreptitiously drop off the lovebirds, then motors back to Bodega Bay. Mitch dashes into the house and sees the gift, then runs out with his binoculars to spot her mid-bay, where she is doing a fetching mixture of appearing to hide and then revealing herself. He sets off in his car in a race with her so he can meet her at the town dock. Just as he is about to touch her hand to lift her out of the boat, the first gull dive-bombs her head, drawing blood.

Think of the attacking birds as maternal Furies, which can be deadly.

After Melanie returns from dinner, Annie admits to her that she was involved romantically with Mitch in San Francisco. When she came up to Bodega Bay one weekend to meet Mitch's mother, the relationship ended. Here is a mother who appears to give free rein to her son (who looks to be in his mid-thirties), yet has the power to veto another woman's entering his life.

> Annie: You know, her attitude nearly drove me crazy. When I got back to San Francisco, I spent days trying to figure out exactly what I'd done to displease her.
> Melanie: Well, what had you done?
> Annie: Nothing. [She shrugs.] I simply existed. So, what's the answer? Jealous woman, right? Clinging, possessive mother? Wrong. With all due respect to Oedipus, I don't think that was the case.

Annie backs off by rejecting the Oedipus comparison. But the rejection of an idea once raised may well mean the idea is worth considering.

◆

I think of Michael as my first serious boyfriend. We met when I was fifteen and he was twenty, at the Sweet Sixteen party of his kid sister Vicki, who went to high school with me. My mom did not seem to disapprove of my having a far older boyfriend, but then she was too heavily medicated to voice disapproval of much of anything.

Just once, I stayed out with Michael until very late—close to two a.m. My mom came out of my parents' bedroom in her nightgown like a walking ghost, and I saw on her face the worried look that managed to break through her sleepy, drugged haze. I began to cry and hugged her.

"Mom, I'm sorry, I'm so sorry, I promise, I won't stay out this late again."

"All right, Sharon. I was worried about you." Then she ghost-walked back to bed.

By this time, I knew that men had orgasms, having learned how to bring Michael off in the backseat of his car. I had no idea that women could have orgasms as well.

◆

At age sixteen, I was still living with my family in Brooklyn. Still sharing a bedroom with my sister, who went to bed early. I liked to stay up late—it was the only way I could have real solitude, sitting in a corner of the living room with my spiral notebook and felt-tipped green pen, writing poems while everyone else in the house was asleep. I felt free at night, staying up past midnight, listening to WBAI, the alternative radio station in New York City.

It was 1972, and the women's liberation movement was the air I breathed. *Our Bodies, Ourselves*, a radical handbook on women's sexuality and health, would be published the following year. It was not long before all of us, every young woman I knew, owned a copy and pored over its pages like it was our new bible.

One evening, listening to WBAI, I happened to hear a show about sex and female masturbation. The host and her guest were talking about the female orgasm. I listened carefully, making sure I had heard them right. *Women have orgasms.* This news came to me as a shocking revelation.

Maybe I should try and see if I can do it. I masturbate right there and just keep going, pushing it a bit further, applying more pressure as I rock back and forth, until a rhythmic sweetness overtakes me, reaches a crescendo, and now I am being rocked by it, by this effortless momentum, which goes on and on and I am being carried into a place beyond myself and I keep going on and on until the jolts of pleasure slowly, oh so slowly, subside, and I look around to find myself on the rug in the corner of the living room, where the sofa curves away from the wall. Now I know this *rocking* has a destination and I know how to get there. At least on my own.

◆

In my early thirties, after a bad breakup with a foreigner, I ran into Michael on a New York City subway platform and we started to date once more. What a relief to go out with someone who had known me since high school. He was divorced, and had custody of his seven-year-old son Pierre. We began seeing each other regularly, having sex the way I had always done, with the man on top, with both of us focused on him having his orgasm and my taking whatever pleasure I could manage along the way. I was about thirty-two.

Michael's younger brother, an entrepreneur, had moved into a mini-mansion in New Jersey and invited the family for a housewarming party to show off his wealth. Michael asked me to go along. When I got into the back of his parents' car, where Michael and his son were sitting, he said: "This is Sharon Dolin." Dead silence. The whole family would have remembered that I went to high school with their daughter Vicki and that Michael had dated me back then. For the entire trip, his mother never said a word to me. Neither did his father. We rode in the back seat in silence.

♦

Our relationship lasted only a while longer. On a Saturday night, Michael came over to my top-floor, ramshackle walk-up in Carroll Gardens, Brooklyn, a large corner apartment with unfinished wooden floors and no room dividers, with windows all around. Lots of light. Lots of privacy even when the shades were up—something I never had as a child and always craved. I had my bed in the tiny dressing room off to the side, the only room with a built-in closet and a door that closed.

I had been talking to a girlfriend about receiving oral sex from a man, about getting up the courage to ask for or just do what I wanted. "Is that normal?" I asked my friend. She reassured me that it was, that she had often ridden a man's face and that men usually liked it.

I am feeling bold when Michael and I get into bed. Does Michael even know what foreplay is? Do I? After some initial kissing, we are about to get straight to what we always do: vaginal intercourse in the missionary position.

"Uh, Michael?"

"Yeah?

"Would you mind if we tried something a bit different this time?"

"Sure, okay, what d'yah have in mind?"

"Lie on your back and move down on the bed."

He gives me a look that I read as "Really?" Then he does as I asked. I attempt to straddle Michael's face, careful not to drop my full weight upon him and making sure I do not squash his nose so he can still breathe. It is my first time and I am clumsy at it. No matter how many adjustments we make, he complains. I feel so embarrassed and self-conscious that I stop. We quickly revert to our usual method, which never fully satisfies me.

The next morning, while reading *The Sunday New York Times*, Michael says, "Oh. The circus is in town. Maybe I'll take Pierre to that." *Why isn't he inviting me to go along with them?* I say nothing. He leaves after breakfast, kissing me goodbye. He never calls me again. I decide not to call him because I understand I have crossed a boundary with him, sexually.

Years later, when we were back in touch once more, and he and I were both married, I decided to broach the subject.

"Um. I have a funny thing to ask you."

"Yeah, sure. Go ahead."

"Do you remember the last time we were dating?"

"Yeah, sure. What about it?"

"Why did we break up? Why did you never call me?"

"Oh, I was too busy being a father. I realized during my marriage, I'm much better at being a father than being a husband."

"Oh. So it had nothing to do with the sex?"

"No. What d'you mean?"

"Well . . . that last night we were together, I . . . I wanted to sit on your face. You didn't seem to like it very much."

He chuckled. "No-no-no-no-no-no-no. It had nothing to do with *that.*"

As I think about our relationship through the lens of *The Birds*, I recall Michael's mother and that terribly awkward car ride, when she would not acknowledge me or say a word to me. She did not approve of me, I don't know why. What power might a mother have to break up her son's relationship?

♦

The gulls attack during the outdoor birthday party for Mitch's kid sister Cathy, right after Mitch and Melanie descend from the bluff and the same two rivals for Mitch's love—the former girlfriend and the mother—give the couple knowing, disapproving, even hostile, looks. Annie watches jealously as the two seeming "lovebirds" descend the bluff with a bottle of wine and two glasses. The next moment Lydia comes out of the house with a birthday cake for her daughter, sees the couple, and her face darkens into a scowl. Then the gulls attack the children. The threat Melanie poses, both to the mother and to the dark-haired other woman, calls forth this jealous, raging plague of birds.

Imagine the frenzied birds as harpies, those winged destructive spirits in Greek mythology—part woman, part bird—who attack during sharp gusts of wind. They also prevent the sating of appetites. Here they seem to be the embodiment of a mother's and former girlfriend's jealous fury, designed to prevent Mitch and Melanie from coupling.

♦

In my late twenties, while visiting with friends in the Bay Area where I used to live, I met a man whose name, now, is not one I can conjure up or would even recognize. The memory of this brief affair is so clouded over, as though caught in the swirling fog coming in off the Pacific. Now, if I squint, I can picture us meeting at a party at his house somewhere in the East Bay, in Oakland. The fog thins a bit. I can make out our two figures going into his bedroom. Shortly after, his girlfriend burst in on us. She had long dark-brown hair tied back with a scarf and she began screaming at him, trying roughly to pull him off of me. He seemed as unfazed by her anger as I was.

How callously both the boyfriend and I behaved. As I write this, I try to summon up the feeling of blocked empathy: a numbness to what she thought or felt, an emotional blindness in the face of my own selfish lust. Not usually the way I think of myself. He and I decided to get in his car and leave, but his girlfriend was too fast for us: she got into her car and physically blocked the driveway, refusing to move, making it impossible for us to go anywhere. Temporarily, she had won. Of course, no one can force someone to be faithful; as I have had to learn over and over, the effort usually has the opposite effect. He and I made plans to meet one afternoon at my friend's apartment in Oakland and a few days later we had the quick, illicit sex we were seeking.

Now the incident makes me smile on behalf of the girlfriend. How clever and resourceful she was. Good, honest, justifiable female rage.

◆

In *The Birds*, I always puzzle over why Melanie instigates the climactic attack. She and Mitch's family have barricaded themselves in the downstairs of the house. Mitch has nailed all of the windows and doors shut with wooden boards and they are sitting huddled together in the living room, as though waiting for the impending attack. What makes her decide to investigate what is making that faint rattling sound? She must know it will only lead to trouble. Why does Melanie feel compelled to go upstairs and open the door to the attic?

Melanie is like Pandora, stung by her own curiosity. She *has* to open that door. She knows she should not, but she cannot control her impulsive urges, just as she could not stop herself from chasing after Mitch or jumping in the fountain in Rome. Curiosity and an attraction to danger compel her.

Hordes of birds that have broken through the roof violently attack her, and practically kill her, before Mitch runs upstairs and drags her dazed, semi-conscious, gruesomely pecked body out of there. It is a brutal scene, still difficult for me to watch.

♦

At sixteen, I dated a boy in my high school named Martin. Martin's father happened to be my family's milkman, who delivered glass bottles of fresh milk before dawn to a metal box outside our front door. Martin transferred to my public high school from an Orthodox Jewish day school, and he looked out of place, the only boy in school who wore a yarmulke. He was very awkward and jittery, with short, frizzy, dirty-blonde hair. Instead of laughing, he sniggered nervously. My Jewish friends and I called religious boys *yarmulke-bops*. We never found them attractive, they were *too* Jewish. Not hip. Martin was attracted to me.

Just a few years before, I had been teased by the boys in junior high for being flat-chested. I had been a despised outsider, and that feeling lingered. It would take years for me to recover my sense of self—many years for me to believe I was at all attractive. In a way, Martin and I had something in common, though I was not consciously aware of it at the time.

For several months we went out—or, rather, we would go in. My father dropped me off by car at his house and picked me up a few hours later. We hung out in his basement. I did not like looking at Martin and I did not want him to look at me. I still have a photograph of me turning my head to hide my face when Martin tried to take a Polaroid. In the photo, I am wearing a blue plaid work shirt over a T-shirt. The long hair that hides my face is kinky because every once in a while I used to braid it while still wet, then remove the braids so my hair stood on end, as close as I could get to Janis Joplin's hairstyle. We made out, though it never went very far. Our clothes always stayed on and I always insisted on it being dark in the room. Perhaps we were both equally tentative in our sexual experimentation and in that way a good match.

One day Martin told me we were both freaks, and we belonged together. That was too much for me to take. I told Martin I did not want to see him anymore. At school, I avoided him, walking away when he approached me in the hallways. My girlfriends also protected me and told him to

leave me alone. For the next few weeks, after school, I would peer out my window and see him standing in front of my house. I refused to open the door and speak to him. I had made my decision.

Martin persisted. He called up and asked me to come over to his house, just to talk things over calmly. Something told me I should refuse, and yet curiosity overcame my resistance. *What can he possibly want to say to me? Maybe if I let him talk to me, he'll leave me alone.*

Martin lived in Bergen Beach, on a dead-end street, a block or two from where some of my closest girlfriends lived, in two- and three-story attached brick homes. I glanced at the marshes across the street, where my friends and I, more than once, watched the cops drag out a dead body someone had found while walking their dog. We always assumed the Mob had dumped them there. I climbed the concrete steps and greeted his mother at the door.

Martin opens the door to the basement, where we have always spent our time together, and I start to go downstairs. He closes and locks the door behind him. Once we reach the bottom, he grabs hold of my arm and tries to fling me to the floor, but I resist him. He starts punching me and shouting at me, "You bitch, *this* is what you deserve!" I struggle with him and scream for help.

Martin is about my height, five-foot-four, with a scrawny frame. I keep screaming for help while trying to avoid his blows. *How is it possible his mother hasn't heard us?* No one comes to the basement door. No one knocks. At last I manage to push him away long enough to run up the stairs. Maybe he has given up, having made his point. I unlock the door, run out of the house and keep running for my life.

♦

I always knew there was something twisted about Martin, some dark, even tortured interior life that I half-sensed. He told me that his parents were concentration camp survivors, but I did not understand what it meant to be the child of survivors. No one did at that time. It felt too frightening and overwhelming to speak about.

The major studies showing that the children of survivors of the Shoah often experienced post-traumatic stress disorder and depression, as well as interpersonal difficulties, were not published until the Nineties, twenty years later. Even if I had understood, as I do now, that trauma is transmitted across generations, would it have changed my feelings toward Martin or the way we treated each other? I like to think I would have had more empathy for him, though I would not have confided in him about my schizophrenic mother. I shared that information with no one.

Perhaps Martin was right. Both of us were *freaks*, damaged in our different ways because of our parents' histories. In a sense, I, too, was the child of a survivor—a survivor, or rather victim, of mental illness. For years, I had covered up my mother's schizophrenia, her drugged-up state, and the shame I felt. Perhaps I was initially drawn to something in Martin that simultaneously repelled me. Perhaps I sensed he was a kindred spirit, a fact that became too dangerous for me to face. In the end, I did not want to be like him: an outcast, someone others shunned, just as I had been shunned in junior high. And so I shunned him.

◆

Hitchcock took five days to film the final scene in the attic, where Melanie is savaged by the attacking birds. He gave Tippi Hedren no advance warning. Trained attack birds were thrown at her continuously until she was cut under the eye and nearly blinded.

Difficult for me not to think there was something punitive in the filming of this scene—as though Hitchcock's own sexual fury at not being able to *have* Tippi taints the action. He was sexually aggressive and controlling with her offscreen. It is impossible to picture Grace Kelly or Ingrid Bergman—two of his regulars—in the role, or to think he would have been able to get away with the same directorial behavior with such seasoned, patrician stars. Tippi Hedren was a working-class ingénue he had discovered from a TV commercial. This was her big-screen debut, and Hitch knew she relied on the income in order to support her mother and young daughter, coincidentally named Melanie (Griffith).

> It wasn't until the very ending of the filming that I starting noticing that he [Hitch] kept watching me, staring at me... He'd be standing, talking to people ... and staring at me. Eventually that becomes almost like stalking. . . the horrible experience of being the object of someone's obsession: it is oppressive, frightening.
> –Tippi Hedren interview, 2012

Hitch had a special obsession for Tippi and she had to rebuff his untoward advances continually, until he became so intolerable to her that she tried to break her contract with him after doing two movies, *The Birds* and *Marnie*. Hitch refused to release her from her contract and threatened to ruin her career, which he succeeded in doing. He prevented her from working for anyone else for the period of her contract—seven years— and thus eclipsed the stardom she had achieved with these two movies.

♦

Replaying in my mind the episode of Jay humping me in his parents' basement while we were watching *The Birds*, I have to wonder: Was there something about the movie that aroused him? Instead of being a turn-off, as it surely was for me, did the violence—aimed mostly at women and children—sexually excite him and spur him on? As I lay there petrified twice over—by the scene on the TV screen of fleeing, screaming children as a murder of crows pecked at them and drew blood, and by the basement scene in which I was, at most, a passive partner— Jay was, it seems, not only aroused, but emboldened to take advantage of the moment.

When I rewatch that scene in *The Birds*, what most disturbs me is that the girl in glasses suffers the worst attack. One huge crow jabs at her back with enough force to throw her to the ground. Her shattered glasses spill across the pavement as she cries out for help, blood streaming down her face. I was a girl in glasses a mere five years older, watching the scene— and being sexually assaulted by someone at my back. So stunned that, at the time, it never occurred to me to cry out or escape.

The girl's helplessness, her victimhood. My helplessness, my victimhood. Is that what Jay was after? Is that what I inadvertently gave him?

♦

I fled the West Coast in the early Eighties because I was a frustrated straight woman in a gay world, only to arrive back in Ithaca where, I soon discovered, single men in their twenties were far outnumbered by teenage undergraduates.

I met Stefano, another Cornell graduate student, in Italian class. Stefano looked like he could have stepped out of the pages of *The Three Musketeers*: He had long, dirty-blonde, matted hair, a small turned-up mustache, penetrating honey-colored eyes that glittered behind gold wire-rimmed glasses, and a passion for fencing. He rolled his own cigarettes and always wore a ratty, black leather motorcycle jacket. He was silent, somewhat brooding and dark, which I found sexy, and it drew me to him.

When we became lovers, I could sense he both desired me and fought his desire for me. Because I was Jewish. As an undergraduate at Columbia, he had lived in the dorms on a floor with many observant Jews, and had become the *Shabbos goy*—the non-Jew who turned the lights on and off on the Jewish Sabbath. I could tell from the rancor in his voice that it made him hate Jews.

Stefano grew up in the same town that William Carlos Williams had lived in—Rutherford, New Jersey—and his parents still lived in the house right across the street from Williams's house. I would write most of my dissertation on Williams, whom I adopted as my poetic grandfather. So, in my eyes, Stefano's romantic mystique only grew.

Stefano wanted me and he hated himself for wanting me. He always wore a gold pendant of Saint Jude around his neck, which dangled between us when we were in bed together. Even I knew St. Jude is the saint of lost or impossible causes and I noticed Stefano never took off the pendant, even while having sex, as though he were wearing a talisman to protect himself from me.

We had been lovers for a while when I noticed my period was a few days late. In bed one night, I told him. His pale skin flushed with rage and disgust, because he realized he could potentially father a Jewish child with me. I told him I would have an abortion. We were both indigent graduate students and our relationship was far from stable. When it turned out I was not pregnant, I suspect even the possibility made Stefano realize he had to end his affair with me.

◆

On one of our last nights together, Stefano wore his white fencing uniform to bed. Drunk, sweaty, reeking of tobacco, and wanting—but not wanting—to be intimate with me, he lay there, restive, half-resisting me, as I undressed him. I felt like Delilah, seducing a young Samson as he swooned beneath me. I think if he could have parried my advances with his épée, he would have, but physical desire overpowered him.

That night I dreamt Stefano and I were on a *terrazza* in Italy, when he turned away from me to look out at the sea, saying, *You are not the only one.*

Though not as tiny as Bodega Bay, Ithaca was still a small enough town, especially on Cornell's East Hill, for gossip about who was sleeping together to circulate quickly. Word reached me that Stefano had begun sleeping with my friend Elke, a Nordic beauty, much blonder than me and not Jewish. Elke knew that Stefano had just broken things off with me and that I was still smarting from the breakup.

In my fury, I went looking for Stefano in Morrill Hall, where he worked as a teaching assistant in the Linguistics Department. I was climbing the stairs just as he happened to be walking down, and I reached him at a landing, where he'd stopped to wait for me. I said nothing. I slammed him into the wall and punched him, knowing I could do no real harm. He stood there, passive as a fencing dummy, and let me hit him, saying nothing.

At the time I lived in a big house on East Buffalo Street, with ten-foot ceilings, tall windows, and wine-colored, ceiling-to-floor velvet curtains. Seated at the large, formal dining room table, I began composing a vengeful letter to Elke, which went on for several handwritten pages. I wish I had made a copy. My tirade ended with a protracted curse something like this: *May the flames of hell burn your flesh for having betrayed me. May you be cursed forever and never find peace in the arms of any man.*

I knew I was being histrionic, yet it felt so cathartic to write that letter. I took such relish in spewing my venom at her. I mailed the letter, imagining her reaction. How giddy I felt, knowing it would give her a guilty jolt—maybe even stop her from seeing Stefano that evening. No matter that it would not be enough to make her break it off with him. I had assumed the role of the jealous harpy and my sharp-beaked words were my best means of attack.

Rear Window:
The Ethics of Seeing
and Telling

What people oughta do is get outside their own house and look in for a change.

–Stella

I FIRST WATCHED *Rear Window* (1954) on television with my parents in the late Sixties. The setting looked so familiar, as though it could have been my Brooklyn neighborhood of Flatlands, where there were always those who looked and those who were looked at: that was part of the urban contract.

Ever since I was five and my father, bankrupt, had moved us—in a reversal of the suburban dream—from Seaford, Long Island to Brooklyn, my family always rented the street-level apartment of a two-family brick home. The owners invariably lived upstairs, away from prying eyes, while we renters lived below. Some message about social class and economic power got communicated to me: The higher-ups lived higher up. Privacy was reserved for the more well-to-do, for the landlords and landladies. To be poor was to rent the bottom floor and to have the threat of spying eyes upon you at all times. To be looked at was a badge of shame we wore along with poverty. To be seen was to be unmasked. To be unmasked was to be caught. To be caught unawares was to be made wary. To be wary and on guard was the price we paid for existence.

♦

Rear Window takes place in Greenwich Village, though Hitchcock had the entire set built on a Hollywood lot. We watch Jeffries (James Stewart), the war photographer (perhaps modeled after Robert Capa, who died the year *Rear Window* was made), incapacitated with a broken leg, spending his time watching his neighbors across the way, particularly the skimpily clad blonde dancer he labels "Miss Torso" (Georgine Darcy), while practically ignoring Lisa (Grace Kelly), his glamorous blonde stunner of a girlfriend who wears a different designer ensemble every time we see her on screen.

"We've become a race of Peeping Toms," the insurance nurse, Stella (Thelma Ritter), complains to Jeffries, lambasting him for spying on his neighbors, saying she can smell trouble. Soon, she, too, gets seduced into watching and trying to solve the murder Jeffries suspects happened in one of the apartments across the way. Even his old army buddy, the ineffectual, scoffing police Detective Doyle (Wendell Corey), gets so distracted by the dancer that Jeffries, in a moment of exasperation, brings him back with a guilt-inducing jolt: "How's your wife?"

In *Rear Window*, the act of looking is often sexual. In what psychoanalytic film theorists such as Laura Mulvey have labeled *scopophilia*, the male gaze focuses on the objectified woman for gratification. And we as viewers—willingly or not—identify with and assume the male gaze of Jeff the photographer.

"We're all voyeurs to some extent," Truffaut says in his conversation with Hitchcock about *Rear Window*. Hitchcock agrees:

> I'll bet you that nine out of ten people, if they see a woman across the courtyard undressing for bed, or even a man puttering around in the room, will stay and look; no one turns away and says, "It's none of my business." They could pull down the blinds, but they never do; they stand there and look out.

Hitchcock may have made this offhand remark (the everyone-does-it justification) in his interview, but in *Rear Window* the ethics of looking gets a more nuanced consideration:

> Jeffries: You know, much as I hate to give Thomas J. Doyle too much credit, he might have gotten a hold of something when he said that was pretty private stuff going on out there. [Pause] I wonder if it's ethical to watch a man with binoculars and a long-focus lens. Do you . . . do you suppose it's ethical even if you prove he didn't commit a crime?
> Lisa: I'm not much on rear-window ethics.
> Jeffries: Of course they can do the same thing to me. Watch me like a bug under a glass.

The ethics of looking, and of acting upon what he thinks he sees: that is what Jeffries ponders when Doyle has momentarily convinced him to give up on his suspicion that his neighbor has murdered his wife. Jeffries has doubts about what he is doing if it proves that his neighbor is *innocent*. If, on the other hand, his voyeurism catches a criminal, then he might well feel justified, he seems to be implying.

Hitch sets up this ethical quandary for his viewers to ponder. If, as viewers, we are hyper-aware of our own watching because it is raised to the second degree (watching Jeffries watching), are we implicated or somehow absolved of any guilt? Does looking at looking cancel itself out? We are, after all, watching Jeff *like a bug under a glass*. What is the ethics of looking if it is looking at what others see? Is it still voyeurism if we are watching a voyeur?

◆

At about age thirteen, I am in my bedroom, doing homework. My mother, sedated as usual, is reclining in bed in the afternoon, reading *The New York Post*. Maybe she has already put the paper aside and started dozing off when she hears a sound at the window, slowly gets up, and pulls up the shade with a *snap!* I can hear it from my bedroom next door.

A pair of eyes—no more than two inches away from hers—is looking right at her. A cat burglar! Both of them startle, she cries out, I hear a yelp, and he runs away as I come running in, asking, "What happened, what happened?"

That night over dinner at the kitchen table, my mom recounts the attempted break-in to my dad and sister, with me piping in intermittently. "Can you imagine the look on the burglar's face," my dad says, "when the shade rolled up and he saw your mothuh's face? Who d'ya think was more scared, your mothuh or the burglar?" He lets out a cackle. My sister and I laugh along with him as my mother smiles nervously through her pursed pink lips.

My mother had gone from having the curvy figure of a Fifties starlet to the dumpy, matronly look of middle age. The drugs she took for schizophrenia made her gain weight and slowed her down. Sometimes I wondered how she had the energy to get dressed, to shop and cook us dinner. Her broad Polish face kept getting rounder and her large nose only more prominent. Her eyes seemed to recede and shrink inside their sockets. She never wore glasses but I often wondered what she saw.

Now I sit here wincing at my dad's cruelty—and my own and my sister's—toward my mom. He must have resented her for how unattractive she had become. I have no recollection of feeling hurt or ashamed for my mother's sake at the time. I needed my dad too much when I was growing up and could not afford to be angry at him. He was too lively, too charismatic, too *normal* for me to risk losing him. I had to laugh along. I loved him too much to judge him.

♦

I spent my teen years talking on the telephone with my girlfriends for hours. My sister had gone away to nursing school while I was still in high school, so I finally had some privacy. I dreamt of getting a Princess phone in baby blue. My parents couldn't afford a Princess, but eventually I did get a corded extension in my bedroom.

I am reclining on my bed, one leg bent akimbo over the other, chatting away with a friend, when I hear a rapping on the side door to our apartment. Our dog MacDuff, a Bedlington terrier, starts barking and I come out of my bedroom to stand at one end of the kitchen. It is rare for us to have an evening visitor.

Our next-door neighbor, who has the strange mother with the bottom of her face missing, is standing at the entrance to our kitchen with a redheaded teenage boy about my age in front of him. I see that the boy is shaking. "I caught this boy peeping in your back window. What do you want me to do with him?"

As I move closer to the doorway, I see that our neighbor, wearing a red plaid hunting jacket, has the barrel of a shotgun prodding the boy's back. I have never seen a shotgun before. I stand there, transfixed. The boy, tall and freckled, looks into my father's face, trembling, silently pleading for his life.

"Shoot'im!" my father says.

"No, please," the boy cries out.

"Get lost," my neighbor says as he lowers the gun. "And if I ever see you around here again, I won't hesitate to use this."

The boy gives him a quick nod and runs off.

Afterwards, it occurred to me that our neighbor was probably talking about *my* bedroom, which had one window facing Glenwood Road and one facing our backyard—both easily accessible from the street. A stranger could have hopped over the low-lying bushes and stood at the windowsill and peered in. Or else opened the unlocked gate to the backyard, stood next to the air conditioner, and searched for a chink of light between the window shade and sash to peer in at me. Which was probably where my neighbor caught the boy, since our backyard faced the side of his house.

The incident left me with the unsettling feeling that I was always in danger of being watched by a stranger through a crack in my bedroom window. I might not realize it but someone could be peering in at me any time the lights were on. It felt like a threatening intrusion—one more thing out of my control. Some guy getting the better of me by spying on me unawares. So I lived as though it might always be happening— always a little uneasy, wondering if I was being watched.

Is that why I have always been fascinated by *Rear Window*? Because it puts at its center the issue of voyeurism, something I lived in fear of all the time: that I could become the unwitting object of some hidden male gaze?

As a girl, and then a young teenager, watching *Rear Window*, I was captivated by the myriad possibilities that exist for women across from Jeff's window: The single woman artist who sculpts a figure with a hole in the middle and calls it *Hunger*. Miss Torso the ballet dancer, with her many admirers. The new bride who has such a voracious sexual appetite, she keeps summoning her husband from the window back to bed with a wail from within: "Haaaaaarry . . ." The bedridden wife of the traveling salesman Thorwald. "Miss Lonelyhearts," who fails miserably at getting a boyfriend until the end, when she is so inspired by the composer's music that she stops herself from ending it all with a bunch of pills. The middle-aged frowzy blonde woman who sleeps on the fire escape with her husband, and who owns the dog that Thorwald eventually strangles to death.

There is also Jeff's frustrated girlfriend Lisa Fremont, who became for this blonde girl watching on her TV set in Brooklyn the paragon of beauty and class. An unattainable ideal.

>Lisa: How far does a girl have to go before you'll notice her?
>Jeff: Well, if she's pretty enough, she doesn't have to go anywhere. She just has to be.

This exchange happens when Lisa is in his arms on the second night. The viewers know, as does Lisa, that she has to do more than just be pretty. The only time Jeff notices her is when she does something risky, like digging in the garden across the way to find something suspicious. She has Jeff's rapt attention when she boldly climbs up the fire escape and enters the bedroom where they both believe Mrs. Thorwald has been murdered.

Lisa has to become an object for Jeff's voyeuristic pleasure, which requires distance coupled with danger. He can *look* at her with love and desire only after she has risked her life for him. Thorwald returns, finds her in the apartment, and a physical struggle ensues that might have ended in her being strangled to death if the cops had not rushed in to intercede. Lisa has to become, symbolically, Thorwald's surrogate wife, even to the point of wearing his dead wife's wedding ring and flaunting it to Jeff across the way, which tips off Thorwald as to where Jeff lives.

♦

On the first night Lisa visits, while she is in the kitchen, Jeff looks out his window to watch the red-headed middle-aged woman he has dubbed Miss Lonelyhearts. He sees she is all dolled up in an apple-green dress and is pantomiming a dinner date with an invisible male guest: first lighting two candles, then opening up the door to pretend-greet him. When she sits down and toasts her invisible suitor with a glass of wine, Jeff raises his glass to her, sight unseen across the way, and toasts her back, right before she collapses in sobs, unable to keep up the act.

On the third night, after applying a great deal of lipstick and drinking a few shots of whiskey, Miss Lonelyhearts, this time wearing an emerald-green sateen dress, goes out to a local restaurant visible from Jeff's window and returns with a man. Jeff's reaction: "Eh . . . He's kinda young, isn't he?"

Which immediately makes me think of the age difference between Jeff and Lisa. When the movie opens and we see Jeffries removing his shirt for a back-rub from Stella, I can't help noticing his scrawny, untoned, middle-aged chest. In 1954, when the movie was released, James Stewart was forty-six, Grace Kelly twenty-five. *Eh . . . He's kinda old, isn't he?* Old enough to be her father. Judith Evelyn (Miss Lonelyhearts) is forty-five, almost exactly Jimmy Stewart's age at the time. When Jeff raises his glass to Miss Lonelyhearts in an invisible toast, he is tacitly acknowledging his sympathy for, though not his identification with, her. Even to this day, an audience takes for granted that Jeff and Lisa are the more suitable match.

♦

In *Rear Window*, Jeffries wrestles with the issue of *rear-window ethics*, as his girlfriend Lisa calls it. In writing this memoir, especially as I move on to episodes in my adult life, how closely do I hew to the truth—the truth as I remember having experienced it?

If the ethical question Jeffries has to wrestle with is his voyeurism, then the ethical question I have to wrestle with is: How do I record the movie of my life—a constantly shifting movie that changes with each projection—without causing damage? Is that even possible? How do I continue to allow others to see into the strange rooms I have visited or inhabited, especially as I move closer to the present? Isn't the stuff of memoir *pretty private stuff*, as Jeffries says? While memoirs and their readers assume creative reconstruction, I like to think there is more than a kernel of truth in what I write.

◆

As a divorced, middle-aged woman, I find myself caught in the hamster wheel of online dating, where male privilege in choosing much younger women still persists. Once, a composer who was close to twenty years my senior contacted me on a dating site. Acknowledging he was out of my preferred age range, he clearly felt he was a suitable match for me. In our email exchange and then on the phone, he impressed me as articulate, charming, and psychologically astute. He read *The New York Review of Books*, he even read poetry. So I agreed to meet him at a movie theater in lower Manhattan. When I approached, I saw a short, fat, bald guy. Not even close to Jimmy Stewart at that age. I ignored my crestfallen heart and did not walk away, at least not for several months.

For the sake of rear-window ethics, I am calling this composer Joel. He had such a protruding belly, it felt like I was reaching over a large workout balloon to find his lips. And since he was impotent (even with drugs), what he liked to do was watch. I would head downtown to his loft in Tribeca. He had partitioned off a section where he did his composing; on the other side of the room was a platform bed with a tufted white comforter. He put on a few dim red lights and then took out of a closet something I had never seen before: his Hitachi, otherwise known as the Magic Wand Massager. The largest vibrator (larger than a free weight) I had ever seen, it needed to be plugged in to an electrical outlet.

I am sure there are some women who (as the many plaudits on Amazon attest) had never had a truly magnificent orgasm until they encountered this erotic barbell. Joel reassured me over and over again that this would be the most intense orgasm I had ever experienced. That one of his girlfriends, who had never had an orgasm in her entire life, found ecstasy under this gigantic, vibrating wand.

I am a good sport. We tried it on low, we tried it on high. It felt like I was taking a large motor, a blender without the blades, switching it on to a very high speed, and putting it up against the most delicate part of my body. I feared it might singe off my clitoris.

◆

Thorwald the traveling salesman and his bed-ridden wife. Something keeps me coming back to them. My father Irving was a traveling salesman and my mother Selma was practically bedridden. I have seen *Rear Window* a dozen times over the last forty years. How could I not have made this connection before?

No matter that Mrs. Thorwald (Irene Winston) looks svelte, much younger, and more beautiful in her white chemise than my mother looked at night in her cotton shift nightgowns. No matter that Thorwald (Raymond Burr) is much less handsome—a bespectacled, heavy, lumbering figure with a full shock of gray hair—than my sprightly, slim, dark-haired, blue-eyed dad.

"Always a smile, always a grin; that's how Irving keeps in trim." My dad often repeated this jingle about himself published in his 1941 high school yearbook.

I am compelled to rewatch the night of the murder in *Rear Window*. This time I notice more details from the vantage point of Jeff's binoculars. In one quick shot, Thorwald is wiping down the inside of his metal sample case and replacing the costume jewelry that he sells wholesale. They look like rhinestone necklaces. I have never paid such close attention before.

When I was a child, my dad sold shoe ornaments. After he'd been away on a sales trip, he would come home, open up his black sample case, and pull out a tray of rhinestone clip-on shoe buckles. Underneath, he always hid small gifts for me to find, such as real Mexican jumping beans. I had no idea there were little worms (moth larvae) inside that made them move.

Rhinestones for women. Two salesmen with their cases of fake glitter, their practically bedridden wives.

In watching *Rear Window* and thinking about my life, I have come to see the relationship between Thorwald and his wife as a darker version of my own parents'. Is it this, and not just the physical and social setting, that has always made this movie feel so uncannily familiar to me? Now I have to wonder how far the similarities go.

Memory is not a static thing. I know I construct it anew each time I remember my past. Several years ago, when I began thinking about *Rear Window* and my life, I wrote a poem containing these lines:

> and memory—that porous
> dream we wake to find is tru[e]
> ly changing? how trust the details
> when they shift
> their tales?

If I were not viewing my parents' marriage through the lens of *Rear Window*, I might not be remembering the same things. But here I am. I must have wanted to do this kind of dreamwork for a reason. When I decided to rewatch *Rear Window* while thinking about my adolescence and my parents, I must have wanted—and felt ready—to face the possibility that my father may have had affairs.

Should I have looked away instead of becoming like Jeff and looking through the window into my parents' bedroom, then into my father's motel bedroom? What are my rear-window ethics when it comes to spying, at least in memory, on my own parents? Perhaps it is only with *Rear Window* as a screen that I am able, finally, to face the unfaceable.

Did my father resent my mother for being schizophrenic, for being lumpish and bedridden so much of the time? Surely there must have been moments when he was so exasperated by her illness, and by her inability to work as he struggled to hold down a job, that he thought of leaving her. And surely a man as lively and handsome as my father must have had no trouble attracting women while he was on the road. Something I never allowed myself to contemplate. Perhaps his ability to take these periodic respites was how he managed to stay in the marriage as long as he did.

♦

For the last five months of my dad's life, I used to visit him in a nursing home in Cherry Hill, New Jersey, after a debilitating stroke left him partially paralyzed and unable to speak. Every week, I caught the Bolt Bus from midtown Manhattan to Philadelphia, which stopped at Cherry Hill. I would glance up at the Tick Tock Diner on the corner of 34th Street and Eighth Avenue, with its huge clock on the marquee, which always seemed to be warning me that time was running out. Helen, my father's domestic partner of over twenty years, would pick me up at the highway bus stop. We would have a quick sushi lunch and then she would drive me over to the nursing home, a plan I agreed to because, as a New Yorker, I hold a driver's license but have never owned a car.

My father had developed an ugly temper after his stroke—not an unusual thing and often caused by brain damage. The stroke was brought on by two surgeries in quick succession to remove tumors from his bladder. He had had to stop taking his blood thinner before surgery. Afterwards, the Coumadin had not built up sufficiently in his body when he fell out of bed early one morning in October 2010 with a massive ischemic stroke.

Along with paralysis on his right side, he had trouble speaking. He uttered what at first sounded like gibberish, but he seemed to understand what I said to him and, with great difficulty, I could often more or less decode what he was trying to say to me. His girlfriend Helen refused to make the effort, and had developed a habit of mouthing back at him whatever syllables he uttered if she did not understand him, which was most of the time. And it enraged him.

"Phphbhslbiph," he would say.

"Phphbhslbiph," she'd parrot back from her chair, a few feet away.

Usually he would begin to hurl curses at her: "Geh the fuck outta here!!" That sentence was clear, even to her. His ugly rage would rattle her and she would get up and walk out. I knew she would retaliate by not visiting him for a while. Though I tried several times, there never seemed to be a way to get through to her that she was provoking him by mocking him with her mimicry. She preferred to play the victim rather than admit to being the tormentor.

◆

What possessed me to try and comfort Helen on one of the days when my dad had lost his temper with her? Maybe she seemed unusually unnerved by his outburst. I wanted to remind her that up until then, he had always been good to her. She'd had a bad marriage previously, having been cheated on by her husband for over ten years, and she and my dad had lived together for over twenty years. In the past, I remembered her chuckling and referring to herself as my dad's common-law wife.

I had spent enough time with them before my dad fell ill to see that Helen had a bad temper and went splenetic over the smallest thing. Once, we were in the car when my dad realized he had forgotten to take his pills along with him. We had driven no more than a few blocks when he realized it and told her they had to turn back. "Irv! What's the matter with you?! Are you stupid or something?! Can't you remember the simplest thing?" She was livid as she turned around and drove us back home. My dad said nothing. And I, too, sat in the back seat, shocked, thinking it was not my place to interfere.

◆

On the day when my dad's outburst has rattled Helen, I turn to her as we are leaving the nursing home.

"You know my dad has always been good to you. He's always been faithful to you."

"Well, he wasn't faithful to your mother!"

Now I am the one who is too unnerved to speak.

On the bus ride home, I kept asking myself, *What made Helen have such an outburst with me? Why would she reveal something so personal about my father to his daughter?* Helen was displacing her rage at my father onto me. She was furious at him for being sick, for becoming a burden to her even before his stroke. He had lost most of his eyesight and depended on her even to pour him a glass of milk. I think she resented the obligation to visit him, which she more and more avoided, though she was retired and lived a ten-minute drive away from the nursing home. By the last few months of my dad's life, she sometimes visited him just once a week, the time I traveled out by bus from Manhattan.

How could I continue to be around Helen when she seemed less and less able—or willing—to control herself around me? Over lunch one day, she began launching into another episode from my dad's past. "I don't want to hear about it," I said. But she continued, blurting out something about my father smoking pot and going up to a woman's room. I rose from the table and went to the bathroom to get away from her.

Blurting out these secrets seemed to be a way for Helen to lash out at my father. And at my mother, who had been dead for twenty years. And at me, as a stand-in for both my parents.

♦

Helen refused to have my mother's favorite oil painting, one of the few possessions my father had hung on to, anywhere but in the garage. I always found this behavior a bit peculiar and vindictive. As though, even dead, my mother posed a threat to Helen. Each time I visited my father (before his stroke) and we pulled into the garage in her car, I would see it sitting there, slowly deteriorating, exposed to the extremes of heat and cold, the paint beginning to blister and flake. "You know you're ruining this oil painting. Even if you don't want to hang it up, at least keep it inside." At which point my dad agreed—or, rather, Helen, who owned the house she and my dad lived in and who apparently made all the rules, allowed the detested painting to shelter indoors, on my dad's side of the study, on the floor.

I grew up with this oil painting in our home. It hung in our living room, in its antique gold frame, next to the baby grand piano and the torchière floor lamp that is now in my living room—a lamp with a marble base, whose warm light shed a creamy glow over everything.

The painting always reminds me of the Mona Lisa: a dark portrait of a woman with long brown hair, dreamily gazing off to the side. She is wearing a Renaissance-looking décolleté dress with a deep, wine-colored shawl spilling over her arms into her lap, while her right hand gestures at a book she holds open in her left hand. This painting, with its darkened patina from age or varnish, must have remained a symbol to my mom of her middle-class ideal of romance and elegance. Perhaps the painting reminded my father of his own idealized, romantic image of my mother from when they were newly married. Once my dad was in the nursing home, I asked to take the painting home with me, and now it hangs in my living room, redolent of my mother and my father's love for her.

♦

Once you know something, especially something upsetting, it is impossible to *unknow* it. For many months, I remained distressed over the things Helen had told me. I would rather never have known of my dad's infidelities while he was on the road.

Now that I do know, it seems patently obvious. My father was youthful-looking, lively, and sexual and he was living with a wife who had sunken into a drugged somnolence, gained a lot of weight, and grown markedly less attractive. I know they did occasionally have sex. When I was a teenager, I would hear my dad get up and close their bedroom door firmly and lock it—a rarity. How responsive could she have been in bed? A question I am too embarrassed to contemplate further.

Would it have been better if he had left her sooner? As my dad said, "I was a good Jewish husband and fathuh. I loved you all too much."

I think my mother was too drugged up to suspect my father of anything and I suspect he limited his affairs to when he was on the road.

♦

My father did eventually leave my mother. I have to backtrack here and remember it was only after my mother broke her leg that she began the downward spiral that made it impossible for my dad to continue living with her. Like Jeff in *Rear Window*, my mom had broken her leg! Not while out in the field risking her life for a photograph, but while sitting in the back seat of my brother-in-law's car.

In the early 1980s, my sister Marla and her husband Paul lived in a house on an oil storage reserve where he worked as an engineer, in a tiny town called Piney Point, Maryland. With my parents in the back seat, Paul was driving them and my sister out of the compound for his birthday dinner. He must have been going a bit too fast to notice a satellite dish that had bounced off the back of a pickup truck and was lying in the middle of the dark road. He hit it, going sixty miles an hour, and my mother was the only one injured. She broke her right leg, was incapacitated, and for the next month lived with my sister, who could take care of her at home while my father went to work.

For the previous five years, my mother had managed to live without taking any medication. I remember talking to my father on one of my visits home from college. My mother had been a zombie for too many years. Perhaps she could go off—or reduce—her drugs and see a therapist with him instead. He agreed. Remarkably, she took herself off her medications (Stelazine and Thorazine) cold turkey and with no immediate ill effects.

After the accident, the fragile equilibrium of my mom's mental state without medication collapsed. She went into shock, lost a lot of weight. Became utterly helpless. I visited my mom at my sister's and watched my sister wash Mom's hair and cook for her while she lay on the couch all day. Finally, my sister had had enough and insisted my dad take her home.

♦

What is wrong with Thorwald's wife? We never really learn why she is bedridden and her husband has to bring her meals to her in bed. We catch a glimpse of her for a few moments in the opening half-hour of *Rear Window*, but she does not look ill. We first see her with a wet towel over her forehead, but it has been a hot day, about 94 degrees by Jeff's thermometer. A slender brunette with a tan, she wears a sexy white one-piece gown with a plunging neckline.

When Thorwald brings her dinner on a tray at night, we hear her mutter, "Well I hope they're cooked this time," as she sits up in bed. He fluffs up a pillow and places it behind her back for support. Then he kisses her hair. She looks at him, then dismissively takes the flower in a bud vase on the tray and flings it away. He retrieves it. He goes back into the living room and begins dialing the telephone as he pours himself a quick glass of whiskey. When she hears him making a phone call in the living room, she is nimble enough to remove the tray, slide off the bed, and tiptoe to the doorway to listen in. "Who was that?" she asks. She walks backwards, perhaps accusing him of an infidelity he thought he had kept hidden, as he hangs up the phone and lumbers threateningly in her direction. She continues bitterly taunting him, laughing openly at him, as she sits back down, elegantly and disdainfully, on the edge of the bed. He hunches toward her, then flaps his wrist dismissively at her and walks out. And she hangs her head on her wrist in mild despair.

In the mid-Fifties, doctors might have diagnosed her condition as neurasthenia, another way of saying she was easily fatigued, depressed, and listless, which is why she has taken to her bed. As to which came first—her husband's philandering or her neurasthenia—the movie is silent.

♦

My mother's mental condition, especially after her broken leg, was far more serious. Unmedicated for schizophrenia, she deteriorated to the point where she could barely function—what psychiatrists label *decompensation*. Now my father had to assume all of the household chores—the shopping, the cooking, the cleaning—as well as working full time as a traveling salesman. When he went out of town, he loaded the refrigerator with prepared foods that she could heat up easily in the microwave. He had been with my mother for over thirty years. For almost all of those years, she had been ill. His own ability to cope was wearing thin.

♦

It is 1982. Twenty-six years old, a graduate student at Cornell, I return to Brooklyn for winter break and am staying at Grandma Rose's house in Manhattan Beach, the same house we used to visit every Sunday during my childhood. My parents have driven up from their home in Seabrook, Maryland for a few days, and they are staying in the upstairs bedroom my mother and aunt shared in their youth. I have to sleep in my Uncle Jay's tiny corner room next to theirs. Nothing has changed since he left home, married, and then died of kidney failure when he was a twenty-nine-year-old lawyer in 1960. It feels too morbid to sleep in his old dusty bed, so I take a pillow and lay some blankets down and sleep on the threadbare gray carpet.

New Year's Eve. My friends have invited me to stay over in their studio apartment on West End Avenue in Manhattan after a late-night party. I call Brooklyn late the next morning to wish everyone a Happy New Year. My grandmother answers the phone in her usual deadpan.

"Hello? Sharon? Here. I'll put cha' mother on the phone. She wants to talk to you."

"Hello Sharon? Your fathuh left this morning and drove back to Maryland without me."

"What? What are you talking about, what happened last night?"

"Nothing. We were all sitting around. We ordered in Chinese food for dinnuh. Everything was fine. We watched a little TV, saw the ball drop at midnight. Then this morning he got up from the kitchen table, he said he was packing up and he left me here."

"What? What do you mean he packed up?"

"Yeah. He just drove away. He went back to Maryland. He left me here, Sharon."

She sounds shell-shocked. He has never done anything like this before. We both know he is not coming back for her. *Now, am I going to be the one who has to take care of my mother?*

I call my dad later that day to hear his version of the story.

"I spoke to Grandma Rose at breakfast, you know how cheap she is, and I told huh, 'Listen, Rose. Your daughtuh Selma needs help. She needs to see a psychiatrist, she needs therapy. And I need help paying for it all.' And you know what she said to me? 'No. I won't do it!' Her own daughtuh! Look, Sharon, I've taken care of yuh mothuh for over thirty years and no one—you know what I'm talkin' about—has lifted a finguh to help me. Granpa Sam, if he was alive, he would've helped me. But Rose? She didn't leave me any choice. So I said *you* try taking care of her for a change. I got up and packed my things and drove back to Maryland."

"Did you plan it?"

"Plan it? I didn't plan anything! I just couldn't do it anymore, Sharon, after thirty-some-odd years."

On the phone with my aunt, I tell her my dad's side of the story. "Then why did he bring such a large suitcase for huh clothes if they were only coming up for a few days?" I have no answer. At the time, I believe what my dad told me: that his actions were not premeditated.

♦

Now I am beginning to have my doubts, as I rewatch *Rear Window* and focus on the shot we see through Jeff's binoculars of Thorwald tying up with rope a large trunk that probably holds all his wife's clothing. Thorwald's alibi is that he has put his wife on a train to visit her mother in the country.

I picture the chocolate-brown vinyl suitcase my dad brought to Brooklyn with my mom's clothes inside. Larger than a carry-on, I see it open on one of the beds in my mom's old room. It has a powder-blue, satin lining and is full to brimming with my mom's clothes. Perhaps the idea of leaving my mom at her mother's was half-formed, in the back of my father's mind, in case things did not go the way he wanted when he asked his suspicious, withholding mother-in-law for money.

As a traveling salesman, my dad could not afford to pay for the medical care my mother required. My grandmother's refusal was just one more of her many rejections over the years. She never trusted my father, maybe because he was married to her mentally ill daughter. He once told me, "You know early on in our marriage your grandmothuh blamed *me* for your mothuh's breakdowns. She said this once in front of a psychiatrist who told huh, 'That's impossible. You said yourself your daughter Selma had breakdowns before she even met Mr. Dolin.'"

Now I replay the scene I imagine took place in my grandmother's kitchen on New Year's Day. I picture my dad getting up from the kitchen table. He is enraged. "I've taken care of huh for thirty years! You think it's been easy? If you won't help me, then *you* take care of huh now!" Then he charges upstairs to pack his things and storms out of the house, driving back to their place on Good Luck Road.

In one of our many phone calls, he says, "Look, I'm turning sixty, I have a heart condition, I need someone to take care of *me* for a change." Part of me does not blame him and part of me is furious with him for leaving my mother with the woman she hates most: her own mother, who has never been able to accept that she has a schizophrenic daughter. This is one of my dad's regrets as well. I can still hear him giving my mother the third degree as we sit on their bed, watching TV: "Isn't it true? Your mothuh always loved Jason best. And after he died, she gave all her love to your sistuh Fran. You know I'm right." He must have been venting his own pent-up frustration that he was stuck caring for a schizophrenic wife while her own well-to-do parents barely helped him. Since my grandfather's death in 1974, my grandmother had refused to help at all, her way of shifting the blame and the burden for my mom's illness entirely onto my dad.

♦

For the next eight years, my mother hibernated in her own mother's house, deteriorating both physically and mentally, sleeping in the musty upstairs bedroom she had shared as a child with her younger sister. The walls were still covered with the same faded green-flowered wallpaper and her own Lincoln High School class photograph from 1944 still hung on the wall overhead as she slept once more in the twin bed of her youth, with its gray-tasseled bedspread, the worn carpeting on the floor the color of stale red wine. It must have been a depressing return for her. How could she not recall the time when she left this room and this house as a newlywed thirty years before?

No one—not my grandmother, who was nearly eighty, nor my aunt and uncle who lived nearby in Sheepshead Bay—did much to help her. No one forced her to see a psychiatrist or a medical doctor, or at least one that did her any good. She dropped down to about ninety pounds.

I used to visit her, only to witness her steady deterioration, to see the cockroaches running rampant in the kitchen. Once I brought over Combat, but my grandmother refused to put the trays down. The unhappy pair of my mother and her mother reminded me of a scene out of *Grey Gardens*.

Once, my mother brought me upstairs to her room and lifted her blouse to show me her emaciated body. "Look at me, Sharon. There's nothin' left of me." She was all bones, like a refugee from a concentration camp. "I'm afraid tuh even sleep in the bed. There's broken glass on it, don'cha see it, Sharon? And you know my mothuh is putting threads in the soup, she's trying to poison me."

My mother continued to waste away, growing thinner, lying in her childhood bed upstairs most days until my grandmother called her downstairs for a meal. My father had been her whole life, especially once my sister and I left home. By leaving her, my father had, in effect, killed her by killing off the only bit of life that meant anything to her: her life with him.

I think she just lay down for those eight years, waiting to die.

Should I have my mother move in with me? But how could I manage—an adjunct professor and editor, barely cobbling together a living? How could I bring her to live in my rundown fourth-floor walkup in Carroll Gardens? I doubt my mother would have been able to climb the eighty-two steps. I was terrified she would overwhelm me, swallow me up. She was no ordinary mother. How could I know how to deal with a paranoid schizophrenic who hallucinated? It was too much for me to take on. Still, I felt steeped in guilt.

Until my sister Marla, who trained as a psychiatric nurse, decided to act. She rescued Mom from my grandmother's house, brought her to her suburban home outside of Princeton, cleaned her up, and let her stay for a few months.

◆

My mother is sitting in the living room in the center of the huge, plush-velvet, semicircular teal couch, soaking her feet in a basin filled with warm water to soften up her toenails before my brother-in-law Paul cuts them. My mom's toenails are so long—one or two inches, literally—that they curl at the end. The color of ivory piano keys, they look like a witch's toenails. I wonder how she ever fit them into her shoes. It is a sign to me of how much her mind has let her body go. Paul clips each toenail carefully, with great tenderness, until my mom's feet look almost normal again.

◆

After two or three months, my sister Marla calls up to say it is time to have Mom hospitalized.

"Sharon, you have tuh be the heavy."

"Why? Why me?"

"Because she'll listen to you. You've gotta get huh to sign herself in."

My mom has to voluntarily check herself in to the psychiatric ward of the local hospital, since she is not a clear danger to herself or to others.

Perhaps my sister senses my mom trusts me more than her, the self-described *cold fish* who rarely shows her feelings.

With my sister driving, my mom in the passenger seat, and me in the back, we set off, stopping at a local Jersey diner for lunch. Mom complains about her food. What did she order—veal cutlets with a sauce? Then she orders some rice pudding for dessert. She puts down her spoon after a few tastes. "Slop. Real slop," she says, and my sister and I look at each other and laugh because she is right and we are nervous about what we are about to do.

When we get back into the car, I realize my mom still has no idea where we are taking her. Marla has not said a word to her. Maybe she thought she might have trouble getting our mother into the car.

"Where are we going?" Mom finally asks.

I breathe in deeply. "We're taking you to a hospital, Ma, because we think you need help," I say as calmly as I can from the back seat, bracing myself for her reaction, all the while feeling the surge of that roiling mixture of guilt and obligation to get my mother the psychiatric help she needs.

"I don't need any help," she says in her sing-song Brooklyn nasal twang. I am surprised by how little resistance she is putting up. The fight has gone out of her.

"We think you do," I reply and all three of us remain silent until we pull into the hospital parking lot.

"And I promise you, Ma, there won't be any electroshock. No more wires. I promise. They won't do that to you again," I say, as we are getting out of the car, knowing that what frightened her most during past hospitalizations was the ECT. It is what frightened me most when I learned about it: sticking wires and electrodes on someone's head and running electricity through the brain. I know now the treatment for schizophrenics has changed and that ECT is used for intractable depression, not schizophrenia.

"Just let me put on my lipstick," she says in the hospital parking lot. Then she opens her purse and stands, leaning over to look into the car's side mirror, applying her hot-pink lipstick before carefully rubbing her lips together. No matter that her eyes are watering, her face oily and grainy, her hair a greasy mess, and that she is emaciated. In her eyes, with her pink lipstick on she will look presentable for her intake interview, when she will try to act as normal as possible and tell them she has no idea why she is there, why her daughters have taken her there. Yet she will agree, first looking up at me for reassurance, to sign herself in.

♦

At the end of *Rear Window*, Lisa gets her man by first risking her life. In the final scene, we watch her recline, initially with the travel book *Beyond the High Himalayas*, clearly meant to impress Jeff, before she switches to the "Beauty Issue" of *Harper's Bazaar*, while Jeff lies napping in his wheelchair, now with *two* broken legs after being forced out the window in his life-or-death struggle with Thorwald.

I have never felt like Lisa, who speaks and dresses and moves like a former debutante. As for myself, to paraphrase an old cigarette commercial: *You can take this Brooklyn girl out of the working class, but you can't take the working class out of this Brooklyn girl.*

When I hold up my life to *Rear Window*, I find I have not managed to see my way through to a happy ending. Though I live on a high floor in a Manhattan apartment building, someone can still look in on my life. Perhaps this writing serves as an invitation to do just that. Recounting my family's story has become a way of learning to live with the shades up.

At times, I have felt like the woman artist working away on her sculpture. At others, like the young blonde dancer with a flurry of handsome suitors. At still other times, like Miss Lonelyhearts, putting my head down to sob at the invisible man across the table from me. Of course, my story is not over.

PART TWO

Strangers on a Train and the Stalked Woman in Glasses

*I particularly liked the woman who was murdered, you know,
the bitchy wife who worked in a record shop.*

–Alfred Hitchcock

WOMEN IN GLASSES never have it easy in Hitchcock's movies: from Midge, the overlooked former girlfriend of Scottie in *Vertigo* to Miriam the "bitchy wife," as Hitchcock deems her, in *Strangers on a Train* (1951). I always find myself identifying with Hitch's women in glasses.

I have had to wear eyeglasses or contact lenses for most of my life.

When I was in the third grade and saw I could not read the eye chart, I memorized it while waiting my turn for the test. The last thing I wanted was to have to wear glasses. I cheated for two years until it became impossible to see the blackboard, even when I was sitting in the front row. I was taking a math test and the teacher had written the questions on the blackboard for us to copy down. I panicked when I realized I could not read them and had to peek at my neighbor's paper to copy down the questions, terrified I would get caught and be accused of cheating. That night, I had to admit to my parents that I needed eyeglasses.

From age ten, I have had to wear glasses: first pointy-edged ones, then tortoise-shell ovals, then gold wire-rims and finally rimless ones. I cried the day I first got glasses. It was a Sunday and we went from the optometrist's office to my grandparents' house in Manhattan Beach, where we went every Sunday. I knew I looked ugly in them. The next day at school, I hid my face, refusing to look at Richard, the boy I had a crush on, who had also gotten his first pair of eyeglasses over the weekend. My shame felt too great to share.

◆

To Hitch's credit, Guy Haines's estranged, cheating wife Miriam (Laura Elliot) does not look or act like a mousy, bespectacled librarian, circumspect and asexual. This woman in glasses is sexy, has a cool job as a clerk in a record shop, and is having so much fun running around with other men, that she has gotten herself pregnant. She refuses to grant Guy a divorce, now that he is a successful tennis player, and is going to milk him, this woman from "Met-calf," for as much money as she can.

As in *Psycho*, the woman with too much sexual prowess—in this case, a sexually avid and uncontrollable woman (perhaps a Jewish woman, given her Biblical name)—will have to pay with her life.

The psychopath Bruno Antony (Robert Walker) is deluded enough to believe he has talked Guy Haines (Farley Granger) into an agreement that each will do the other man's murder ("criss-cross," as he puts it), though all Guy Haines thinks he has done is humor him. Bruno begins to stalk Miriam, Guy's "bitchy" (read noncompliant) wife, by going to Metcalf and waiting outside the boardinghouse where she lives until she runs out with a guy on each arm, headed on a bus to Leeland Lake for a nighttime carnival. Licking her vanilla ice cream cone and talking salaciously about her cravings, she spots Bruno, standing conspicuously a few yards away, smoking a cigarette.

"Hey, are we gonna go to the Tunnel of Love?" Miriam asks her two male companions. As they set off, Miriam looks back to see Bruno following them. That look. Her pleasure in being pursued by a stranger, while she has a man in tow on either arm. The voracious woman who eats so much, one of the guys can't figure out where she puts it all.

When it is time to "Strike a Rail" with a hammer to win a Kewpie doll, only Bruno can make the bell ring. Right before he does, he looks down at his hands, the same ones his mother had just finished manicuring for him, the ones that will soon strangle Miriam. Now Miriam is watching Bruno and he looks at her, raising his eyebrows with a silent look of recognition, showing off his prowess for her. Or so it appears. He does not take a Kewpie doll. She will be the doll he takes.

There is something mythical in the way Miriam looks back, reminding me of the way looking back is often connected with death. When Orpheus looks back at Eurydice as they are both climbing up out of the underworld, he loses her forever. Lot's wife looks back while she is fleeing Sodom and is turned into a pillar of salt. When Bruno follows the threesome to the isle, he jumps into a boat called Pluto, named after the god of the underworld. His intent is clear.

The whole time Miriam is flattered by Bruno's attentions, thinking he desires her. She thinks *her* look is the lure, not realizing that she is misseeing, that her glasses are no help, that *his* look is the lure. The woman in glasses might as well have been blind.

When Miriam's boat enters the tunnel, we hear her frightening screams. Now we are the ones who cannot see, and we might assume the worst—that she has been killed while in the tunnel. Instead, it is as if her death cry precedes her actual murder, when she will be strangled and unable to scream. They all emerge from the tunnel as Miriam is wrestling and resisting the advances of one of her nameless male companions, with Bruno's boat right behind them. When they all get out at the shore, Miriam plays at running away from the two guys she is with, who momentarily lose her and call out for her, as she turns and runs toward the camera, toward the one who is watching her: Bruno. He flicks on the lighter he borrowed from Guy on the train, illuminating her face: the flame twinned and reflected in her glasses, he asks, "Is your name Miriam?" She barely has time to respond with a breathless "Why, yes . . ." before his hands are around her throat.

We watch her strangulation reflected in one of the lenses of Miriam's fallen, broken eyeglasses on the grass. Her failure to see the deadly intentions of this stranger gets her killed—an act that is reflected in the lens by which her vision should have been corrected. Then Bruno takes the smashed eyeglasses and gives them to Guy as proof that he, Bruno, has murdered her.

◆

Since my late teens, I have worn contact lenses. Even when I am wearing them, I still feel like I am the one in glasses: the studious one, the unglamorous one, the vulnerable one. The one who is trying to see, but somehow failing to see, before it is too late.

It was the fall of 1978. After college, I lived for several months with my grandmother in Manhattan Beach. I had a job as an editorial assistant at a small publishing house specializing in genre books: westerns, mysteries, romance novels, all the categories of books I never read. Some nights I stayed out late, past midnight, in Manhattan.

I considered it safer to take the D train to Sheepshead Bay and grab a bus from there than to go to Brighton Beach, which was lonely and had become somewhat dangerous after nightfall. Some blamed the crime on the wave of Russian immigrants, those with mob connections. This was also the late Seventies, when New York City was a dangerous place. When I did walk down Brighton Beach Road in the early evening after work, one of the few young women on the street, men in cars would occasionally stop and try to proposition me, assuming I must be a streetwalker. The smell of crime was in the air.

On some nights, I grew impatient waiting for the bus and chose to walk home: down Sheepshead Bay Road, which was well lit, to where the road dead-ends into Emmons Avenue, then across the wooden footbridge to the other side of the bay, where I would walk the lonely two-and-a-half blocks to my grandmother's house on Dover Street.

♦

On one of these nights when I have decided to walk home, I step onto the gray wooden footbridge and begin walking across it, the streetlights on either side of the bay and the lights of the swaying fishing boats reflected on the moving, darkened water. It must be around one a.m. I am the only one on the bridge. I continue across, feeling a bit anxious because there is no one in sight. It always surprises me how desolate some neighborhoods in Brooklyn can be at night compared to Manhattan. As I draw close to the far side of the bridge leading into Manhattan Beach, I spot a man in an unmarked van slowly cruising east on Shore Boulevard, the street that hugs the side of the bay where I am heading. He turns his head, notices me, then slows down and turns the van around. *Uh-oh. This is a very bad sign. Is he after me?* What can I do but go forward? I turn around: it looks just as lonely and deserted if I head back toward Sheepshead Bay. And this guy can just as easily drive his van around and catch up with me on the other side. *I'm trapped. All I can do is run.*

I start running as fast as I can, jogging left to Dover Street, which is one block west, praying I will reach the house door and get inside before the van catches up to me. I am racing on panic followed by the adrenaline rush that pushes me to run faster and faster down these ghostly blocks of single-family homes.

What's gonna happen to me if this man catches up with me? What if he grabs me and pulls me into his van? If I scream, will anyone hear me on these deserted streets? Or come out in time to help me?

I keep going, flying as fast as I can. I choose to run down this one-way street going the wrong way so if the man in the van is still chasing me, he will have to ride down a different street and decide how many blocks to go before cutting over to ride back up. That is, if he chooses to obey traffic signs. I am counting on that.

Without catching sight of the van again, I reach my grandmother's house and race up the two steps to the side door. Put the key in the lock and I am home. Slam-close the heavy gray wooden door and slide the deadbolt in place. I have managed to escape from who knows what bodily harm. I will never know if the man in the van was chasing after me, but why else would he turn his van around so suddenly after seeing me? I vow never to walk home from the subway at night again. I also make a promise to myself to find my own apartment by New Year's. My grandmother remains sound asleep upstairs.

◆

In *Strangers on a Train*, there are two women in glasses: Guy's wife Miriam, who fails to see Bruno for the demonic, calculating killer he is, and Guy's girlfriend's kid sister Barbara, nicknamed Babs (played by Hitch's daughter Patricia Hitchcock). With her glasses on, Babs sees what others initially miss. Here is a study in contrasts.

At the cocktail party her father the senator throws, Bruno shows up and begins flirting with an older society lady named Mrs. Cunningham (Norma Varden) by asking her what she thinks is the best method for committing a murder. It's an irresistible return-to-the-tools-of-the-crime when Bruno holds out his hands and then playacts strangling her at the cocktail party. But he goes a bit too far. The carnival music flares up—in his head, we recognize—and when Bruno is forced to remove his hands from the now blubbering, half-choked Mrs. Cunningham, he faints.

Babs walks away with the stunned realization that Bruno is Miriam's murderer, and that he was briefly hallucinating himself back at the carnival, killing Miriam all over again—his hands around Mrs. Cunningham's neck, his eyes fixed on Babs.

Shaken up, she tells her sister, "He looked at me. His hands were on her throat . . . and he was strangling me."

"How do you mean?"

"He was looking at her first, then looked over at me and he went into a sort of a trance. Oh it was horrible. [She looks down and sobs, then looks up at her sister.] He thought he was murdering me. [Then she removes her glasses and loses her vision.] But why me, why me? What did *I* have to do with it?"

The glasses. Her sister Ann (Ruth Roman), Guy's lover, the clear-sighted one, sees instantly.

◆

From 1986 to 1995 I lived in Carroll Gardens, Brooklyn, then a working-class Italian neighborhood, and for several years I used to take three trains to the Upper East Side to see my therapist. After one such session, I headed for "The Lions"—my name for the main branch of the New York Public Library at Fifth Avenue and 42nd Street, where a pair of distinctive stone lions flank the main steps. Requesting an out-of-print book of criticism about William Carlos Williams that I need for my dissertation research, I had a photocopy made of a particular chapter.

It is a warm day in late May and I step outside the library's main entrance. Before the renovation of Bryant Park, there used to be a small kiosk and several tables and chairs just down the first set of steps on the Fifth Avenue side. I sit down at one of the tables to read.

Then I notice him. Tall and a bit stocky, with medium-length auburn hair and some light freckles on his cheeks. Probably in his thirties. He has gotten himself a beer and chosen a seat at the table catty-corner to mine, where he has a good view of me. This man is a stranger and yet he looks vaguely familiar. I look him over without turning my head or making eye contact. Then it hits me: I saw him on the subway platform this morning. He probably lives in my Brooklyn neighborhood and he must have gotten on the same F train with me.

Though I am careful not to let him see that I have noticed him, my heart begins pounding. What are the odds that he would end up exactly where I am, when I've made so many stops? Something feels terribly wrong. I quickly calculate how many places I have been. He must have spent the whole day following me—from the F train, to the A train, to the 6 train, then waited until I was done with my shrink appointment, then boarded the bus I took to the library. And all along, I was too busy reading to notice him.

Or else he just happens to be at The Lions, having a drink outside at the same time I am. An innocent coincidence.

I am being stalked. I get up and begin to run: down the few remaining steps of the library, across Fifth Avenue. I turn around once to see he has gotten up as well and is moving in my direction. A large, hulking figure. I keep running, I have always been good at outrunning danger, I have done it before. *Should I cry out? Find a cop? Should I continue my day or not?* I am in the middle of midtown on a sunny afternoon with plenty of other people around. *Why not keep going to do my next errand?* I run all the way to the Pan Am World Airways office, where I need to exchange an airplane ticket that someone has sold me (at the time, airline tickets are transferable). I duck inside, figuring if he has managed to follow me, I will be safe anyway inside this office. Time passes as I exchange my ticket. I have lost him.

Theorists of memory make a distinction between "observer memories," in which you view yourself from the outside, and "field memories," in which you see the episode from your own viewpoint, as if you were still participating in it. Of this stalking episode, I have both types of memory. When the stalker sits down at the table, I am inside the memory, re-experiencing it as though it is happening right now. A field memory: I can still see him pouring the beer into his tilted glass, slowly, as though this were the most natural thing for him to be doing. And it is the way he takes his time, the slow confidence of his movements that alarms me most, as though he is contented with how his plan is working out. When I flee across Fifth Avenue, it's an observer memory: I see myself as though from an overhead pan, running across the street and glancing back at his broad steps, like a giant's, striding after me. The memory is so clear that I still feel I could pick him out in a lineup—though with time and age and the tricks of memory, I know this would be unlikely.

How can I be certain he was stalking me? What if his appearance outside the library was a fluke and he chose a table near mine by chance? Or perhaps at that moment he recognized me from the neighborhood and just wanted to chat me up. How does someone know when she is in danger? As a woman, I believe I just knew. I felt it on my skin.

Growing up in Brooklyn, I would often hang out with friends who lived on a dead-end road in Bergen Beach, where lost drivers on their way to the airport often turned up. Several times men beckoned a bunch of us girls over to their car window, pretending to ask for directions while they exposed themselves to us. We soon learned to stop going over to strange cars.

In order to survive in New York City, I had developed my radar for danger, as women must do. I will never know if I was seeing clearly or not when I got up and ran for my life. It was a visceral response. If I were prone to paranoid fantasies, if I saw stalkers everywhere, I might be more skeptical of my reaction. I still believe he was out to get me in some way that I did not want to be gotten. And I was not about to stick around to find out whether he meant to do me harm or not. When he got up just after I did and seemed to be coming after me, hurrying in my direction, that clinched it for me.

Why do I remember this incident after so many years? Perhaps because this memory feels so Hitchcockian, with its iconic setting, the New York Public Library—not unlike Mount Rushmore in *North by Northwest* or San Francisco's Legion of Honor in *Vertigo*. Or like the Jefferson Memorial in *Strangers on a Train*. The British-born Hitchcock loved to film in iconic American settings, as though landmarks might lend their weight to the unfolding personal story. Or perhaps there is something just as American about being stalked or being on the run for one's life as there is about these landmarks.

In *Strangers on a Train*, there is the quick, terrifying moment when Guy is walking in Washington, D.C. with the man who has been assigned to trail him, Leslie Hennessey (Robert Gist), when Guy spots Bruno on one of the top steps of the Jefferson Memorial. It is a long shot, but Bruno's stance, in a suit and hat, with his right arm slightly extended, probably holding a cigarette, is unmistakable to the audience and to Guy, who quickly suggests to Hennessey that they both jump in a cab.

With a Hitchcock lens, I see myself back then, in front of the New York Public Library, as a more-knowing Miriam who was being stalked by a malevolent man. I was not interested in luring a stranger. There have been few times in my life where I felt myself in real physical danger. This was one of them. And I got away.

◆

Bruno stalks Guy throughout much of *Strangers on a Train*, from the time he has strangled Guy's wife and now expects Guy to murder Bruno's father. Like many psychopaths, Bruno is very clever. When Guy is waiting on the tennis field to practice at the club, he spots Bruno in the audience, by scanning the crowd, watching everyone's head turn from one side to the other, following the tennis play. Only one man's head remains fixed, staring at Guy, waiting to catch his eye: Bruno. After the match, when Guy goes upstairs, he finds Bruno laughing and joking in

French with an older couple along with Ann, Guy's girlfriend. He has been able to insinuate himself into this social situation and, initially, to charm people, including Babs, who at first sight views him as an available single man and rushes over to introduce herself.

♦

When I lived in the Bay Area in my early twenties, I went to a party in San Francisco and met a young Frenchman named Marcel. Straight men were such an anomaly back then that it was easy to find him charming in conversation, and so I accepted his invitation to visit him across the Bay in Oakland where he lived.

I take BART from San Francisco to the East Bay one late afternoon to the address in Oakland that he gave me over the phone. He greets me at the door and shows me in. He is thin, with dark straight hair, and he smells strongly of perfumed bath powder, the kind a woman might use. In the afternoon light, he looks very pale, ghostlike. *Has he also powdered his face with it?* He quickly explains to me that he lives with an older woman who happens to be out of town. I do not ask him more because I do not want to know more. I sense he is a kept man who is cheating on his benefactor while she is away. There is something creepy about him now that I did not pick up at the party the week before. I ask to use the bathroom and find the powder there. *A bit odd. It must be the woman's bath powder.*

We sit down at the dining room table and he brings out a bowl of fruit. I glance at the bowl and see a mixture of overripe peaches and bruised apples, the kind of fruit my grandmother might have offered me back in her filthy, roach-ridden house in Brooklyn. This is California, where fresh produce is as easy to come by as a slice of pizza in New York. I start feeling uneasy, a bit queasy, but pretend everything is normal and just say no thank you. Marcel proceeds to tell me a story, a dating story, I suppose apropos of our date.

"I thought you would like this story. There's a woman I have a correspondence with in L.A. for six months. She put a personal ad in the *L.A. Times* looking for a woman. So I decide to answer her and I am calling myself Marie. We've been writing letters and talking on the phone a lot and I am thinking she is falling in love with me. We've never met, of course. Every once in a while, she is asking to me to come up north and visit. And when she calls here, it's happened two times already, I change my voice and I tell her Marie is out of town. It is sad, is it not?"

Why is he telling me this story? And how am I supposed to respond? I do not remember saying much. I begin feeling a sickening mixture of fear and repulsion. I glance down once more at the rotting fruit. I have seen and heard enough. I get up and tell him calmly that I have to return to San Francisco. I can see he understands and he leads me to the door.

Up until now, I have never understood why Marcel felt compelled to tell me his secret and sabotage our meeting. Now I see he probably could not help himself from revealing how perverse he was. The way Bruno could not help himself from talking about murder with Guy on the train, after initially charming him by recognizing him as a tennis star. Or from talking about murder and then almost strangling a woman at the senator's party. If there is something twisted or pathological in a person, it will usually reveal itself soon after the initial display of charm.

What mixture of narcissism, passivity, and subterranean attraction prevented Guy from getting up and leaving the car where he had seated himself with Bruno by chance? Or even after lunch, when Bruno, no matter how persistent, revealed his sick plan for them to do each other's murder: "Now, you think my theory's okay, Guy. You like it." "Sure, Bruno, sure," Guy says, before leaving the train. Why respond this way to a psychopath, who will see it as a sign of encouragement and assent, rather than a case of being "yessed at" in order to get away gracefully? Now I wonder why I lingered as long as I did at Marcel's house. What mixture of passivity and fascination mingled with disgust had, however briefly, gotten the better of me?

♦

Just recently, a female stalker entered my life. I do not know her name—
or even if we have ever met. She called up two of the places where I
teach and demanded to speak to me or to be given my email address.
According to the people who received the call, first she tried to enroll
in my course and then she went on a rant about what a terrible person I
was. Finally, growing more and more upset, she accused me of stealing
her boyfriend of seven years. During her last call, she threatened to slash
my face. I am a bit old for that kind of talk and I never ran in such circles,
even as a teenager, which made the threat feel even scarier.

One night, an anonymous caller—I have to assume it was the same
person—called my home every two minutes, but I never picked up. I
figured out how to block anonymous phone calls altogether. The next
day I called the police and tried to file a report. One of the institutions
where I teach tried to do the same, but because neither of us could supply
a name or phone number or other information that might identify the
caller, the police would do nothing. If she ever shows up where I live or
work, that will be another matter.

The power to make someone paranoid: Perhaps that was all she wanted.
Or to sully my name at my workplace. I was amazed at how easily I began
to feel defensive over something I had not done. It felt crazy-making. For
a few days this stalker succeeded in making me feel paranoid: Looking
behind my back when I walked the dog. Glancing around in fear at the
people in the supermarket. Then I calmed down, reminding myself that
I live in a doorman building. I will have to hope that her inability to get
through to me or wreak much havoc made her go away.

I wrote about this most recent stalking incident and then deleted it, feeling
nervous, superstitious—yes, even paranoid—that I would invite more
stalking from a person who seemed to have stopped. *Paranoia strikes deep
/ Into your life it will creep*, sang Buffalo Springfield, when being paranoid
was part of the anti-war, countercultural movement in the Sixties. In
those same years, I was growing up with a schizophrenic mother who
was overcome with paranoia every time she had a breakdown. Someone
was always out to get her, she was certain. It has taken me many years to

acknowledge and accept that I am not like my mother. That I will never become like her. One of the ways I can continue to mark my difference from her is by putting this recent episode back into my story. I may wear lenses, but I refuse to let paranoia cloud my vision.

Nevertheless, what if being a woman requires me to live life with a modicum of paranoia? What woman doesn't turn around to check, if she suspects she is being followed, and quickly plot a route of escape? Perhaps the term *vigilance*, without the stigma of pathology, is a better way to describe what I believe I was exercising during those stalking incidents. Was I seeing clearly? No one has perfect vision when it comes to detecting danger. When it comes to knowing whom and how much to trust, especially in love: *that* is where my vision has often failed me.

To Catch a Thief
and How I Married One

Hughson: *You know I thought you'd have some defense, some tale of*
hardship: Your mother ran off when you were young,
your father beat you or something.

Robie: *No. I was a member of an American trapeze act in a circus that*
traveled in Europe. It folded and I was stranded.
And so I put my agility to a more rewarding purpose.

WHAT COMPELS ME to rewatch *To Catch a Thief* (1955)—not a Hitchcock thriller so much as a romantic comedy about a retired jewel thief named John Robie (played by a tanned, dashing Cary Grant), and a rich, spoiled, American heiress named Francie (played by Grace Kelly, Hitch's ideal of an aloof, sexy blonde), set against the brilliant Technicolor backdrop of the French Riviera? It must be that the Mediterranean setting, coupled with the idea of thievery as love and love as thievery, conjures up my own love affair with a foreigner and a thief over thirty years ago.

When John Robie first meets Francie and her mother, he appears to be a charming, wealthy stranger, an American it turns out, who introduces himself as Conrad Burns. All four of them (Mrs. Stevens, Francie, Robie, and the insurance detective investigating a string of jewel heists) are having drinks together. Francie sits there silently, coolly, in profile, unamused by the flirtatious banter between Robie and her mother Jessie (Jessie Royce Landis). Jessie *is* suspicious of this American's background, and goes so far as to ask why he has not flirted with her daughter. She asks about his lumber business in Portland, Oregon, the phony life he has invented for the occasion:

"Mr. Burns, would you mind if I had you investigated a little?"
"Not at all. With what object?"
"If I were Francie's age, you'd sound too good to be true."

Why does everyone else trust this debonair liar and seasoned crook who, in the opening scene, sports a navy-blue-and-white-striped shirt and a red bandana around his neck (so faux American in Paris)? Why does the Lloyds of London detective H. H. Hughson (John Williams) believe John Robie (formerly known as "The Cat") is not the current jewel thief, even going so far as to entrust him with catching the copycat jewel thief and, to that end, providing him with a list of potential targets—the first ones being this rich American heiress and her daughter? What powers of suasion this man has. From the first moment, the viewer is never in doubt that Robie is a reformed thief, and that a shrewd copycat is committing the current jewel thefts.

♦

I met Carlo in Bradley's, a small, neighborhood jazz club on University Place in the West Village. My friend Cindy and her boyfriend took me there, partly because they enjoyed the idea of finding me a man. Bradley's was a casual, friendly place with a handful of small tables. Most people stood or sat at the wrap-around bar, holding their drinks, listening to two- or three-piece jazz ensembles and chatting in between sets. Tommy Flanagan may have been on piano with Ron Carter on bass the night I walked in with my friends.

I look over to see an olive-skinned man in his late twenties, about my age, standing at the bar, and I am completely smitten once I overhear him speaking Italian. Somehow, we strike up a conversation. I can be bold, so I may have spoken to him first. "Oh. So you are Italian . . . and Jewish, too!" He nods his head, purses his lips into a coy, boyish smile, and I smile back at him. What a perfect combination of the exotic and the familiar! He has dark eyes behind gold, wire-rimmed glasses, and thick, wavy black hair. I glance down. He is wearing beautiful Italian shoes and tight black jeans and an olive-green leather jacket. Too good to be true.

On our first date, he takes me to El Internacional, an arty tapas bar and restaurant in Tribeca with an elaborate mosaic-covered entrance. Over dinner, he admits he is actually Spanish Catalan and not Italian. "Oh, I am telling to you now my real name is Carlos. In an Italian restaurant it is easier to get work as a waiter and not a busboy if my name is called Carlo. Especially because I speak in Italian." I smile over his awkward English. What he says makes sense and from then on I call him Carlos. He is still European, still Jewish after all, so what does it matter?

♦

Early on in our dating, Carlos said he had to leave town for a few days. At the time I was sharing Cindy's two-bedroom apartment on Prospect Park West in Park Slope, Brooklyn. Mid-week, I found myself returning to Bradley's, one of the few Village bars I felt comfortable visiting alone as a single woman. Walking in, I spotted Carlos sitting in the corner with his back to me, talking to a woman. I slipped out before he could see me. The next time we met I asked him what he was doing in town, why he had lied to me.

"Are you a lady's man? Because something tells me you are."

"What is this? Man's lady? Lady's man? I don't understand."

I knew he understood perfectly, was feigning confusion, but I let it drop.

I was in my late twenties, working at *The Villager*, reviewing theater and handling the arts listings, banging them out on a manual typewriter in the small, East Village storefront. Soon I would move to a part-time job as a copy editor at *The Village Voice*, thanks to my friend Rita who was managing editor. I considered myself to be a poet and I thought I had found the ideal man for me—a Spanish Jew who was training to be a clarinetist, working as a waiter at night and practicing all day. I pictured the two of us together: the artist couple.

♦

Once Francie figures out that the man she has been spending time with is none other than John Robie, The Cat, she experiences a frisson of pleasure at her discovery.

"I've never caught a jewel thief before, it's so stimulating," she says as she brags to Robie about how she figured out his real identity, which he keeps on resisting.

"I can only be myself, Miss Stevens."

"Then *be* yourself, John." She runs with her fantasy, suggesting they plot together to pull off the next heist: stealing the jewels of Lady Kenton, the woman who lives in the mansion Robie has just been surreptitiously casing out with her, pretending he is on a real-estate hunt for a new home. "The Cat has a new kitten. When do we start?" she persists.

The thrill, the romance, the exoticism of being lovers with a famous jewel thief. Now Francie finds Robie so much more appealing than he was as Conrad the Oregon lumberman. There is something so erotic in the exotic: the allure of the Other, the mystery, danger's sexual charge. Especially when one has lived a safe, sheltered life.

Even Francie's mother is elated by the discovery that Robie is a former jewel thief rather than "a simple woodcutter from Oregon," once her own jewels have been stolen and Robie has to come clean about his identity in order to help catch the current thief: "My real name is John Robie. I used to be a jewel thief . . . several years ago." She responds, "Well, what a wonderful surprise!"

♦

Carlos initially told me his father dealt in antiques. Later, he admitted that they were a touring father-and-son acrobatic act—Carlos and Carlitos—and traveled all over Europe performing in circuses. They had lived in Milan for five years, which is how he learned to speak Italian so fluently. He and his father appeared on the Ed Sullivan Show twice: in 1965, when Carlos was a boy of eight, and in 1970, when he was thirteen. I suppose that dealing in antiques seemed more respectable to him than being part of a world-class acrobatic pair. How could he understand that for me, as an American who had grown up watching the Ed Sullivan Show, his having appeared on the show was far more glamorous? If not a famous jewel thief, he was a formerly famous acrobat—more famous, presumably, than Robie had been in his circus days. *Well, what a wonderful surprise.*

Later on, once I got to know Carlos better, he told me that his father used to beat him and slam him into the wall if he made a mistake while rehearsing their acrobatic routine. I understood, then, that there was trauma and little glamor in his memories as an acrobat. Carlos told me his mother fled because his father used to beat her even worse, and that she tried for years to get him away from his father and bring him to Spain, but failed.

♦

Carlos made me Spanish tortilla late at night. When he was not working as a waiter in an Italian restaurant, he practiced his clarinet and took private lessons with a teacher who trained world-class musicians. Carlos complained that he could not practice on a full stomach, so we always ate dinner after he had finished practicing, which often meant after eleven o'clock at night. Practicing meant he sat erect for hours in a straight-backed chair, running his fingers up and down the keys, doing scales. I can still see him fussing with the reeds, licking them, cutting away at them with a pocketknife, and licking them again. The art of the reed, I learned, was as much a part of learning to play the clarinet as how one pursed one's lips to blow a stream of air into the ebony column or how one fingered the steel stops.

The poet and the musician: that element of romantic fantasy continued to shape my view of our relationship. In my notebook at the time I wrote: "this dream I am calling our life together." In another:

> our bodies—the arched bow of
> an instrument the other has become—
> and I have heard you play
> though there were no notes to catch
> and in my breath is a reed
> and in yours are the stops

At making tortilla the traditional Spanish way—with eggs and potatoes baked in the oven—Carlos was an expert. Also, as I slowly began to see, at concocting lies.

Carlos and I met in February. By May, I received word that I had been awarded a Fulbright Scholarship to Italy. I felt anxious about going to Italy alone for a year, even though I had always dreamed of doing so. Now there was Carlos. He offered to take over my room in Cindy's apartment, promising to wait for me to come back from Italy in a year. I didn't believe him. I knew that if he remained in New York while I was away for a year, he would charm some other woman and I would lose him. He had to come with me.

One night in bed, I blurted out: "Hey, why don't we get married?"

"Uh, sure, Teeta." That was his nickname for me.

"Then you can come with me to Italy."

"Okay . . . sure. I guess so."

"You don't sound like you want to."

"Oh no, I do. I just worry to leave the country. I don't have my Green Card. They won't let me back in."

"Don't worry, you're marrying an American. I promise, we'll do whatever it takes to get you one."

No matter how many times I reassured him, I knew he continued to worry about being able to return to New York. I knew it was also his attempt to get out of going with me. He had lived in Italy with his father and it held painful memories. New York had become his safe haven from his past, where he could be anybody: Italian, Spanish, even Jewish, who would know.

We started looking for a synagogue for our marriage ceremony, and found one with beautiful stained glass windows on the Upper East Side of Manhattan. The congregation was Orthodox, but the rabbi was willing to allow us to have the ceremony there. He just needed proof that we were both Jewish. He never questioned me, never asked for any proof. I may have mentioned my mother's maiden name or the Jewish cemetery my grandfather was buried in. From Carlos—a foreigner, a Spaniard—he needed some proof.

"Let me give your mother a call," the rabbi says to Carlos, when we meet with him in his study.

Carlos shakes his head and seems edgy. "No, I'm afraid it is not possible. She is living in Barcelona and has problems with her nerves. I don't want to upset her."

I look at him, feeling puzzled.

"Well, what about her rabbi then? Just give me the number of her rabbi and I'll talk to him. She doesn't even have to know."

Carlos shakes his head again. "No, I am sorry. It will not be possible."

"Well, you'll have to figure out some way of confirming that you're Jewish, at least on your mother's side. Why not go home and think about it, and give me a call when you're ready to. I can't allow you to get married here unless I have proof."

In bed, in the middle of the night, Carlos breaks down.

"Sharon, I have to tell you, I'm really sorry, I'm so so sorry, the reason we can't call my mother, she has no rabbi, I'm not Jewish."

"What? But you told me you were."

"I wanted for you so much to like me and you asked me right away if I was Jewish so I said yes because . . . because you wanted me to be Jewish. And I wanted to be. I promise, if you want, I'll convert. I'll convert right away."

Who was Carlos? Why did I trust a man who had led me to believe he was a charming Italian Jew, when in fact he turned out to be half Spanish and Catholic (on his mother's side) and half Egyptian and Muslim (on his father's side)? Who would lie about such things? Who would pretend to be Jewish?

The will to believe is stronger than anything. Sometimes I wonder if it was the movies I'd watched—on Flatbush Avenue, or propped on my elbows in my parents' bed—that first taught me to suspend disbelief so readily. Or was it just a case of magical thinking: I wanted to believe who Carlos said he was, and so I quickly overlooked anything that threatened to break the spell. I was in love with him, but whom was I in love with? We believe what we want to believe, so I continued to believe that the lies stopped there, that he had peeled off the last mask, his last false self.

When I thought about Carlos back then, I pictured him as a piece of raku pottery, formed by being thrust into a fire of burning straw: beautiful to behold, but with deep cracks on the inside. That was how I saw him: beautiful and damaged by his father's daily beatings. I thought my love could somehow repair those cracks. Unlike the cracks in my schizophrenic mother that I could never do anything about.

When I look back to our initial meeting in Bradley's, I realize Carlos must have been picking up cues from me as to what would please me, and like a cuttlefish that can change its colors and textures to fit into its background, he became the image of what he thought I desired. He must have been practiced in the art of reading people and I fed him all the necessary lines. I recognize that behavior now as something children have to learn early on when they feel unsafe with a parent; he had, after all, grown up with a father who beat him, unless he was making that up as well. I, too, as a child, had to learn to read my mother for subtle changes in her behavior, which might signal the start of a schizophrenic episode in which she might turn irrational or even violent.

Instead of ending things, I felt even closer to Carlos. I saw how he had backed himself into a corner because of his desire to please me. And so I forgave him. I was set on marrying him. I needed to believe there would be no more lies to uncover.

It was already late May and there was no time for Carlos to convert before we left for Italy at the end of August. We found a reformed synagogue, Garfield Temple in Park Slope, and a Reform rabbi who agreed to perform a Jewish ceremony.

A month before our wedding, I attended my college friend Jody's ultra-orthodox wedding at Lincoln Square Synagogue on the Upper West Side. On the stairs, I bumped into Rabbi Meir Fund, with whom I had studied Kabbalah. I told him about my impending marriage, my Fulbright to Italy, and Carlos's bedroom confession that he was not Jewish. "Don't marry him now. Go to Italy. Don't rush things. Give it time. You can marry him when you return," he said.

Now I think back on that sage advice, advice my father should have given me. But would I have listened? I was stubborn, impatient, and eager to marry, since I was turning twenty-nine that summer. And somewhere inside I knew: If I didn't take him with me to Italy, I would lose him.

Why do I have to learn the lesson over and over again: that when I grasp someone too tightly to me, it always fails? Hidden inside the urgency of my tenacious hold is my fear that it is impossible to possess someone and my refusal to recognize that impossibility.

I realize now I am a liar, too. I deliberately lie to myself through willful blindness. How many times have I practiced avoidance, like a child's game of peek-a-boo? If I don't look or probe, the painful thing will disappear. It never does. All I have managed to do is defer the pain, which only increases. When I finally do choose to face what I have been avoiding, I suffer twofold: the pain of my failed avoidance along with the pain of whatever it is I have been avoiding.

◆

To trust or not to trust John Robie, The Cat: that is Francie's question. After she seduces him in her hotel room, knowing full well his identity as a notorious jewel thief, the scene cuts to her asleep on the divan in her white gown and glittering fake diamonds, the open window an invitation to thieves and a portent of what is to come. When she awakens to discover that her mother's valuable jewels have been stolen, she enters Robie's room, where the hall light falls upon him awake in the chair, and accuses him of the crime. "Give them back to me—Mother's jewels!" Enraged, Francie engages in a physical struggle with him, then searches his hotel room and summons the police.

Instead of fleeing, Robie visits Jessie's hotel room to look for evidence, and to reveal to her his true identity. Even then, Jessie doesn't suspect Robie of stealing her jewels. Why would he, after all, return to the scene of the crime? Francie will have none of it, and produces the list she found in his jacket pocket "of everyone on the Riviera with jewels worth stealing," including her and her mother. To Francie, it is incriminating evidence. To her mother, the only thing Robie is guilty of is love. "Since when is love a crime? His name is Robie and for my money he's a real man." Now Jessie is the one who is seduced by Robie's considerable magnetism while Francie, feeling hoodwinked, calls him "a low, worthless thief!"

How does Francie know what to believe and whom to trust? While the viewer is fairly certain Robie is innocent and a reformed thief, how is Francie to know when this suave charmer is telling the truth? Surely there is a thief to catch, but it will take several plot twists before she trusts him and before Robie, with her assistance as well as her mother's and the insurance agent's, is able to catch the copycat thief.

♦

I did not know I needed to catch a thief until I had done so.

Two years into our marriage, when Carlos and I had returned from Bologna and were living in Carroll Gardens in Brooklyn, our relationship began to fray. Working as a book editor in Soho, I had put my dissertation on hold. Carlos was working nights as a waiter and taking clarinet lessons and practicing by day. He had begun conversion lessons with the local rabbi. After several months, he stopped, making vague promises about starting up again.

Carlos had taken to returning home late, often with another friend, Franco, from the restaurant, and the two of them would stay up talking. Often, they both crashed in the living room on the couch and floor. I never liked Franco, with his rheumy eyes and the vulgar way he talked about women. I know he had been trying to convince Carlos to buy a gun. I half-sensed that Carlos was using Franco as a shield to ward off sleeping with me. I said nothing and would fall asleep alone in our bed, hearing their muffled conversation through the flimsy room divider.

Now I see how practiced I had become in the art of self-deception, of looking away at whatever felt too painful to face. It is a kind of sleepwalking, until I am ready to wake up and see what is hidden in plain sight.

In the fall, Carlos tells me he needs to take a trip out West to visit his uncle. This is the first I hear of his having an uncle, let alone any relative, in the States.

"So I'll take some vacation time and come along with you."

"You can't."

"Why not?"

"My uncle is very anti-Semitic."

"Oh."

Carlos leaves for a week, putting all his expenses on my American Express card. When he returns, I ask him about his trip. "First I visited my uncle in Texas. Then I went to California with him. Then we flew to Las Vegas."

I do not allow myself to question or think much about the distances he has traveled or the vagueness of his answers, though he has charged thousands of dollars (I discover later) on my credit card. He has told me his uncle is anti-Semitic and I feel so shamed and wounded by this that I hesitate to question him further. I do not want to know. He has already gotten away with so many lies, why bear down on this one? I am not ready to know.

Perhaps I was enacting some version of my mother's behavior: when my father, the traveling salesman, returned from weeks on the road, she never questioned him. She, of course, was too drugged up to harbor any suspicions (or for paranoia to take hold of her, which might have encouraged suspicions). In my case, I was afraid to know. I needed Carlos and his need for me, so I let the incident drop.

♦

The following spring, I flew out to Los Angeles on a business trip and arranged to fly home from San Francisco, so I could stop off and visit with old friends in the Bay Area. Among them was Jody, my Orthodox friend from college who now lived in Berkeley with her husband and two children. I had always felt ashamed in front of her because I assumed she judged me for marrying someone who was not Jewish. I stayed with her overnight in Berkeley and, once she made clear she was not about to judge me, opened up to her about the strains in my marriage.

"It's not that he wasn't Jewish that bothered me," Jody said. "It was that he lied to you. It made me wonder what kind of father he would be. It made me wonder what else he was capable of."

What else was he capable of? Those words stayed with me on my flight home to New York City. Before I left, Carlos had promised to pick me up at JFK on his motorcycle. He said he wanted to try and make things better between us; we both agreed we needed a fresh start. So where was he? I waited a little while at the airport until I realized he was not going to show up.

◆

When I enter our fourth-floor walk-up apartment, around midnight, no one but our black-and-white tuxedo cat is there to greet me. *Where is Carlos? Didn't he remember he was supposed to pick me up at the airport?*

The answering machine with its lone, blinking red eye glowers at me. This machine is attached to a secondary phone line Carlos had installed because (he said) he wanted to start a catering business. For the first time, I switch it on to hear the messages.
    Beep. "Hi Sweetheart. I miss you. Please call me."
    Beep. "Hi Carlos. The holidays are coming up. I hope I get to see you soon. I love you."

So *this* is his catering business: two intimate messages in the voice of an unknown woman. The clues are left out in plain sight: as soon as I wish to uncover the subterfuge, I can do so almost instantly.

I decide to look through his things. I find his large black notebook, in which he likes to scrawl notes to himself. In one of his recent entries I read: "Una bolsa para Amy. Algo para Sharon." A purse for Amy. Something for Sharon. That says everything. *Is he with her right now?*

Who is Amy? Carlos works nights as a waiter at Lusardi's on the Upper East Side. I know the restaurant is closed by now, so he cannot be there. I decide to check the phone bills. In the 1980s, people still use phone booths on the street. Imagine having to carry around all that change. Instead, Carlos often charges his calls from the street to our home number—an expensive, lazy alternative. Our phone bill lists where he was calling from and the number he was calling. When I scan the bill, I see one number he has called repeatedly after midnight. I jot it down and pick up the phone.

"Hello, Carlos?" a woman's voice quickly breathes.

"Hi."

The woman hangs up.

I dial again. She picks up.

"I'm Carlos's wife," I say quickly.

This time she stays on the line: I have caught her attention. She says nothing, waiting for me to speak. "Are you sleeping with my husband?"

We have a short conversation. She won't say who she is, nor will she respond directly to my questions, but her silence gives me the answers. She stays on the phone because, evidently, she had no idea of my existence, no idea she has been seeing a married man. *Didn't she think it was suspicious that he never brought her to his place?* He probably slept over at her apartment while I was away on my California business trip.

That night I wait up for Carlos, who comes in well past one o'clock, carrying his black-and-red motorcycle helmet.

"Where were you? You were supposed to pick me up at the airport. Why weren't you there? Were you too busy screwing your girlfriend?!"

He is speechless for a moment. "What are you talking about?"

"Get the fuck out of here! Get out!" I push him out the door and lock it.

Three days later, he returns. I open the door. He has not shaved for several days and looks disheveled, so unlike him. I can smell the slightly fetid odor of someone who has not showered for a while. "Oh please, please, Sharon. I've been sleeping all night on the trains with the bums. I have nowhere to go. Please let me in." I feel sorry for him, he is so good at looking pathetic, so I let him back in.

He sits down on our bed and begins to cry. "Now I've lost her. Amy broke up with me the next morning, right after you spoke to her."

I say nothing. *Does he really expect my sympathy?*

"You would like her. She is Jewish like you, very intelligent. She's a lawyer on Wall Street. When she found out about you, she refused to see me. Refused to talk to me after you called her. She hung up on me. I feel like throwing myself out the window."

"Go ahead."

For days, he stays in the house, holding himself hostage there, refusing to leave.

"You remember that time I said I went out West?"

"Yeah, right. To visit your anti-Semitic uncle." It is still a painful subject. "Why are you bringing that up now?"

"Well, I went to a dude ranch with her in Wyoming and I fell off a horse and sprained my wrist. It still aches when I play the clarinet."

"Oh. So *that's* how you spent my money."

Why did I let him back in? Desperate to get him out of the apartment, I call up my landlord, a tall, older Italian man we have always suspected of having Mob connections. He drives over from Bensonhurst and, by the sheer threat of his presence in the doorway, compels Carlos to leave once more, agreeing to pick up his belongings in a few days.

I know there must have been other women. I call another number from the phone bill. This time it is an out-of-town area code: New Orleans. In the background, I hear the screech of parakeets. I ask her if she knows my husband. She says they are friends, nothing more. I hang up, as a wave of nausea comes over me.

I feel as if I am leaning over a very deep well. Though there are probably more women whose voices might throw back an echo if I called out to them, I know I have to pull myself away. That I have heard enough to know I do not need to know more.

"Go through all his things," my friend Alicia, a primal scream therapist, urges me. "You'll probably find more lies there."

I walk over to the clarinet case that still rests on one of the bookcases in the hallway. This is his prized possession: Where else hide something but there? I open it up. How many hours have I watched him spend carving a reed, fitting it onto the clarinet's mouthpiece, and carefully screwing it into position. There each clarinet piece rests, nestled in rich, wine-colored velvet. I look through all the compartments, lift up the velvet lining. Underneath, I find a folded-up sheet of paper. I open it up and recognize at once it is an official document with a seal on it. A New York Certificate of Marriage Registration: "This Is To Certify That . . . Carlos Cabrera . . . and Mary Clifford . . . Were Married . . . on July 18, 1984."

Can this document be real? Could he have married someone else a year before marrying me and never told me about it? I call him up at his friend's where he has been staying.

"Hey. You know what I found? Another marriage certificate! Were you already married to her when you married me?!"

Pause. Silence. "Where did you find it?"

"In your clarinet case. What's it doing in there?"

"It's mine. It's a fake. Put it back," he says in rapid fire.

Or else he says, "It's a fake. It's mine. Put it back."

In whichever order he said them, I am certain that these were the three clipped sentences he spoke to me because when uttered together, they formed a ludicrous contradiction. Finally, his lies were transparent—like those of a panicked little boy. Finally, I had learned it was impossible to believe anything he said. So I hung up, knowing that the next morning I would take the subway to Lower Manhattan to visit the City Clerk's Office and find out the truth.

"I need to know if this is real," I tell the woman behind the dingy gray counter, holding up the paper and pointing to the two names. "That's my husband, but that's not me." The clerk looks at me for a moment, then down at the document. I wonder how strange my question seems to her. Her face remains impassive. At her job, she must have seen everything.

"It looks real to me. Wait here while I go back and check the records." She takes the certificate with her and disappears. After several minutes—

several very long minutes, though I feel fairly certain I already know the answer—she returns and says, "Yep. The marriage is legal and on the books in New York State."

I have married more than a pathological liar, a cheat, and a thief. I have married a bigamist.

I leave the City Clerk's Office, feeling like my life has become unreal—or all too real. Now I am the one who feels like a somnambulist. Lines from Calderón drift into my head:

> What is life? An illusion,
> a shadow, a fiction. . . .
> All life is a dream,
> and dreams are just dreams.

I have been awakened from the dream of my marriage with an official slap. I *thought* Carlos and I were married. I picture those summer days, roughly three years before: How ecstatic I was at finding a vintage lace wedding dress for $30 in a thrift shop near *The Village Voice*, where I was then working. Our Jewish ceremony at the Garfield Temple in Park Slope, and the dancing at the wedding party afterwards. Dancing with Carlos, then dancing with my friend Isaac, who got terribly drunk and went reeling out into the street with a few bottles of vodka that he had emptied. My frail, emaciated mother attended the wedding, as did my father and sister, my aunt and uncle and cousins, and many more relatives and friends. I still have the photographs.

I picture the two of us living in Bologna that fall: the rich winter-squash soups he would make for us; the Spanish tortillas he would bake; the *pizza tre stagioni* we would share, a vegetarian variant on the usual "four seasons"; the small squares of polenta we would buy to eat at home, so we could save money. The two of us taking the overnight train to Genoa, a port city, as we had been advised to do before flying home, so we could get him the Green Card he so desperately wanted. How easy it had been because he was—or so I thought—legally married to me, an American.

I realize it has all been a circus act. He has done a trick with my life, and I have been his unwitting partner and now, his shocked audience.

♦

"Your marriage is not legal. We need to get you an annulment, not a divorce," my lawyer explained when I told her the news.

"He's not Jewish. It's a liaison, not a real marriage, so you don't need a Jewish divorce," my rabbi said.

No one officially considered us married. I was the unsuspecting partner of a sham, a fraudulent marriage, in the eyes of the state and in the eyes of my religion. A pseudo-marriage: that is how I refer to it even to this day, which always raises eyebrows and elicits questions. But it feels closer to the truth than saying simply that I was married.

There were more discoveries. In a crack behind the built-in wardrobe in the small dressing room I used as my study, Carlos had tucked away two original photographs by Robert Frank. So this was how he was spending his cash while I paid our rent and utilities. One photo, from Frank's series *The Americans*, was *Rodeo - Detroit* (1955), a profile of a man in a cowboy hat smoking a cigar with two women beside him; the other one, from his *London* series (1951-52), was of a man in a top hat rounding a corner in the London fog.

I looked around at our barely furnished apartment. We had no rug, not even a real desk for me: I was still using a door laid over two filing cabinets from my graduate school days. My sister and brother-in-law had given us the four Breuer cane chairs for our dining room table. We slept on a futon on the floor. *He was probably planning to take those photographs out of the apartment, maybe when he moved in with this new girlfriend. So then he could have three marriages on the books!*

Then I remembered him telling me his father liked to collect expensive photography equipment, even when they had no money. So Carlos resembled the parent he hated. I took the photographs, stashed them with a friend, and eventually sold them back to the gallery where he had bought them to help pay off my debts, including my lawyer's fee.

While packing up Carlos's things to leave outside the door, I discovered a shabby peacoat of his hanging in the closet, one I had never seen him wear. He much preferred the Italian black-leather bomber he had paid a wad of cash for. This old, navy-blue coat, which had hung in the closet, unworn, since we moved in, was strangely heavy when I lifted it off its hanger. It was weighed down by dozens of silver dollars sewn into the jacket-pocket lining.

Dozens of Lady Liberty heads in profile, like the dozens of women he might have slept with. Had he ever really felt at home with me, if home is where you finally empty your pockets of fear?

I recalled his argument for why we had to leave Italy early: *We'll come home with one hand in front and one hand behind.* To hide our nakedness. To hide his nakedness. That was how he saw himself: always in danger of being exposed, of being thrown out of Eden, naked and destitute.

Here was a man who was so afraid of having nothing that he could never shed the paranoia of an illegal immigrant, a transient, who might be stripped of everything and either deported or jailed. He had to be prepared to flee at any moment with his valuables hidden in his jacket. At least he would have silver with which to bargain for his life.

How sad and futile were my efforts to love him, to make him feel secure. Nothing I had done had changed his core feeling of distrust and fear—first instilled, no doubt, by his father's beatings. Unlike John Robie, another former acrobat, he really did have a history of hardship and trauma that explained, if it did not fully excuse, his life of deception.

Though he owed me several thousand dollars from his trip out West, I left the coins where they were and folded up the coat, putting it with his other clothes and CDs outside the door for him to retrieve. I wanted him to have the CD of Mozart's *Requiem*. A death mass. That's what our marriage felt like and I was throwing it out.

♦

I am writing about this period of my life while visiting Barcelona for the second time. The first time was twenty-eight years ago, with my bigamist-husband. Like *To Catch a Thief*, which is set in Cannes and Monte Carlo, two jewels on the French Riviera, part of my story takes place on the Spanish Mediterranean coast during the winter holidays of my Fulbright year in Bologna. We stayed for two weeks in Barcelona at the apartment of one of Carlos's friends, an American musician in the Barcelona Symphony, and we visited Carlos's mom and her second husband often.

♦

In *To Catch a Thief*, Francie parades through the lobby of the Carlton in glamorous black-and-white beach attire: her hair in a black sheath, she wears a large white sun hat, a black sleeveless catsuit, and an open white linen skirt that parts as she strides. She looks as though she could have stepped out of the pages of *Vogue*. Blonde. Confident in her cool perfection. Poised and assertive, as she was the night before when Robie walked her to her door, and she leaned over, pulling him toward her to give him a lingering kiss, gazing at him with bedroom eyes before closing the door. Francie, the seductress who leaned her "diamond" necklace toward him, coaxing him to steal it—though he immediately knew it was a fake—as the fireworks, like a pulsating sex show, were bursting in the background.

♦

Carlos's mother was that kind of polished beauty, a bleach-blonde with expertly penciled lips and white eyeglasses that swooped up into rhinestoned points. She wore dramatic black eyeliner past the upper edge of each eye, as if preparing to go on stage. She had perfectly manicured fingernails and was confident in her elegance, her sense of fashion. I remember being shocked when I first met her at how white-skinned she was beside her olive-skinned son. Carlos must have resembled his father, whom I never met.

During our visit with her, Maria often complained about her nerves: "Ay, mis nervios," she would sigh. Over dinner, she talked openly about going to her psychoanalyst, an unusual topic in Barcelona in the mid-eighties and perhaps even today. "Ay mis nervios, mis nervios." In our conversations, she told me several times how guilty she always felt over having abandoned her abused son when he was a small boy.

"I tried everything to get him away from his father," she said. "I had to go. His father beat me. I thought he was going to kill me. I couldn't take Carlitos with me, you see, he was on his father's passport. His Egyptian passport. I had my Spanish passport. For years, you must understand, from Spain, I tried everything. Lawyers, but nothing worked. Ay, mis nervios. You see what it has done to me. My health is destroyed. You know Ernesto my husband, my husband now, he wanted I have a child with him, but how can I? How can I have another baby when I left my boy? No one understands. All the time, I was thinking, crying about Carlitos."

There were tears in her eyes as I sat on the sofa beside her. "When he was fourteen, Carlos, he ran away from his father and came here to Barcelona and found me. He lived here with us until he finished high school."

Those few weeks we stayed in Barcelona and visited with her, she took pity on me, this poor American woman who, in her eyes, did not know how to dress. One evening, she laid out on her bed a variety of clothes for me to choose from. One bullfighter-red, box-knit sweater stands out in particular—or this may have been her Christmas gift to me. A pullover that closed at the neck with two silver clasps sewn on a rectangle of black suede on the left side of the collar. I wore that sweater, with its archetypal Spanish red and black, for years in New York. It always reminded me of her theatrical elegance and fragility.

♦

Almost thirty years later, at the same time of year, I have returned to Barcelona alone to write this chapter of my life. What memories will resurface from my renewed contact with this city?

I climb to Park Güell, where Carlos and I had climbed so many years ago. That first time, I had gazed at the large mosaic dragon halfway up the monumental steps. The two of us sat in the Teatre Grec, where performances used to be held—a Greek-style amphitheater rimmed by a sinuous stone bench covered in particolored mosaics by Gaudí's collaborator, Josep Maria Jujol. The park was empty then; now it is filled with tourists taking photographs of each other on their cell phones. Back then, we gazed out at the city of Barcelona in the distance, into our as-yet-unknown future, before I had discovered a level of deception and betrayal I could never have imagined.

I am counterposing my memory of the scene with the present: like a stereopticon, in which two images shot from slightly different perspectives form, when looked at together, a three-dimensional view of a scene. Of course, I have added a third ingredient: Hitchcock's movie. Am I giving my experience greater depth and nuance this way? Or am I distorting the view? We all read our lives through multiple lenses, whether we are conscious of it or not.

Now is the best moment, I read on a storefront. *Now* may be the best—only—moment we have, but no one lives without the constant inrush of salt spray from the past, mixing in with the freshwater present. Every one of us with a memory lives in briny water. *Homo reminiscens.* Humans are memory creatures.

I find a figure today I do not remember seeing the first time I was in Park Güell: the caryatid of *La Bugadera*, the washerwoman. She stands under a portico in rough-hewn stone, her right arm at her side, her left arm raised to hold a huge stone basket atop her head. As I watch, a pigeon comes to rest on her right shoulder, another on her raised left hand. In front of her I feel able to stand with no shade from the past. She is the figure of now. My now. The woman in a stone skirt and stone blouse with sleeves rolled up past her elbows. The worker woman. The one who endures despite the hardships. The one who believes, because what else is there to do but believe, in the future and in the ability of life to renew itself.

Perhaps that is why I love cities such as Barcelona, Rome, and New York. They are capacious enough, with enough layers and neighborhoods and views to absorb different lives lived by the same person. In a city such as this, a thief, a cheater, a liar can never steal my ability to write and transform loss into a new self.

♦

Where does this last memory belong? Is there ever really a last memory? Are we ever finished with the past? "One is always at home in one's past," wrote Nabokov in *Speak, Memory*. Doesn't a memory still breathe inside of us if, once, it was deep enough to make a wound?

I realize that every time I summon a memory, I am reconstructing it anew—pumping it up with air, like the man I see on the street during the days before Christmas in Gran de Gràcia, who blows up balloons and twists them into living shapes for children.

While Carlos and I were staying in his friend's apartment in Barcelona, we planned on taking a short trip to Madrid to visit his father, the man I had heard so much about but never met. His father had remarried and had a daughter, Carlos's half-sister. One morning, we arose early, ready to go. Or so I thought. I knew Carlos had many apprehensions about seeing his father. I had sat with his mother in Barcelona as she flipped through a photo album, showing me picture after picture of Carlos as a small boy with his father. This fantastical story of their being a father-son acrobatic team was indeed true. One photo in particular stood out: Carlos as a toddler standing on his father's shoulders, about to perform a somersault. How precarious Carlos's life was from such a young age, dependent upon this man who, at any moment, might beat him or throw him into a wall. Back in New York, Carlos had already told me about his father's brutality. How he was hit on the head so many times, he feared he might have brain damage.

We are about to leave the apartment to catch the train to Madrid. Carlos tries to open the door, which is locked with a key from the inside. He turns the key but fails to open the door. He turns the key over and over and still the door will not open. He is struggling with the lock but I see it is an internal struggle. This goes on for at least ten minutes. We are locked in. Carlos has locked us in out of sheer terror over seeing his father once more. His struggle continues, becoming more and more desperate and more and more futile.

"It's okay. We don't have to go to Madrid. We can stay here in Barcelona," I say. He calms down instantly. A few minutes later—late enough for us to have missed our train—he opens the door with one turn of the key. I look at him and say nothing. I know we will never go to Madrid. There is no point in asking him if there is a later train.

◆

On my last evening in Barcelona, I go to see the masterful artist Pep Bou in a show called *Bombollavà* ("Bubbles" in Catalan), in which he creates illusory forms out of soap bubbles. As I watch this artist create more and more elaborate yet transitory shapes with bubbles whose skin catches the multicolored lights, it reminds me of the kind of beautiful, yet ultimately illusory, world I had tried to create for myself with Carlos. The clarinetist and the poet: the artist couple. That is how I saw us. Even the Brooklyn apartment we rented—whose previous tenants were a visual artist and a musician—fed this dream.

The question I still ponder: What made it possible for me to be so thoroughly deceived? Love-induced blindness? Was there something about my childhood that set me up for such an experience? At the time of the breakup of my pseudo-marriage, my friend Alicia said two things to me over the phone in her clipped, no-nonsense voice.

"You know you married your mother."

What could I say? All I could do was take it in.

"You're how old . . . thirty-two? It's time for you to start wearing foundation."

I followed her amusing but practical bit of cosmetic advice. About the former, I think she meant I had found a broken person, like my mother, whom I thought I could fix, the way, as a child, I may have hoped but failed to do with my mother. Perhaps Alicia was right in her blunt assessment, though I always find such analyses somewhat facile and reductive.

Since I was raised by a drugged-up, schizophrenic mother and a childish, overburdened father, I never had the guidance I needed: at least one parent to teach me how to protect myself, when to be wary and when to be open, and how to put my trust in another person slowly, carefully. Of course, I was not the only one this charismatic, pathological liar had fooled.

Trust, belief, credulity. I trusted Carlos to trust me. What I had not counted on was that he would not—could not—trust anyone. It occurs to me now that on the spectrum from paranoia to blind trust, my mother, in the midst of a psychotic episode, occupied one extreme and I, perhaps in reaction formation, have inhabited the other. Or at the very least, the vigilance I exercise when I think I am being stalked by a stranger seems to vanish when a man poses, convincingly, as a lover.

Of my three major relationships with men thus far—this one with Carlos being the first—I have found the men themselves and their form and style of deception so radically different that this first experience did almost nothing to prepare me for what was to follow. I have found it difficult, nearly impossible, to be a good student of the past because each time the new situation is just different enough so that I fail to recognize a pattern.

Just as in the art of the bubble master. He creates now a swirling rainbow helix, now a string of pulsing baubles on a line. And now a cloudy sphere pumped with a smoky spray so, unlike the first two, the enormous bubble rises like a helium-filled balloon.

Spellbound: The Scar of Who You Are

My dear girl, you cannot keep bumping your head against reality and saying it is not there.

–Dr. Brulov to Dr. Petersen

WHICH OF US CAN SAY we have never been under the spell of anyone or anything? Obsession feels so interwoven with what it means to be alive. No wonder Hitchcock's movies are so preoccupied with obsessive memory and the memory of an obsession—often for another person. No wonder, even upon repeated viewings, I continue to be obsessed by these movies, to find they still cast their spell over me.

Like a good neurotic who repeats the same action, hoping for a different result, I watch Hitchcock again and again, suspending my memory of what happens in order to reenter the opening frames afresh, hoping certain things might happen differently than they do. As with this chapter of my life I am reentering here, I wish that it, too, could turn out differently in the retelling.

In the opening minutes of *Spellbound* (1945), Dr. Edwardes fixes his gaze on Dr. Petersen and she in turn gazes up at him, the camera lingering over each of their faces in a reaction shot. I am instantly drawn in, just as they have been drawn to each other. Their eyes—especially hers—are preternaturally lit up, and with that one look they have fallen under each other's spell.

Dr. Edwardes (a tall, slim Gregory Peck) has arrived at Green Manors, a mental asylum, in order to take over as its new director, but he himself has his first delusional spell a few minutes into lunch, just after he and Dr. Petersen (Ingrid Bergman with her earnest, liquescent eyes) have met and tacitly sealed something between them. As Dr. Petersen describes a swimming pool to be built for the patients' use on a spare plot of ground, she draws her fork down the tablecloth to indicate its shape, leaving indented dark lines on the white cloth. The eerie quaver of the theremin swoops in as Dr. Edwardes bursts out, "I take it that the supply of linens in this institution is inexhaustible!" Moments before, Dr. Petersen experienced a powerful attraction to this tall stranger, which visibly rattled her; now, a blatant warning that he is suffering from some form of mental disorder.

Even so, Dr. Petersen feels so magnetically drawn to Dr. Edwardes that she does something quite risqué that first evening. On the pretext of fetching Dr. Edwardes's latest book, *Labyrinth of the Guilt Complex*, from his study, she is compelled to open the door leading into his adjoining bedroom, where he is nodding off over a book. He looks up with a disarming smile.

> Dr. Edwardes: I know why you came in.
> Dr. Petersen: Why?
> Dr. Edwardes: Because something has happened to us.
> Dr. Petersen: But it doesn't happen like that . . . in a day.
> Dr. Edwardes: It happens in a moment sometimes. I felt it this
> afternoon. . . . It was like lightning striking. . . . It strikes rarely.

The dialogue and the sentiment might sound dated and hackneyed. Nonetheless, they capture the frisson of shared, sudden love. Something I, too, have felt.

♦

What is it about Robbie that captivates me from the first moment I see him: a tall, thin, full-bearded man standing several rows in front of me in synagogue? Perhaps it is the way he glances back and fixes his eyes on me. I happen to be wearing a short skirt and I watch him take in my face, my torso, my legs in a feverish, undisguised, up-down look. I can feel him devouring me with his gaze.

It is the Jewish festival of Sukkot at Kane Street Synagogue in Brooklyn. The congregation has begun the ritual of marching around and shaking the lulav (palm, myrtle, and willow branches) and etrog (citron), while singing *Hosannah* ("Save us"). Someone passes a set along to me, and I enter the procession. As I pass by this compelling stranger standing in the pew and grinning at me, I have the urge to hold the etrog up to his nose and say, *Sniff this.* I want him to breathe in its soapy, citrus scent, the citrus scent of me. I restrain myself. We have not even met.

After services, we gather next door in the sukkah, a temporary wooden structure built for the holiday, with a covering of branches designed to let in starlight. In early fall, the sukkah attracts lots of bees that hover inside and dive into the dishes of honey that are set out for dipping in slices of apples and challah. The light itself is honey-colored as it stripes its way through the look he gives me, the look I give him. Somehow, I stammer out hello. Somehow, we introduce ourselves to each other. What we talk about is lost. But I can feel the entire congregation buzzing far in the background as I fall under the spell of attraction between us.

◆

On one of our first dates, a Sunday afternoon in early fall, Robbie and I are strolling through the Brooklyn Botanic Garden and have stepped into a greenhouse to admire the bonsai collection.

"Why are you walking over there?" He sounds agitated, even annoyed.

"What do you mean?"

"You know what I mean."

"No I don't."

"You do this, why do you have to do this?"

"What. What do I do?"

"You know. You're ignoring me."

"I'm not. I was just looking at the bonsai."

"But we're not here to look at the bonsai."

"No? I thought that's why we came in here."

"No! You're impossible. You see? You see?! You're doing it again. What's wrong with you?" He comes at me, menacingly, with a wild look in his eyes.

"I'm sorry, I'm sorry. I didn't mean to upset you."

"Upset me? You've ruined the whole afternoon!" He stomps off.

What have I done? What can I do to make it stop?

Where did this first outburst from Robbie come from? I tried to remember, but I was never able to explain to anyone what I said to precipitate Robbie's rages. Not to my therapist, not to my friends, not even to myself.

After the annulment of my marriage to a foreign bigamist a few years before, I thought I was being careful about whom I chose to date. Hadn't I learned the right lessons? *Don't go out with a foreigner. Date another American. Another Jew. Not someone who pretends to be Jewish just to please me.* How much better could it get than meeting a man in my local synagogue? How much more *haimish*?

♦

How much better could it get for Dr. Petersen than meeting another psychiatrist, the man who was to take charge of the sanitarium where she works? How much better could it get for her, a woman who has never been in love? While Drs. Edwardes and Petersen are together in his room, he receives an emergency call from the operating room. Both doctors rush to the OR, where Dr. Edwardes is struck almost immediately by another attack because of the lights. He removes his operating mask, struggles to breathe, and shouts incoherently about the lights being out, the darkness, and a man murdering his father. At one point he lashes out at the other doctors: "Fools, babbling about guilt complexes . . . what do you know about them?" Then he faints and the next scene finds him bedridden, being tended to by Dr. Petersen.

Here, the woman in glasses gets to remove them to become the desired woman (I'll call her Constance now), then puts them back on, at Dr. Edwardes's bedside, in order to solve the mystery of his mental illness. When she opens up the book he has supposedly written, she finds the first clue: comparing the signature in it to a note he had written to her earlier that day, she notices that the handwriting does not match. She realizes that *this* Dr. Edwardes is not the same one as the author. "Who are you?" Constance asks, with a look of wary skepticism. Only *after* she has fallen in love with him.

♦

Who are you? A question to which, in the case of Robbie, I thought I knew the answer.

Robbie and I discovered we overlapped by three years as undergraduates at Cornell University. We even had a few friends in common. I did not remember meeting him in college but he remembered me. "You even stopped by our house once, looking for someone. I remember I thought you were very cute in your overalls and I tried catching your eye. But you completely ignored me."

"Yeah, that sounds like me." I wanted to believe it was true, that we occupied the same small orbit in Ithaca.

Robbie looked like a young, slim Robin Williams. Once, in a lingerie store on Long Island, the sales person mistook him for the actor, whom she had dated years before he became famous. Robbie had wavy, thinning brown hair, a full, thick mustache and beard, a long nose and mischievous brownish-green eyes.

In my favorite photograph of the two of us, we are wedged into the stern of a skiff in waters off the coast of Jamaica near the Green Grotto, holding each other, our bare legs touching. Robbie is grinning with such boyish delight as he lightly holds the fingers of my left hand on his lap, and my right hand grasps his forearm. He leans his body and face toward me. We are both in our mid-thirties. We look happy, complete, as though relieved at having found each other at last.

What I remember most about Robbie are his eyes, their moist sweetness and desire. Their affectionate, passionate—even maniacal—intensity. His voice, slightly gravelly, often teasing or on the verge of chuckling as he recounts an election story. As a lawyer he worked in politics, running campaigns since he was a teenager. Like Robin Williams, Robbie had his own manic charisma. It was hard not to fall in love with him.

◆

Robbie was late picking me up for our first date. Was he hesitant about being with me, despite—or because of—the power of our attraction for each other? I waited downstairs, leaning against the mailboxes, feeling anxious, until his car pulled up. I had tickets to a puppet theater show at the Brooklyn Academy of Music, a show that hinged on the love of a grandfather for his grandson. I had just learned that Robbie, though raised by two parents, always felt closest to his maternal grandfather. During the performance, as the plot became clearer, Robbie turned and smiled sweetly at me, as though I had somehow intuited he was meant to see this show.

Our relationship was filled with such uncanny moments. It felt for both of us *bashert*, as though we were fated to be together. After the play, he drove us into Manhattan to Florent, the all-night diner frequented by bohemians and crossdressers, and we sat in a booth talking for hours. This was the fall of 1991. I was thirty-five, Robbie was thirty-four.

◆

"I remember now. Edwardes is dead. I killed him . . . I took his place. I'm someone else, I don't know who. I killed him." That's Dr. Edwardes's response to Constance's question, "Who are you?" He gets up and paces while smoking a cigarette. "I have no memory. It's like looking into a mirror and seeing nothing but the mirror. And yet the image is there, I know it's there. I exist. I'm there. How could a man lose his memory, his name, everything he's ever known and still talk like this, as if he were quite sane?"

Constance figures out that this imposter Dr. Edwardes is actually a medical doctor. He labels his own condition: "Amnesia. The trick of the mind for remaining sane. You remain sane by forgetting something too horrible to remember. You put the horrible thing behind a closed door." What is the horrible thing he wants to forget?

Constance notices a scar on Dr. Edwardes's hand—a physical trace and a clue to his childhood trauma.

◆

In the case of Robbie, there will be no physical marks for me to discover.

Early on in our dating, Robbie and I exchange family secrets, sitting on my couch in my Brooklyn apartment.

"Robbie, I feel I have to tell you something. It's very difficult for me to share this with anyone. But I do want you to know. My mother is schizophrenic. I grew up with her that way. It's been very hard to deal with my whole life. I've hidden it from friends and boyfriends and I don't want to do that anymore."

Robbie listens and nods, and looks at me as though he understands. He reaches over and grasps my hand. I can tell he won't judge me. He waits for me to continue.

"Yeah. She used to have nervous breakdowns and was in and out of mental hospitals. Then for years she was very drugged up from all the medications she was on. That was hard to live with, too. And just earlier this evening, I got a call from my sister that my mom is in the hospital."

"Oh, I'm sorry. Another breakdown?"

"Nah. This time it has nothing to do with that. Something with her blood, the doctors don't even know yet. I have to go out to New Jersey and see her this weekend."

"I hope it's nothing serious."

"Yeah, me too." I want to change the subject. "And what about you? What's your family like? Normal, I'm guessing."

"Well, yes and no. I grew up thinking my parents were my real parents, but something always felt wrong. When I looked at baby pictures of myself, they never went all the way back, but only started when I was around two years old. I asked my parents, but they would never tell me anything. But I always felt they were keeping something from me. When I was twenty-three, I finally needed my birth certificate so I could get a passport. I was going overseas for the first time to visit a friend of mine in Thailand. I remember my dad hesitated at first when I asked him, then he gave it to me. It was the first time I had ever seen my birth certificate. I always thought I'd been born in New York, out on the Island where I grew up. It turns out I was born in Lincoln, Nebraska and another man's name was listed as my father—not the man I grew up calling Dad."

"Wow. What a story. And you only found out in your twenties?"

"Yeah. Unbelievable, isn't it."

"So who was he?"

"I asked my mother and she finally had to tell me. She'd been married to this man, a Jewish guy, and moved to the Midwest with him for graduate school. While she was pregnant with me, she found out he'd been cheating on her. So right after she gave birth, she left him and flew home to her parents back East. With me as an infant."

"Why did your mom feel she had to lie?"

"I don't know. I guess getting divorced back then wasn't so common. And when I asked them why they never told me, my dad got angry: 'I could have had the name and place changed on your birth certificate, but I didn't!' That's what he said to me. He worked for the city so I guess he could have done it. My mother never wanted me to know. Of course I still love him like my father but I deserved to know the truth."

"Yeah. Of course you did. That must have been such a shock." A pause. "So did you ever meet your father . . . I mean your biological father?"

"My parents were both against it—they even tried to stop me—but I tracked him down. I flew out to Chicago to meet him. He's a poli-sci professor at a local university and he's remarried. He has two other kids, I guess they're my half-siblings. He was happy to meet me."

Once Robbie has told me his story, I let it recede into the background, not imagining I will need to use it to decode his life and behavior.

◆

The fall of 1991 will be a season of new love intertwined with death. In Yehuda Amichai's poem "A Man in His Life," he quarrels with Ecclesiastes (*To every thing there is a season*):

> A man needs to love and to hate at the same moment,
> to laugh and cry with the same eyes.

Amichai was right. In life, there isn't enough time for separate seasons. A time of passionate love and a time of grief: I cannot think of one without thinking of the other.

At summer's end, I returned from a month in Italy to find my mother in a local hospital in New Jersey, where she had been checked in because of cellulitis on one of her legs. The doctor ordered a series of routine blood tests, only to discover my mom's blood levels—red cells, white cells, platelets—were all extremely low.

As I enter her small room in the local hospital, I take one look at her as she wheels herself over to sit opposite me. She looks emaciated; she cannot weigh more than 85 pounds. Her hair is greasy, her nose still the most prominent thing on her face. Her eyes are tearing up, though she is not crying. I notice pinpricks of blood on her arms and face.

I know instantly, when I look at her, that she is going to die, that she will not recover from whatever illness she has.

"Hey Mom. How're you doing?" I am trying to sound upbeat.

"Hi Sharon. Not so well."

"And the doctors? Did they say what they think is wrong with you? Why they're keeping you here?"

"I don't know, Sharon, they won't tell me anything. Just all these blood tests they keep doing on me."

"Oh."

"Let's talk about something else. So how was Italy?" She is right. What more is there to say?

"I brought these photos I took for you to look at."

I hope I can distract her with a bunch of photographs of Siena. In one, I am wearing a magenta, flowered sundress and squinting up into the sun from the bell tower overlooking the Piazza del Campo, where the Palio takes place each year. I have just given Robbie a copy of the same photo, writing on the back:

> Here I am looking up
> at you
> before I knew
> that I knew you.

"I also got you some Baci, Ma—you know, those Italian hazelnut chocolates with little fortunes inside." She takes them from me and I notice the blue veins in her hands stand out even more than I remembered. As a child, I used to play with her hands, pushing down on the veins that came right up to the surface. Her hands are shaking as she unwraps one of the chocolates.

◆

As my mom's condition worsens, my sister has her transferred from the small local hospital to the Robert Wood Johnson University Hospital in New Brunswick. Her blood levels keep dropping and she receives numerous transfusions. The doctors finally take me and my sister aside and explain that my mother has *aplastic anemia*. They never say why her bone marrow stopped functioning and is no longer making the components of her blood. She is too old (nearly 65), too feeble, the doctors continue, for a bone marrow transplant.

"So is she going to die?" I ask the doctor in charge of her case.

He does not give me an answer.

◆

After visiting my mom in the hospital, I took the train back to New York. I mentioned casually to Robbie which train I would be taking. When I stepped onto the platform at Penn Station, he was standing there. Such a simple act of kindness. This was the core of Robbie: his goodness, his empathy, his ability to talk to anyone. No wonder I was falling in love with him.

It is a custom in my family to wash our hands after leaving a hospital. Back in my apartment, I want to get the smell of sickness and death off my entire body, the same body that is now with Robbie.

"Will you wait while I take a bath? I need to get the hospital smell off of me."

"Yeah. Okay. I'll sit out here and read the paper." He is always reading the newspaper to keep up on politics.

Once I am in the tub for a while, I call out to Robbie and ask him to come into the bathroom. We have yet to have sex or see each other naked. I want him to see me, to see my naked body shimmering beneath the bath water. With Robbie, I often feel these urges. I want him to see me and desire me. A primal feeling.

We make love that night. We hold each other, caressing each other and kissing. It is one of the few times I am naked with him in bed. Showing him my naked body, I am to learn, is not the way to make him desire me.

◆

In *Spellbound*, Constance seems more or less blind to the dangers posed by J.B. (his real initials). They have fled to her old teacher's house in Rochester, once J.B. has been framed for the murder of the real Dr. Edwardes. Constance is in love with J.B. and she is determined to cure him.

J.B. awakens in the middle of the night, goes in the bathroom to shave, and falls into a trance when he sees the bristles of the brush swirling in the cup of shaving foam, then the white of the bathroom fixtures. He holds an open razor in his right hand and veers toward the couch where Constance is sleeping, then turns and goes downstairs in a fugue state. Asleep, Constance does not see that his illness might endanger her. Once awake, she refuses to see the threat. "We know that a woman in love is operating on the lowest level of the intellect," her old teacher and analyst Dr. Brulov (Michael Chekhov) warns her.

◆

On a weekend we spend in Montauk, Robbie becomes upset with me, his temper flaring up, because I don't want to go shopping in a lingerie store with him. Finally, I relent. It seems to be the only way to calm him down. At the shop, he hands me black lace corsets, a garter belt, black stockings, and I begin trying things on for him. His mood brightens as he brings more and more things to me in the changing room.

"Which ones do you like, Sharon?" Robbie asks. In the haze of all that lingerie, his feverish desire overwhelms me, making it difficult to know. We return to the inn where we are staying and I try on everything he bought me. "No, no," he says. "Pull up the stockings like this . . . from the toe." He sits down beside me on the edge of the bed and shows me how to ravel each sheer stocking into a meshed nest, slip my toes in and slowly unravel the stocking up my calf, all the way up my thigh. As though he were practiced at watching the ritual done just so by a woman bent on pleasing him.

Robbie likes me best in a black lace corset, with stockings held up by a garter belt. I feel uncomfortable, self-conscious, and prefer being naked—the way he is. Yet I want to please him. *Maybe I'll get used to it and even like it someday.*

I see him standing at the foot of the bed in his basement bedroom, beginning his ritual of lighting up a joint, toking on it with one hand, making himself hard with the other, while watching me writhe in bed in whatever lace things he fancies.

◆

Robbie is driving us home from a meal in Chinatown. He has had a few drinks. We are on the Manhattan Bridge and another car cuts him off, which enrages him. He speeds up to pass the car, but instead veers over as though trying to knock it out of its lane. He is driving like we are riding in bumper cars.

"Please, please stop it," I cry.

He pretends not to hear me and continues threatening the other car, riding as close as possible to it.

"Stop it before we get into an accident!" I am terrified he is going to crash into the car from the passenger side where I am sitting. "Stop. Please. Robbie. You're going to get us both killed!"

He continues, ignoring me completely. He is possessed, a maniacal gleam in his eye. It only ends when we turn left to exit the bridge and the other car takes the right exit ramp.

◆

Dr. Brulov tries to warn Constance: "We are speaking of a schizophrenic and not a valentine." "We are speaking of a man," she replies. How does she know he is a good person? "I can't feel this way toward a man who was bad."

How many times have we women been wrong? A man can be a good person, yet still be so damaged he can cause real harm.

◆

In brilliant October light, on one of my visits to see my mother, I exit the train and walk up the long hill to the hospital. I stop off in the hospital cafeteria, to steel myself with a Diet Coke. It is close to Halloween and the cafeteria walls are strewn with skeletons and pumpkins. I put my head down, trying to block out the skeletons with their grim foreboding of death.

On this afternoon, both my sister Marla and I are visiting and my mother asks for ice cream. That is all she can eat. At this point, Tegretol (the pharmaceutical drug my mother had taken to control her schizophrenia) has fully left her system.

"It feels like there's something sticking in the roof of my mouth," she says.

My mother has the shakes, and must be bleeding internally. I do not want to picture her face. Marla comes back into the room with a cup of vanilla ice cream and hands it to her. Mom is shaking so badly she is barely able to guide the spoon into her mouth. She puts it down on the metal tray in front of her. Turns to my sister. "It's you! It's your fault I'm here! I could never trust you. You did this to me!"

On and on she rages. *So this is what she is like without medication.* In numbed shock, I watch my sister step back and leave the room without saying a word. I stand there. I have never heard my mother like this before.

I remain with Mom until she calms down. She does not rage at me, she has never raged at me. I say goodbye and take the train home to Brooklyn. I think Marla and I stay away after that, afraid of the raving woman we might encounter if we visit her.

◆

The next time I visit my mother she is in a private room, unconscious, hooked up to oxygen, her eyes closed, breathing heavily. I can hear her wheezing; her breath sounds like it is moving through flaps of sandpaper. She has caught pneumonia, which is inevitable since her body is not producing white blood cells for fighting off infection. My sister and brother-in-law are already in the room, preparing to leave.

"There's nothing to do, Sharon. Let's just go. She's unconscious anyway," says my sister.

"No. I want to stay here and say goodbye."

"She can't hear you, you know. You really should leave." The two of them walk out.

I sit down beside my mother, beside what is left of her, a package of skin and bones, her face grainy, her small eyelids clamped shut. The pinpricks of blood are gone. Her wheezing mouth is the most active thing about her.

I read somewhere that hearing is the last thing to go when a person is unconscious and dying. *So perhaps she still can hear me, or at least sense me here.* I want to believe it is possible. I take her right hand and squeeze it, and I feel her lightly squeeze mine. I remain there with her, holding her hand. I believe she knows I am there. At one point she opens one eye very wide and looks right at me, like a blasted sea captain, then closes it. *She saw me. I felt it. She saw into me and clutched my hand.*

"I love you," I say, because that is what I want to tell her. The only thing I want her to know. And I hear her wheeze, with the same three beats, "Vuh-vuh-vuh." An incomprehensible rasp, but I can tell what she means. These are her last *words* to me.

◆

My mother died that night, hours after I said goodbye. I knew I was not responsible for her illness, nor for her death. And yet. *Couldn't I have done more? Done differently?*

I helped my sister bring my mom to the hospital's psychiatric unit a year or so before. I acquiesced to my sister when she decided our mother should live in a halfway house in Jamestown, New Jersey. I visited her there once. It was too painful to see. A bed. A nightstand. A chest of drawers. In a room with other beds, nightstands, identical chests of drawers. That is what a life can be reduced to. I gave her a small, framed portrait of me holding up Dante, my black-and-white tuxedo cat. There was nothing else personal in the room. Perhaps a picture of my sister and her husband.

I had ceded control to my sister, who was a psychiatric nurse, and to the doctors who prescribed the drug that eventually killed her. Let me be more accurate: My mother died of pneumonia due to a weakened immune system brought on by aplastic anemia, a fatal condition that was brought on by the drug Tegretol, which has the rare side effect of destroying a person's bone marrow, where all our blood cells are produced.

Did I also feel guilty over my sense of relief? Now I did not have to worry about what to do for her. I did not have to decide whether to see her or not see her, or to feel the attendant guilt. Guilt, too, that my mother had raged at my sister and not at me—something my sister and I have never spoken of.

Here is a poem I wrote six years after my mother's death, acknowledging—with its clear reference to Lady Macbeth—that I felt steeped in guilt:

True Yahrzeit

Midway through
writing a Yahrzeit poem
for my mother
the ink gives out

so I have to stop and find
the hand-mixed ink—a blue somewhere
between the Mediterranean and her eyes—
turning and turning until the nib falls
into the ink bottle
impossible to retrieve with tweezers
my pointer and thumb
I have to pour the ink
into another bottle shake out the nib—
blue, blue, sea-sky hue everywhere
my fingers, the porcelain basin
berried

it's one o'clock in the morning
and I'm scrubbing with Ajax and a sponge
when I realize *this* is the poem this laughing to myself
this washing and washing my fingers
stained with the blue blood
of my mother—her death—my ink
the only thing that saves me
the only link to her I can keep.

♦

The doctors never explained anything to us about the cause of my mother's death. My mom's cousin Muriel, who did research in environmental health, told me over the phone that aplastic anemia has to be caused by a toxic exposure, either in the environment or to something my mother had ingested.

WARNINGS
APLASTIC ANEMIA AND AGRANULOCYTOSIS

APLASTIC ANEMIA AND AGRANULOCYTOSIS HAVE
BEEN REPORTED IN ASSOCIATION WITH THE USE
OF TEGRETOL. DATA FROM A POPULATION-BASED
CASE CONTROL STUDY DEMONSTRATE THAT THE

RISK OF DEVELOPING THESE REACTIONS IS 5 TO 8
TIMES GREATER THAN IN THE GENERAL POPULATION.
HOWEVER, THE OVERALL RISK OF THESE REACTIONS
IN THE UNTREATED GENERAL POPULATION IS LOW,
APPROXIMATELY SIX PATIENTS PER ONE MILLION
POPULATION PER YEAR FOR AGRANULOCYTOSIS AND
TWO PATIENTS PER ONE MILLION POPULATION PER
YEAR FOR APLASTIC ANEMIA.
         –Novartis

My mom had blood work done every three months. By the time the doctors discovered her condition, it was too late. My mother was one of the anomalous few that pharmaceutical warning labels are written about in order to protect drug companies from lawsuits. Thanks to Tegritol, her risk of getting aplastic anemia had been raised to between thirty and forty-eight in a million. I have to assume that many of the cases (including my mother's) go unreported, and so the mortality risk is probably much higher.

♦

Robbie met my family after the funeral, back at my house, where everyone gathered. I had made lentil soup, the traditional food for Jewish mourners, and everyone stood around having soup and bagels in my dining room.

That night—because what else is there to do—Robbie and I have sex. And I come, in the grieving light of my apartment, with the tall mourner's candle sitting on the dining room table, shedding its sallow flickering along the walls all week long. During *shivah*, the Jewish week of mourning, friends drop by to sit with me a while, to hear stories and look at pictures of my mother when she was young and beautiful. After they leave, Robbie comes over, and in that same light, we have sex. It is the only way to manage the grief—to have it interrupted by short pangs of pleasure. I can feel her all around me. During that week, Robbie tells me he is certain my mother's ghost visited him in his basement bedroom. That she was a benign presence, just there, wanting to see who he was.

A month after my mother died, Robbie invited me to go away with him for a weekend to Mohonk Mountain House, a beautiful old lodge in upstate New York. We climbed the craggy mountain in the bleak, cloudy, late-November light. We had no need to say much. I felt he understood my loss. He was there for me the way he was there for me at the train station. Back in our room, Robbie sat on the porch in a wooden rocking chair, smoking pot and looking out over the lake.

We had sex eight times before dinner. I know because I counted. Robbie climaxed eight times. It all felt too rushed, too frenzied. Too urgent, even desperate. Not pleasurable at all for me. I felt relieved when it was over.

♦

Now, twenty-five years later, the spell of Robbie has lifted enough for me to see how much of his behavior—his irrational fits, his temper, his sexual voracity—probably had something to do with cocaine. He must have been high on cocaine or experiencing withdrawal from it. He told me he had quit and I believed him. But coke is colorless, tasteless, and odorless. He could have been doing coke in my presence without my ever being aware of it. At Mohonk, had Robbie dipped into the bathroom and snorted some coke?

Cocaine, I learn now from the National Institutes of Health, not only stimulates the pleasure centers of the brain but can also cause psychotic episodes: anxiety, paranoia, delusions, even violence. Similar to my mother's paranoid schizophrenic breaks. Is that why it has taken me so long to see it? Do we become blind, or inured, to the things we are most familiar with?

And what is it about traumatic or sad experiences? Why do I remember them better than anything else? Why do these memories of Robbie haunt me still?

Psychologists speak of a *negativity bias*: our tendency to react to and remember negative feelings and experiences more than positive ones.

Everyone agrees there is something called post-traumatic stress disorder. And even though positive life events cause stress, as indicated on the Holmes-Rahe Stress Scale, I have yet to hear of anyone having *post-ecstatic stress disorder.*

My friend Susan says I have a Velcro problem: I let the bad things stick and I let the good things slide off me. It turns out it is human nature to let the bad things stick.

I grew up loving my mother, feeling deeply attached to her and at the same time feeling traumatized by her. Now that she had died, I transferred my love to Robbie, who also traumatized me. What a familiar feeling. Consciously, I detested his behavior, but I couldn't walk away from him. Unconsciously, did I find comfort in Robbie's bouts of violent, irrational behavior? Was staying with Robbie a way of keeping my mother alive?

"We don't remember days," wrote Cesare Pavese. "We remember moments."

Sometimes a short terrifying scene that lasted only a couple of minutes persists in my memory, the way nightmares do. Like the time Robbie was driving us back from Long Beach and became furious with me. I could never understand why. He slowed down, pulling to the side of the road, and stopped the car. I felt that familiar feeling of terror. He threatened to let me out at the side of the road. We were in the middle of nowhere, and it was late at night. *What did I say? What could I possibly have said to make him so angry?* For a moment I was terrified he was going to physically force me out of the car and drive away.

♦

I recently found a typed, single-spaced, five-page signed letter I wrote to Robbie. Even then I seemed to understand his destructiveness, his threatening, violent moods, and to reject his tendency to blame it all on me.

August 31, 1992

Dear Robbie,

. . . I think, more and more, our relationship has turned into an abusive one in which I am vilified by you.

. . . .

I think you are incredibly needy. I think you love me but need to have me be for you exactly what you need. But I can't fulfill all your needs. Especially when you don't know how to be there for yourself. I think that your inability to cope with stress, as manifested by your addiction to marijuana and other substances, leads you to act out with me a lot of the time. You have so much anger bottled up inside, that I become your private shooting gallery. . . . Let me remind you, you had the drinking binge in which you were terribly abusive to me (not for the first time) and put our lives at danger in the car. Unlike you I think that your abusiveness and rage at your lover is a pattern for you. Unfortunately, the pattern with me is to be with someone who has that kind of rage and for me to be so fearful of it that I will do or say anything to placate the person. The one time I didn't do that was in the Berkshires. I got as mad as you were. And you couldn't take it. That's why you almost left me up there—another incredibly cruel act to threaten me with, given that I don't drive and was feeling as freaked out as you were. That too is not the first time you've exhibited that behavior. Out on Long Island you almost dumped me by the side of the road. Or have you forgotten?

Twenty-five years later I still flash back to these episodes. His rage attacks that seemed to come out of nowhere. His threats. My cowering. I never mailed him the letter. I was probably afraid of his response.

♦

Constance knows that some trauma from J.B.'s childhood has given him his "guilt complex," which is so powerful that he would rather imagine he has killed Dr. Edwardes than face this trauma from his past. She convinces him to return to Gabriel Valley, where he remembers he skied. Approaching the precipice, with Constance skiing right beside him, he has a flashback to an early childhood memory: he is a boy sliding down the outer edge of some outdoor steps and yelling at his younger brother to get out of the way. His brother does not budge. J.B. slams into him and he flies into the air, landing on the sharp point of the railing, which impales him. However implausible, it is a case of involuntary manslaughter.

♦

What was wrong with Robbie? I thought I understood him once he told me about his parents' deception. When he described going in search of his biological father, I thought he had worked through the pain. Now I see he grew up breathing a lie, and it had created a fault line inside him that never healed.

Was childhood trauma what led Robbie to cocaine? From a young age, he worked in politics. Working on political campaigns can be like working on Wall Street: long hours, the adrenalin rush of the work, and cocaine to keep himself going. I remember one of his old friends saying, "I'm not surprised he did cocaine. We all did it ten years ago. What surprised me was that he was *still* doing it."

♦

Once, just once, I return from a dinner party with other poets around eleven in the evening. Robbie has invited me to come over afterwards, no matter how late. He lives in a brownstone in Cobble Hill that he and a law school friend co-own. Robbie has the downstairs bedroom, a bathroom, and a front room he uses as a home office.

I find him in his bedroom, in his gray-and-white striped cotton bathrobe, frenetically pacing back and forth, making jerky, speeded-up movements like a figure in a silent movie. His calico cat twitches her tail as she lies beside the spring poking through the gold-colored upholstery of his antique chair.

I watch him pace for a while before he notices me. He looks possessed by a demon, his hair sticking out, uncombed. He is sweating and pacing, pacing and sweating, in a tight diagonal, back and forth in his basement bedroom. He stops when he catches sight of me at the door, gives me a wild-eyed look, then continues his pacing.

"What's going on? What's wrong with you?"

"I'm okay. I'm okay, Sharon. I . . . I just took some . . ."

"What? I'm leaving. I told you I won't be around you if you take that stuff!"

"No, no, don't go. Please, please, Sharon. I know how to calm down. Please don't go, I promise I'll calm down. Just . . . just give me a few minutes."

I glower at him and perch on the edge of his bed. First he swallows a Xanax that he takes from a bottle in his nightstand drawer. Then he unties his bathrobe, lets it drop to the floor as he goes to take a very hot shower. I can see the steam pouring out through the half-open bathroom door. When he steps out in his long white terry bathrobe, his pale skin flushed from the hot shower, he seems a bit calmer. He sits down on the bed next to me and reaches for my hand. Gradually, as the Xanax takes effect, I watch him return to some semblance of himself.

♦

Now I realize I must have been witnessing Robbie's routine when he was having a bad reaction to cocaine. When I look back, I see how ritualized his actions were, as though he had done the same things before and had come to depend upon them. He promised me that he had stopped snorting coke, that he had slipped this once because he missed me. So I stayed over, not happily, but I stayed. I wanted to believe him.

Was that my mistake? Shouldn't I have seen then that he had a serious drug problem? Or should I have told him, "That's unacceptable to me," when, early in our courtship, we were at the Prospect Park Zoo, strolling around, and he said, "I just want you to know that I have given up coke. But I also smoke pot every day and I will never give it up. You should know that." Something inside of me clenched, but I was too smitten already to let any warning stop me. *Okay, I can live with that. It's not ideal, but I guess I can live with that. As long as he's stopped doing coke.*

◆

Robbie's—dare I call them—psychotic episodes continue. We fly to Israel on vacation. In a hotel in Eilat, he locks the door and comes at me, menacingly. I cower on the bed as he threatens me. "It's *you*. You're the one who's done this to me!" He paces back and forth around me like a tiger circling its prey. He could strike me. He could do anything to me. I see he is capable of real violence. His eyes flash and he puts his fingers through his hair and pulls hard. He is flushed. Raging. "You crazy bitch. How dare you look at me like that!" On and on he rants. I am shaking. He comes close and I am sure he is about to strike me, he looks so wild.

Finally, I ask him to unlock the door. The whole time, I keep thinking, *I should go. Book a flight and go home.* I stay. My dependency on Robbie, my bond with him, is too strong for me to break. From the shock, I fall ill with strep throat as we drive out into the desert.

We visit the huge crater Mitzpe Ramon in the Negev. Feverish, a pink keffiyeh wrapped several times around my neck, I look over the edge. I could be on the edge of a different planet. Why did I let this episode—so many episodes—pass?

I look up the symptoms of withdrawal from cocaine. One of them is paranoia. *In extreme cases of paranoia, the person may also become psychotic verging on violent.*

◆

Each time Constance tries to talk to J.B. about the root of his trauma, he has a tantrum. "Don't start that again. Don't stand there with your wiseacre look. I'm *sick* of your doubletalk!" But it passes. She knows his angry resistance to her is part of the treatment. She is not afraid he will hurt her, though Dr. Brulov does raise the possibility, especially after seeing him descend the stairs in a trance, clutching an open razor: "There is no use taking chances with a possibly dangerous case."

Though Constance is a doctor, she has no objective distance because she is in love with her patient. Ethics aside, when Dr. Brulov, the voice of reason, urges her to turn J.B. over to the police, she refuses: "The mind isn't everything. The heart can see deeper sometimes." Impossible for me not to hear the echo of Pascal's aphorism with its indisputable ring of truth: "The heart has its reasons that reason knows nothing of." No matter that following the heart can lead one into danger.

◆

Robbie and I are having dinner at our favorite vegetarian restaurant, Nosmo King, right off Canal Street. He sometimes drives us into the city from Brooklyn just to have a meal there (we are both vegetarians). Out of nowhere, he begins berating me, turning on me with one of his dark moods. This time—the only time—I stand up and walk out. *I'll show him I'm not going to take it anymore.* I take the F train home.

Later that night, I get a phone call from Robbie. "I . . . I got into an accident with the car coming home after you left."

"Are you okay?"

"Yeah, but it was a close call. I was almost killed. Why did you leave me in the restaurant like that?"

"Ohhh. I'm sorry."

His equilibrium is so delicate that some harm might come to him, and it will be my fault. This is his message to me. I dare not walk out on him again.

♦

This is the part where I should step forward and stop being the passive woman. The part where I should have figured out Robbie was an addict, and needed to enter an inpatient drug treatment program.

In this way, too, Robbie reminds me of my mother, who never thought there was anything wrong with her, who resisted being hospitalized. Robbie knew he had a problem, and didn't know he had a problem. He lied to me. He lied to his therapist, who believed he had stopped using cocaine. He lied to himself. Sometimes a person can get away with lying for only so long.

♦

In August, 1993, when Robbie and I had been together for almost two years, he invited me to go away with him to Monterosso in the region of Liguria, Italy, where I had been the summer before I met him, the summer before my mother died. There, in the town that the poet Eugenio Montale used to summer in as a child, the largest of the Cinque Terre, we stayed at Porto Roca, a small hotel perched on the cliff edge overlooking the sea. The proprietor kept a large green parrot in a tall cylindrical cage on the patio. Each day we grabbed towels and climbed down the steps cut into the steep cliff face to the sea. One day we decided to hike the path to Vernazza, the next town down the coast, the town I had been to by myself two years before, where I had watched the fishermen night-fish from the pier with their small bobbing lights and had made a wish I would return there with someone I loved.

The path between the two towns takes about ninety minutes to hike. On the way, we looked over at the terraced cliffs to our left, where an occasional farmer tended the cliffside vineyards that produce the sweet wine called Sciacchetrà, and the sea to our right. The whole time, whether because it was humid or because of something else, Robbie was cranky with me, unhappy, in a way I did not understand. That I never understood.

Something was off. Something was always going off between us.

By the time we reached the small village of Vernazza, both of us hot and sticky, I wanted to take a dip in the sea to cool off. I have always been thirsty for the sea in summer, the way some are thirsty for cold beer.

"I have to go to the bank."

"Okay. Let me get in a quick swim before lunch since you don't like to swim. You can meet me down by the water. It's right there," I said, pointing to the small beach.

His face darkened and I could tell one of his episodes was about to begin, one that had the potential of spoiling the entire day. To ward it off, I agreed to go with him to the bank and go for a swim after lunch.

After lunch we both strolled to the sea, alongside the beach by the rocks, where a few local boys were diving off the cliff edge. I jumped in feet first. The water felt cool and delicious, especially after our sweaty hike on a humid day. It was what I had been waiting for. Robbie watched me swim; he usually preferred not to swim himself, and I had learned to curb my disappointment. When we were in Eilat, I swam with the dolphins while he took a photo of me in the water.

This time, after I had been swimming around for a while, he stood up and jumped into the sea. His pale body shimmered under the turquoise water. He was treading water with a bit of difficulty, the sun in blinding white patches around him, as he lifted his head, straining a little to keep his face and beard from getting wet. He grinned at me, his eyes catching the glint of sunlight in them, with a look that said, *You see, I'll do anything for you.* This was the Robbie I loved. Why was it always this way with him? Perfectly sweet or perfectly horrid.

That evening after dinner we stood at the railing, looking out over the Mediterranean from our private terrace, gazing up at the stars and at each other. The next night, we stood out under a darkening sky and watched the moon descend, leaving its milky luminescence far out on the sea, the stars shining bright as aluminum specks in the sun. Robbie pulled out a ring box.

What words did Robbie say to me that night? *Will you marry me, Sharon? Sharon, I brought you here because I thought this was the most romantic place to propose . . .*

♦

In many Hitchcock movies, the conundrum or crime relies on an object. In *Strangers on a Train*, it's Guy Haines's monogrammed cigarette lighter that Bruno keeps and that he intends to plant at the scene of the crime to incriminate Guy in the murder of his wife. In *Spellbound*, the imposter Dr. Edwardes pulls out a large, monogrammed silver cigarette case from his bureau and shows it to Constance. The initials J.B. become the entryway into solving the mystery of his identity.

♦

The diamond ring Robbie gave me on the terrace overlooking the sea in Italy held the secret to his identity, and his undoing. The ring had been his mother's. I half-wondered, later on, *Was Robbie in too much debt to buy me a new ring?* But no, he wanted me to have this particular ring. It had been his mother's and he had asked her for it to give to me. It was a ring with a troubled history: the one his mother had received from her first husband, Robbie's biological father, whom she had fled from and hidden the existence of for over twenty years. She held on to it, unworn, for all those years. Thirty-six years, Robbie's current age. What a complicated piece of faceted light.

Robbie wanted me to have his mother's ring, I sensed, because it was a way of healing, of repairing all that had gone wrong in his past. And in his mother's past (the two were intimately connected). If I wore this ring and married Robbie, it would heal the fracture between his mother and his biological father. Looking back now, I think Robbie hoped it would heal the fracture inside himself: the anxious, desperate place that was a legacy from his mother, helped along by her years of deception and exacerbated by his cocaine habit.

This was the ring he gave me. A ring fraught with history. With bitterness and betrayal. A ring of promise and a ring of sorrow.

When we returned from Italy at the end of August, I called up my friend Susan to tell her the news.

"He proposed to me as we stood looking out over the Mediterranean one night. I half-expected it to happen; we went to the same hotel he had recommended to a friend of his who got engaged there."

"But what did you say?" I could hear a note of alarm in her voice.

"I said 'yes' of course. Why?"

"Sharon, you know how crazy he gets with you. I'm really worried. Remember the time he came to meet us at the Indian restaurant? Do you remember the look he gave you? He looked at you and plugged into you like you were a drug. It frightened me. And what about what happened when you were up in the Berkshires? How you said one thing to him and he ended the entire trip?"

I fell silent. I had almost forgotten that episode. I had been behind the wheel, a rarity, when Robbie made some cutting remark about my driving and I snapped back, "I *saw* the car." In a fury, he told me to drive back to the lodge where we were staying. "That's it. You've ruined our trip. We're going home." We left, having been there barely a day.

Susan's words disturbed me. I probably *was* a drug to Robbie. And I found the intensity of his desire for me—the way he fixed his gaze on me, whether fully clothed or in disarray—too potent, too magnetizing, to give up. Yet his moods with me, the way he turned on me unpredictably at some slight remark I made, had me more and more frightened. Frightened and worried enough that I began to think we should see a therapist together—something I never got the chance to suggest.

When Robbie raged at me, I felt lost, terrified, helpless—yet I clung to the very person who made me feel that way. A very old feeling. The dynamic between Robbie and me had tapped into the roots of the childhood trauma I had felt with my mother. Now that she had died, I clung to Robbie all the more. It was as though I transferred the intensity of my attachment to my mother, no matter how fraught, to Robbie. The bond was so primal that I didn't think I had a choice.

As I revisit this time from my past, I see, as I never fully saw before, that Robbie had to have been an addict for the entire two years we were together. His outbursts of rage and depression were a result of the coke he had taken or else were symptoms of his withdrawal—like the time we vacationed in Israel, when he couldn't risk bringing any coke or marijuana through customs.

After it was all over, I found out that Robbie was in debt for $100,000. When we went to Italy, he asked me if I could charge the hotel room and other major expenses to my credit card. He promised he would reimburse me. *How could he have been in so much debt?* He did take us on extravagant vacations. But he worked as a lawyer, co-owned his brownstone and rented out the top floor. Now I have to admit that he probably snorted his way through more cash than I earned in five years as an adjunct assistant professor.

◆

I am writing down some of these memories while sitting on Plaça del Diamant, in Barcelona—a plaza that contains one of the few remaining bomb shelters from the Spanish Civil War. Here is where women and children, mostly, hid themselves for several hours when the alarm sounded the warning that aerial bombing by the Italians or Germans would begin in minutes. There is a bronze statue on the square with a screaming woman's naked torso and her right hand and leg poking through a barrier. She is fleeing and stuck there forever. A visual embodiment of what it feels like to live with harrowing memories.

I thought I would have to return to Cobble Hill, to stand in front of the brownstone where Robbie lived. Instead, I have had to leave New York City to have this full realization, the one I have fled from for so long: Robbie was not using coke occasionally. More than likely, he was using it all the time. Right under my nose. Right into his nose.

◆

Now comes the part I have dreaded the most. The part where I have to relive the last days of Robbie's life. How many small details from that week seem fixed, like shots in a film. I conjure up that Tuesday, when we went to flamenco and I watched the male dancer. "He has real duende," I whispered to Robbie. Afterwards, I talked with him about duende: that particularly Spanish idea that true art must be passionate enough to include—even embrace—death.

Thursday evening, on the Jewish holiday of Simchat Torah, we were standing in the street in front of Kane Street Synagogue, where we had met roughly two years earlier on the holiday of Sukkot. There, outside, it was traditional to dance with the velvet-covered Torah scrolls, to celebrate the end of the yearlong reading of the entire scroll before commencing once more. There is where I still see Robbie in his suit, standing in the street, waving a small Israeli flag and biting his lower lip while grinning.

He slept over that night. Friday, I arose early for a class I was teaching on Greek tragedy to my Cooper Union freshmen. He grabbed my stockinged leg, hoping to pull me back into bed, as I bent to kiss him goodbye. He had that pleading, hungry look. I had to resist him. I was running late already.

I was teaching *Antigone* and introduced it by talking about the final chorus of Sophocles' *Oedipus Rex*, with its injunction to "count no man happy till he dies." I explained the ancient idea that until you know how a person dies and you can measure an entire life, you can't call that person happy.

Afterwards, I went to Macy's and bought a cardigan sweater the color of raspberries. What did Robbie say to me on the phone later? I was complaining about being unable to find anything to fit me. "That's because you're more attractive than most women." Later, I could not wear the sweater because its red reminded me of the color of freshly dried blood. I asked Robbie if he would like to come over for dinner; I was about to buy some salmon. He said, "No. Go ahead. I'm supposed to meet my friend Sid. I'll see you tomorrow as planned." So I shopped for myself, buying one salmon steak and some broccoli. Stopped off to rent a video at the local rental store. I chose *JFK*.

Around midnight, Robbie called. In a pleading voice, he asked me to come over. I said no, I was already in bed, watching a movie. We already had plans to see each other the next day at Shabbat services and have lunch together afterwards. I hung up the phone and continued watching the movie.

I woke up late on Saturday afternoon, and called Robbie. His answering machine clicked on and I left a message. "Hi Robbie. I overslept so I don't think I'm making it to services today. I'm still planning on coming over for lunch. Call me." By the time I was dressed and ready to go, it was about three in the afternoon. I tried his line again. His answering machine clicked on once more. *Strange not to have heard from him.* I scarfed down a small can of tuna to fuel myself for what was to come. Something told me it would be a while before I ate again.

I headed up Court Street to his house on Warren Street, about eight blocks away. When I turned onto his street, I noticed a police car double-parked a little farther down the block and my heart jumped. An officer's head was poking out of the window to talk to a woman. I climbed the flight of steps to Robbie's front door and tried the lock with my key. It opened two inches, no further. A latched chain on the door barred my entry. *Hmm. This is strange. Why would he chain the door?*

I went downstairs to the street-level door leading directly into his basement office and was about to knock when I saw all three newspapers sitting on the mat. *Something is definitely wrong.* I knew Robbie's routine. The first thing he did each morning was grab the papers from outside and flip through them while sitting on the can. As a part-time lobbyist in Albany, he wanted to be up-to-date on politics, so he read everything. *What's going on? Has Robbie still not left his bed so late in the afternoon?* I climbed the stairs once more and tried ringing the doorbell again. No answer. *Why would he chain me out? He knows I have the key.*

Who should I call? My father? No, he won't be able to handle this, and he lives all the way out in Pennsylvania. My uncle will know what to do. He's stronger. And he really loves Robbie.

I called my aunt and uncle from a phone booth.

"Aunt Fran, this is Sharon."

"Sharon, what's the mattuh?" She could already hear the note of alarm in my voice.

"Uh. I don't know what's going on. I went over to Robbie's and tried to get in, I have the keys, only the door is chained from the inside. We were supposed to have lunch together and it's already 3:30. He didn't answer the phone when I called, either."

"Hold on. Bob! Bob!" I heard her calling my uncle from the other room. "Something has happened with Sharon and Robbie. We have to go over and help her. Shaaaron?" She came back to the phone.

"Yeah?"

"We're coming now. Wait for us. We'll be there as soon as we can."

My aunt and uncle lived in Sheepshead Bay. I calculated it would take them at least half an hour. Afterwards, my aunt told me that my uncle warned her as they were driving over: "Frannie, this isn't going to be good. Prepare yourself. We may have to miss the theater tonight."

My uncle tried the door, saw the chained lock, and asked me to go to a nearby hardware store to buy a file. With the file, my uncle tried to cut the chain, but soon gave up. "We should call the police, Sharon." I did and they arrived in eight minutes.

"Do you mind if I break this chain?" the officer asked me, once I explained the situation to him.

"No. Of course not."

He closed the door, then with one quick blow he jerked it open with the force of his body and broke the chain. The two officers and my uncle were about to go inside.

"His bedroom's downstairs," I told them.

My uncle turned to me. "I think it would be better if you waited out here, Sharon honey."

I walked down the front steps and stood outside with my aunt, who held on to me tightly.

My uncle emerged first. His face was solemn. "He's gone, Sharon. There's nothing we can do to save him."

A crack opened up inside me. Here my memory fails. I must have screamed or cried out.

Next I was sitting in the police car with one of the officers, who wanted to know where I had been that day and last night. When had I seen Robbie last. Only later, I realized he was ruling me out as a murder suspect.

I never saw Robbie's dead body. I never wanted to see it—though, months later, I had the thought that it would have made his death more real to me. I entered the house after the ambulance had taken his covered body out. It looked as if there had been a violent struggle. The chairs in the kitchen were overturned. One was even smashed and broken. Someone had torn an Israeli poster from the living room wall and ripped it up. *Downstairs. I have to go downstairs.* On the wall above his bed I saw a fist-sized hole punched into it. *Who did that?* His bed was still made. It looked like he hadn't slept in it. Did I—or did one of the officers—open the nightstand drawer filled with bloody tissues?

Only later I learned my uncle and the cops found Robbie lying naked on the bedroom floor, face down, a bruise on his forehead where he had fallen. The shower running. The hot shower to calm him down, probably after downing a Xanax. The hot shower he never managed to reach.

I called his mother but no one answered. I was relieved not to be the one to tell her. I reached his sister and told her Robbie was dead. *Better his mother should hear it from his sister than from me.* A sort of calm, a sheer practicality took over for a brief while as I did the things I needed to do. When Robbie's mother showed up with his dad, she, too, seemed lucid, even pragmatic. She went downstairs and looked through his drawers until she found his tallit—his white satin prayer shawl with navy blue stripes on the edges—to bury him in.

Before his parents arrived, one of the officers had given me a blue-and-white oval Dutch tin that once contained chocolates. "Here, you might want to do something with this before his parents show up." When

I opened the tin, I saw it stored all of Robbie's drug paraphernalia. I was with Robbie when he bought that tin in August on our way home from Monterosso, after he had proposed to me. There was a stopover in Amsterdam. I remembered the way he ate chocolate truffle after truffle, as though he had no ability to control himself. Just like with sex. Just like with pot. Just like with coke.

Then the cop handed me a stack of Polaroids. "Here. You probably want to take these, too." They were erotic Polaroids of me wearing various pieces of lingerie—probably what Robbie gazed at on the nights we were not together. I took them home. Held on to them for a few weeks. Then scissored them into shreds in the trash, along with the lingerie I used to wear. His stash of marijuana: I flushed down the toilet. Any pipes, papers, matches: I threw in the trash.

♦

The delusion I seem unable to free myself from is that my life would have been different, happier, more fulfilled, had Robbie lived. If we had married. If we had had children and a life together. It seems to be the one fantasy I cling to the most tenaciously. The *if only*.

In part, it is because I grew up on such movies as *Spellbound* and *Rear Window*, where the man, however troubled or difficult, resolves his issues with the help of the woman who loves him and they live (we presume) happily ever after. As Constance says to convince Dr. Brulov, "I can save him." Then she does.

♦

How little of my life has worked out like Hitchcock's endings. Many of his thrillers, even, end with a happy romance. I have found man after man, some more troubled or filled with obstacles than others. Surely I have obstacles inside of me as well. One of them takes the form of blindness—of desire shading into belief that I can *heal* the man I love. Each time I have hoped and trusted that the impediments to love will dissolve through my patient devotion. And I have failed each time.

Because I am not a therapist. And even therapists fail their patients. Because change—radical change—is more difficult.

"People think that in falling in love they make themselves whole? The Platonic union of souls? I think otherwise. I think you're whole before you begin. And the love fractures you. You're whole, and then you're cracked open," wrote Philip Roth.

"You were lucky, Sharon," my father said. "What if you had married him and had a ten-month-old, and *then* he did that and died? You'd be in even worse shape." Those wise words never found a place to take permanent root inside of me, never grew into a conviction that I was—am—better off without Robbie. Even now, I can mouth the sentiment, but it means little. Those words say that what happened *had* to happen, that it was inevitable. My cousin Jackie told me she had a premonition of Robbie's death when we all stood in the cemetery at my mother's unveiling (about a year after her death, when the tombstone was uncovered). For my part, I refuse to believe anything is inevitable, predestined—certainly not a thirty-six-year-old man's death.

♦

I should not emulate the example of *Spellbound* but the reverse. I have fallen into playing the trusting, loving Constance too many times when I need to be the more skeptical Dr. Brulov, who asks, "And how do you know what his real character is?" How could I know Robbie's real character, given the scars from his childhood, the lies he had been fed all those years about his father, and how coked up or in withdrawal he probably always was? How could I know my mother's real character, when she was either under the influence of drugs or subject to a psychotic attack?

♦

In my dream life back then, Robbie and my mother were connected. As in this poem:

Ménage

When he untwined
his legs from mine
and rolled toward her

I got up
went downstairs
where the waves from the window
rose higher and higher—
was it too risky to swim?

Just then a wave rose up
tall as a theater curtain
crashed through the windows
flooding everything

smashed
my mother's girlhood
photo album in half

tore a corner
off my book of days

Picking them up
weeping, weeping
what could I do
ankle-deep in water
bereft of my lover
and a motherless daughter

In *Missing Out*, Adam Phillips argues that "our unlived lives—the lives we live in fantasy, the wished-for lives—are often more important to us than our so-called lived lives and that we can't (in both senses) imagine ourselves without them." Perhaps it is impossible for me to give up on the fantasy of the unlived life I might have had with Robbie. It is constitutive of who I am as much as the experiences I have lived—maybe even more so. And of all the hypothetical futures I might have had with him, who is to say which one would have come true?

I started out writing these memories, aided by Hitchcock, in order to give shape to my life—to purge myself of these ghosts that continue to haunt me. But perhaps there is no such thing as purging memories, least of all for a writer. "[P]eople's memories," wrote Haruki Murakami, "are maybe the fuel they burn to stay alive." Maybe the memories of what might have been, I would venture to add, are the most potent fuel of all.

Rebecca and My Haunted Marriage

You know I . . . I wish there could be an invention that bottled up the memory like . . . like perfume and it never faded, it never got stale, and whenever I wanted to, I . . . I could uncork the bottle and live the memory all over again.

–Young American woman

IF ONLY MEMORY were something you could bottle up and store like perfume. But this image is as wrongheaded about memory as is that of a computer file. Every memory we retain depends upon the network of synapses between neurons. And these synapses are highly mutable. In the very act of recalling a memory, which is a dynamic process, we may unintentionally alter the memory or—to use the young woman's metaphor in Hitchcock's *Rebecca* (1940)—change the scent of the perfume.

So here let me daub the *Rebecca* perfume on my life.

The first time I saw *Rebecca* was after my divorce, while living in the aftermath of those years when I had assumed the role of the naïve wife to my widower-husband. Now I am trying to make sense of what transpired by viewing my life through one of Hitchcock's lenses. I find myself constructing the memory of that time anew, rolling the film so that the picture of my marriage bears an uncanny resemblance to *Rebecca*. No wonder the movie haunts me still.

◆

In the opening scene in Monte Carlo, the young American woman (Joan Fontaine) stumbles upon the brooding English widower Maxim de Winter (Laurence Olivier) when he is about to plunge off a cliff into the sea. When she cries out, "No! Stop!" she breaks his suicidal spell. From then on he is attracted to this ingénue, whose childish naïveté revives his own will to live. She describes herself as a "paid companion," a position she assumed after the death of her father the previous summer. In so many ways, she finds in Maxim yet another father, and he finds in her the youthful innocence he lacks. In the Hotel Princesse where they are both staying, Maxim insists she have lunch with him at his table after she has spilled over a small bud vase at hers—the first of her many clumsy accidents. Then, intent on driving her in his car to some place where she can sketch, he orders her to finish her lunch. "Oh come on. Eat it up like a good girl." She looks at him docilely, then down at her plate, and does as she is told like an obedient child, looking back up at him for approval. In this short encounter, they have established both their attraction for each other and the father/daughter dynamic of their relationship.

Maxim's dead wife Rebecca begins to haunt the young woman on this first day, even before she has any thought of marrying him. She overhears her employer, the brash, tacky American, Mrs. Edythe Van Hopper (Florence Bates), talking to a nurse about Mr. de Winter and his late wife, who drowned "while she was sailing near Manderley. . . . She was the beautiful Rebecca Hildreth, you know. They say he simply adored her." Those last two sentences return to echo and torment the young woman's dreams that night, as she tosses and turns in bed. For much of the movie, this young, working-class, nameless woman, soon to be the new Mrs. de Winter, will spend her time fretting over her inability to measure up to the beautiful, aristocratic Rebecca—a fear first instilled in her by the cruel and petty Mrs. Van Hopper once she learns that Maxim intends to marry her paid companion immediately.

Mrs. Van Hopper berates the vulnerable young woman: "I suppose I have to hand it to you for [being] a fast worker. How did you manage it? . . . You haven't the faintest idea of what it means to be a great lady." She clinches her attack by saying de Winter is marrying her not because he loves her, but because he "just couldn't go on living alone" in that big empty mansion. After looking her up and down dismissively, she harrumphs disdainfully: "Hmm! Mrs. de Winter." These are her parting words on the young woman's precipitous rise in class through marriage.

♦

I married Grey when I was thirty-nine. By then I'd had a previous marriage to a foreign bigamist annulled, only to feel "widowed" five years later by the death of my American fiancé. Yet I still felt like an ingénue when I moved into the apartment that was to become my home for the next twenty years.

I moved into Grey's apartment on the Upper West Side ten months after his wife died. We had been dating since the previous September. I forget when he proposed to me. We decided—or, rather, I sense that he felt—it would not be right to marry until after the first anniversary of the death of his late wife in September. The first time I saw his apartment was after the funeral service, when I rode uptown in a cab with his good friend, an older Park Avenue blonde.

Grey's smart, accomplished third wife, Lisa, a successful city planner, had died tragically in a plane crash while returning from a business trip in the Midwest. My husband kept a photograph of her in his study throughout the twelve years of our marriage, prominently displayed beside an urn that once held her ashes and a small cross-legged, black stone Buddha. She stands in a garden, with her arms comfortably crossed, each hand holding the opposite elbow. There is an air of composure and self-possession about her. She was an accomplished woman, having come from a suburban, intellectual family.

Though educated at Cornell and Berkeley, I felt self-conscious about my working-class, Brooklyn roots. My father never went to college and my mother had to drop out of NYU when she had her first nervous breakdown and was hospitalized. I went to college on a full scholarship after graduating from South Shore High School, known more for its race riots than its academics. I always felt I had to study harder to catch up with most of my classmates. I spent hours in the library, reading such classics as *Paradise Lost* for the first time and looking up words in the dictionary, unlike the many graduates of prep schools and good suburban high schools for whom the classics were old news.

How could I ever measure up to Grey's late wife? That was the perfume I breathed: the fumes of failing to measure up.

◆

My close friend Susan introduced me to Grey at a friend's photography opening, saying he had an interest in poetry. At a dinner party afterwards we took seats near each other. I'd had a traumatic experience earlier that day and was relating the episode to him and the others at my end of the table.

"I was doing a freelance editing job for a famous radio personality. I had gone over to his apartment to deliver the disk along with a hard copy of my work. He said he couldn't pay me right away until I incorporated myself—there was some tax issue, I didn't understand it. So here I was about to leave his apartment without a check and with no real proof of my work. So I asked him for a receipt and he asked me, 'Why do you want one?' And I said, 'Because I need to pay my rent.' This money was not pocket money, but a few thousand dollars that I was counting on to tide me over until I began teaching again at Cooper Union that fall," I explained to the table.

"Well, he wrote out a receipt, put it on the glass cocktail table in front of me. I picked it up and said 'Thank you.' And he flew into a rage. 'Thank you? Thank you?! You don't think I'm gonna pay you? How dare you!' Then he went over to the table by the elevator and picked up a tall blue crystal vase and with two hands and raised it over his head and heaved it into my open knapsack on the floor. 'Here! You want something! Take *THIS* as collateral.' I took the vase out of my pack; it was heavier than I had imagined and thought to myself, *This guy could have killed me with it if he'd struck my head instead.* I couldn't help myself from saying, 'You have a problem with anger.' And he screamed at me, 'Do you have Ph.D. in psychology?!' 'I don't need a Ph.D. to figure it out.' As I was talking, I was inching toward the door, deciding I had better not say anything else to further antagonize him. The whole time, I realized, one of his assistants was cutting up vegetables in the kitchen and she never came out to say a word. When I finally got out into the street, I broke down completely. By the time I got home I was running a fever and there was a message on my answering machine from his assistant to call back with my social security number so she could send me a check."

Grey listened calmly, with a sphinxlike smile. "That's an interesting story. But tell me: Why do you expect people to treat you well?" His eyes sparkled impishly behind his glasses. The comment both disarmed me and made me pause; it was so unexpected. I took it in and mused over it before responding. He had said it without malice, matter-of-factly. An odd remark—one that I will never forget, and that would return to haunt me years later.

"Because I do," was all I could muster. I still feel that way. Expect the best of someone and you are more likely to get it than if you expect the worst. It reminds me of a game I play sometimes while riding the subway. I look at each person and ask myself, *What is ugly about that person?* And find it. Then I ask, *What is beautiful about that person?* And find it.

There was something attractive about Grey. His eyes continued to twinkle behind his gold wire-rims as he smiled at me. Perhaps it was the way he listened so attentively to me. He had light-brown curly hair with some gray in it. A long face. Not a beautiful face, but attractive in its intelligent engagement with me. He was tall and lanky, somewhat freckly, and bore a strong likeness to the composer Gustav Mahler. An intelligent face. *That's my kind of man.* But the thought passed quickly—I knew he was married and I had become engaged to Robbie in late August, only a few weeks before. Later on, once Grey and I were together, he would tell me he'd had the same thought: *That's my kind of woman.* Who knows if he was telling the truth.

♦

A few weeks after the opening, on October 8th, my fiancé Robbie died from an accidental drug overdose. I went into a dark place from which I did not emerge for many months.

In the spring, Grey and his wife Lisa invited my friend Susan out to dinner for her birthday. She invited me along as her "date" (we were both single, straight women in our late thirties), since neither of us had a boyfriend at the time. This was in May, eight months after the death of my fiancé. Susan used to invite me along to many places; she knew I battled prolonged grief (mourning which did become melancholia, as Freud aptly put it) and she often tried to include me, to bring me out of my self-imposed isolation. I remember little else of our meeting.

In July, I invited Grey and his wife Lisa to my birthday party at Nosmo King, the vegetarian restaurant below Canal Street where Robbie and I had loved to dine. Grey showed up and said his wife was out of town. I was talking about my "Chevy body." That's what Dr. Shen, my Chinese doctor of herbal medicine, said about me, explaining my weak life force: "You've got a Chevy body. Some people are born with a Cadillac body. You were born with a Chevy body. No chi. No chi." Grey chuckled as he sat across from me, one of two men among a dozen women friends at the dinner party. Later, once we were together, he told me, "You know, if I had been single then I would have mailed you a tiny model Chevy car. Just for fun."

♦

I saw Grey and Lisa one other time, when they came up to Saratoga to celebrate Lisa's birthday. They stopped by to visit me at Yaddo, the artists' colony, in August of 1994 and I offered to take them to the Saratoga Race Course for a brief visit. Lisa stood by the entrance to the racetrack. She had long, thick light-brown hair that she clipped back from the sides of her face with barrettes. She had a sweet smile, with a long nose that dipped just above her lips, and she wore granny glasses. She could have stepped out of the Victorian era, with her long pastel-flowered skirt and the large sun hat she held gracefully in her hands.

♦

In early September, I received a phone call from my friend Susan. "Sharon, I've got really tragic news to tell you. Grey's wife Lisa has just been killed in a plane crash. The memorial service will be held on Tuesday at the Plaza Chapel. I thought you might want to go. I know you only met her a few times, but Lisa was an amazing person. I know you two would have become good friends."

I put down the phone. Exactly eleven months to the day after my fiancé Robbie died, Grey's wife Lisa died in a plane crash. I do not believe in fate and I do not know why these two events occurred as they did. And yet they did happen that way.

♦

Grey is now single and I am now single. How unlikely this scenario was. I had to act. I had been so unlucky in love. Would this be a chance for me to be with a stable, decent man? His wife had just died. But I knew that most men don't remain single for long. I had needed to grieve for nearly a year. *Women mourn, men replace.* Perhaps the old saw had an element of truth to it.

♦

I attended the memorial service, feeling a bit awkward about being there. After all, I had only met Lisa a few times. I drove back uptown in a cab with one of Grey's close friends, a wealthy woman—an American aristocrat, if such a thing exists—and I felt distinctly outclassed. During that first visit to the apartment I remember a huge coffee percolator and a maid dressed in black with a white apron preparing and serving food. This was the kind of home I had only seen in Woody Allen movies: a comfortable apartment filled with oak bookcases and warm carpeting. It was so far removed from my shabby rental in Brooklyn.

That week I called Grey up and invited him over for dinner. I told him I had invited Susan as well. I thought we would both be more comfortable that way. He called me back.

"Thank you for the invitation. If it's all right with you, my inclination is for just the two of us to have dinner."

"Okay, if that's what you prefer."

Grey comes over to my apartment in Brooklyn, with its worn, unpolished wooden floors, no room dividers, and a futon from my San Francisco days. Though I have put up bookcases wherever there is a spare wall, I see my apartment still looks like a graduate student's, with my makeshift door-and-file-cabinet desk the first thing he sees as he steps into my living room.

I have decided to cook risotto for the first time. Unlike most people, I don't test out recipes before making them for my guests. As he stands around the small kitchen with me, he comments, "You know you should have heated up the broth first." After dinner, when he is getting up to leave, he tries embracing me and he grabs my behind. I push his hand away. "I think it's a bit too soon for that."

♦

Grey and I began to date about two weeks after the funeral of his late wife. "Far, far too soon," said my therapist, who warned me that he was on the rebound and I would only get hurt. I knew that Susan would also disapprove. She seemed to be in deep mourning for Lisa, though I don't remember them as being particularly close. I knew that if Susan knew I was already dating Grey, she would view it as a betrayal of Lisa, which, in a way, it was.

Years later, when I asked another poet why she would never accept his friendship, she said: "Why, someone would have mourned longer even for a dog!"

♦

In *Rebecca*, while Mrs. Van Hopper stays in bed in her hotel room with a three-day cold, being tended to by a nurse, the young woman goes out on the sly with the brooding Mr. de Winter. She feigns to her obstreperous employer that she is taking tennis lessons as she goes off with him to sketch in the countryside. It is the kind of lie a young girl might tell a prudish, disapproving mother or auntie. On the third day, while they are out driving, the young woman, reacting to Maxim's aloofness and her own diminished sense of self, finally gets up the nerve to ask him why he is spending time with her. "You've blotted out the past more than all the bright lights of Monte Carlo," he replies. He has just scolded her for biting her fingernails and made her cry by almost forcing her out of the car. He asks her to promise him "never to wear black satin or pearls. Or to be thirty-six years old." In effect, he is asking her never to grow up.

♦

Early on, when our dating was still a secret, I lent Grey a bright red, wool scarf after he had slept over at my apartment. That day he bumped into

Susan on the street, and she kept complimenting him on the scarf. As though she knew. More than once, he made sure to stop us on the street right outside her apartment, to kiss. Something illicit about this amused and excited him. And I laughed along. As though Susan had become the stand-in for Lisa, his late wife, whom he was cheating on.

I did not understand that I was part of a pattern: that the way he got from one wife to the next (I was to be his fourth) was by betraying the former one. When I asked him why he divorced his second wife, he said, "She was always very angry. I felt I was wasting myself on her." I did not learn until much later, after I had found and read the court documents from their divorce trial, that he had publicly shamed her by carrying on openly with another woman while they were still married.

At the time, I did not view his quick courtship with me as a betrayal. He was, after all, a widower. He assured me he was able to mourn for Lisa on one track and move on in his life with me on another track. *Was this really possible? To ride the train of mourning while simultaneously riding the train of courtship?* I trusted Grey. As a doctor, he had an air of authority. I had mourned for almost a year over the sudden death of my fiancé; by September, I felt ready for a new relationship and a new life. I was thirty-eight years old. It was time.

Grey invited me to move in with him. Here was a man who said he valued domestic life. We still had time to have a child together.

I would be moving into upper middle-class comfort, exchanging my fourth-floor walk-up in Carroll Gardens for an elevator building on the Upper West Side. Stately Arts and Crafts oak furniture. Original art on the walls. I gave away my five white, particle-board bookcases from Ikea. They had no place next to glass-fronted Stickley bookcases full of signed first editions.

◆

On July 1, 1995, I move in. "I'm only asking you to do one thing. Could you please remove Lisa's picture from the bedroom?" It seems like a reasonable request. How can he expect me to sleep in bed with him, have sex with him, with his late wife standing there with her arms folded, looking on? First Grey's face goes grim, which I know means grave disapproval. Then he says simply, drily, slowly, "I'll do it, but you should not have asked. You should never have asked."

It is his warning to me. I have reached—even overstepped—the boundary of what is possible for me to assert in this new home. And I pull back, though somewhere inside of me there flickers the knowledge that I am right and he is wrong. I should not have had to ask; he should have known to do it. Just as he knew we should buy a new bed and discard the one he had slept in with her.

◆

Maxim proposes to the young woman while he is busy getting dressed in a separate room. When she thinks he wants "a secretary or something," he snaps: "I'm asking you to marry me, you little fool!" His proposal is about as unromantic as if he were hiring a wife. When she says she loves him "desperately," he says, "Bless you for that. I'll remind you of that some day. You won't believe me. It's a pity you have to grow up." We never see Maxim and the young woman kiss on the lips. To consummate their "engagement," he kisses his own finger before placing it on her forehead. A paternal kiss if ever there was one.

Maxim and the young woman have a perfunctory marriage ceremony at the *Mairie*, the Mayor's office in Monte Carlo. No bridal gown or veil, no tuxedo. Sensing she probably wanted more, Maxim, as an afterthought, hastily buys her a big bouquet of flowers from the street vendor outside.

◆

Over dinner at Gramercy Tavern, Grey proposes to me, holding out a box from Tiffany's containing a small diamond necklace. He never gives me a ring. Somehow, he has gotten it into his head that I do not like rings. I think that subconsciously, he does not want me to be seen wearing an engagement ring less than a year after his late wife's death. Too showy. A diamond necklace could mean anything. I have never liked diamonds and have to pretend to love this one, whose tiny point periodically digs into my upper chest. I wear it all the time, which seems to be what he expects of me.

Grey knows I want a wedding with my family present, but this will be his fourth marriage and, scarcely a year after his wife's death, he does not want a public ceremony. Grey has rejected his suburban Jewish upbringing and wants nothing to do with Jewish ceremony, but I insist on a Jewish wedding.

"All right. But let's have a private wedding. With just you, me, and the rabbi."

"I think you need to have witnesses."

"Are you sure? Call your rabbi friend Ron. Maybe he'll find a law that says it's okay."

I try explaining to him that a wedding, especially a Jewish wedding, is a public event. When I speak to my rabbi, I am relieved to learn that a minyan (a quorum of ten Jews) must be present for the marriage to be legal.

"All right. So let's get married in her study. And you can have your family there. I just don't want mine."

"Why?" At the time, his mother and father, both elderly, are still alive.

"I think they'll be bad luck. They've been through this with me several times before."

I take him at his word. In time, though, I come to see the real reason is his utter disdain for them.

◆

On a Sunday, I take Grey to meet my family at the home of my sister Marla, who lives with her husband and child outside of Princeton, New Jersey. My father has driven in from Cherry Hill with his longtime partner, and my aunt and uncle and two cousins are there as well. They talk in loud voices and drink gin and sing along with my sister as she plays show tunes on the piano. They are uninhibited, unself-conscious, and are enjoying themselves. My father is thrilled at the engagement. Finally, there is someone who can take care of me; that is all that matters to him. So what if Grey is cold and aloof? He is a doctor with money.

On the train ride home Grey says, "You know, I think it would be better if your family didn't attend the wedding ceremony, either."

"What? I thought you said it was okay."

"Yeah, well, I changed my mind. My parents might find out."

He has a way of saying things with grim finality, so I know it will be futile to argue with him. I also know that the real reason he doesn't want my family there is that he finds them déclassé. An embarrassment.

Here were my father, my sister, my aunt and uncle, who had all seen me through the most painful year of my life in the aftermath of Robbie's sudden death. My aunt and uncle had acted like second parents to me, and now Grey would deny them the joy of being at my wedding. Not even my own father would have the honor of being present in the rabbi's study. As the weeks wore on and I tried dissuading Grey from his decision, he said, "No. I said I don't want any of them there. Not your family or mine." I knew that if I insisted, he would call off the wedding. I thought about my first marriage that had to be annulled. *Well, I had a real wedding in Brooklyn the first time I got married, but did not have a real marriage. Now, maybe I'll get to have the real marriage. That's more important than the wedding, which only lasts for a day.*

Grey and I got married in mid-October, under a chuppah in the rabbi's study at Kane Street Synagogue in Brooklyn, with ten random members of the synagogue present as our witnesses.

Grey promised we would have a party on each coast for our friends and family. Right after the ceremony, we flew out to San Francisco. There we had a dinner party with my friends and one old buddy of Grey's, who decided to bring out wedding photos of Grey with his first bride, a woman I had never met; his friend had been the best man. I found it disturbing but said nothing. It felt as though he were saying, "Wives come and go but I remain your friend." I had no idea I, too, would be temporary.

Back in New York, we held a dinner at Sparks Steak House in Manhattan with family and friends from both sides. No dancing. With Grey, there could never be music or dancing. I wore a cranberry-colored tulle dress that I had had custom-made for me by a designer down on Houston Street. Why wear white and pretend it was my first wedding, or his? The dress still hangs in its plastic sheath in my hall closet, worn once. We toasted ourselves. We had a big steak dinner. Then we went home.

♦

When Mrs. de Winter (for that is the only name she gets) is on her way with Maxim de Winter to Manderley for the first time, it suddenly begins to rain, and since they are driving in a car with the top down, he reaches in the back and gives her his raincoat to pull over her head. "Do I have to put it on?" she asks. "Yes. You can't be too careful with children," he responds. So she arrives, cloaked by him and his name, this child bride, somewhat bedraggled when she has to formally meet all the servants upon entering the mansion, including the formidable housekeeper Mrs. Danvers (Judith Anderson).

When the new Mrs. de Winter first walks into Manderley, she is awestruck by what she sees: the grand front entrance, the luxurious rooms. When she sits down for her first dinner in her new home, she takes the napkin off her plate to put on her lap. It bears the initials *RdeW*, short for "Rebecca de Winter." We see those initials on many items in the house, a sign of all the ways the new Mrs. de Winter will be haunted by her predecessor.

♦

The napkin. For a Jewish wedding ceremony, even one held in the rabbi's study, it is customary for the bridegroom to step on a glass wrapped in a napkin and break it. Is it a symbol of the broken hymen? Or of the destruction of the Temple (even at a happy occasion, there must be some remembrance of that sadness)? I watch Grey, ordinarily a bit slapdash with everyday activities, very carefully choose a napkin from the drawer, first picking up a mauve one that would have been there when Lisa was alive, hesitating before casting it aside and then selecting a periwinkle blue napkin from a set I have brought with me from Brooklyn. *Ah. So he doesn't want to use a napkin from his days with her.* Especially not for a ritual sealing his marriage to someone else.

Grey had to have been aware that I was stepping into an apartment suffused with memories of his previous marriage. I knew that many women in my position would have refused, would have insisted upon moving to a new apartment. Or at least that everything—all the furniture—would have to be changed. Somehow, I knew neither of these things would happen. I had tacitly agreed to live in this apartment with a dead woman's things and the memories of her intact. Grey expected me to fit in, to assume the role of wife, to be grateful to him for rescuing me from my meager Brooklyn life. I had risen in rank, married into the comfortable upper middle class, and I would never be looked upon the same way again.

♦

After Mrs. Danvers catches the new Mrs. de Winter wandering through Rebecca's room, which had seemed to the new bride a forbidden sanctuary, Mrs. Danvers proceeds to shame her by showing her all the ways she will never measure up to Rebecca, even down to the sheer black negligee still lying underneath the pillow on the bed. Mrs. Danvers opens the window and leans her face close to the distraught young bride, coaxing her to kill herself by jumping from the window. She almost does jump—until she is startled by the flares in the sky and the hubbub caused, she will learn, by the discovery of Rebecca's boat and her dead body within the hold.

♦

I had no evil housekeeper. No one banished me from any rooms when I first moved in to the apartment where my husband had lived with his late wife. Yet most of her things were still there. Her clothes, unlike Rebecca's, had all been given away quickly, too quickly, so that her friends, even her sister, had no opportunity to keep something of hers as a memento. But her books? Her papers? Her furniture? One of the first things my husband did after I moved in was to buy one more Stickley bookcase, to add to the two large ones already lining one wall in the living room, and cram it full with all his late wife's city-planning books. Her drawings. Her fine art books. Her dead plans. A sturdy, oak-paneled bookcase with glass panes and a brass lock. This bookcase, heavy and expensive, proclaimed: *Herein reside valuable relics of the revered late wife.* Not like my worthless paperbacks, which were banished, like those of an interloper, to the small closet-like room that became my study.

On the night we were married, I sat on the toilet off the master bedroom and thought of killing myself. What was there inside of me that felt like dying? Already I saw how strictly I would have to conform to Grey's style, Grey's choices, Grey's way of doing things. Perhaps I felt dead already.

♦

My memory of the movie *Rebecca* is flawed. I keep forgetting that Rebecca was actually evil and that Maxim detested her, that she was not the best-loved wife. As I keep forgetting that Lisa, the late wife whose things lived on in the apartment I shared with my husband, was not really loved any more than I was. But it is the power of things—and actions—that overpowers. My husband's first, most urgent act was to buy that Stickley bookcase for his dead wife's things. Not for mine. Just as, at Manderley, Rebecca's room—the only one, Mrs. Danvers explains, that faces the sea—was preserved just as it had been when Rebecca was alive. Surely Maxim was complicit in this arrangement.

♦

I could not bear to move into Lisa's study and make it my own, because it had been hers. Her papers, her office supplies were all still there (for years I guiltily used her greeting cards, even her postcards). I was optimistic enough to think I might get pregnant and this room would be the right size for a baby's room. For several years it remained a spare guest room (though we had few guests), and I chose for my study what had once been a storage room that I lined with both Lisa's and my bookcases of cheap, serviceable pine; what more could I need for my books, inherently lacking in value? Not signed first editions, like the ones my husband housed in the living room in the other oak, glass-paneled bookcases. How could I not feel at every turn that I was the lower-class upstart?

♦

213

One year, for my birthday, Grey gives me a card that contains a torn-out page from a copy of E. M. Forster's *Howard's End* that I have owned since college. He has pasted it into the card, circling a paragraph he particularly likes: "Only connect! That was the whole of her sermon. Only connect the prose and the passion, and both will be exalted, and human love will be seen at its height. Live in fragments no longer." I seethe but say nothing. He has destroyed my book and given me this torn fragment as a gift. He never understood that my paperbacks might be valuable to me—that monetary value is not the only kind there is.

The best I could hope to do was to become an acolyte and help him in the service of preserving Lisa's memory. Never changing the kitchen. Never changing anything but the bed frame and mattress in the bedroom. We could add some furniture—he would order a new cherry wardrobe for me—but nothing could be taken away. Her grandmother's Biedermeier mahogany dresser, severe as a German dowager, stood in our bedroom. Her deep-red Persian rug covering the floor in the hallway caught my steps each time I entered the apartment.

♦

On the new Mrs. de Winter's first morning at Manderley, a servant named Fritz teaches her, in effect, the late Mrs. de Winter's routine of doing her correspondence and making her phone calls in the morning room; he even has to point the way to the room. She is literally and figuratively lost in this huge mansion. On the desk are the diaries, stationery, and address book with a big letter "R" on each. When the phone rings, she picks it up and says quickly that Mrs. de Winter is not there, that she has been dead for over a year. She knows she is not the real wife, at least not yet. When Mrs. Danvers appears and asks her to approve the lunch menu and to fill in the sauce she wants, she is flustered, and tells Mrs. Danvers to choose the one that the late Mrs. de Winter would have chosen. Returning to the books, she accidentally knocks over a figurine, guiltily picks up all the pieces and, in a panic, hides them quickly in a desk drawer behind the stationery.

The clumsiness of the new wife. Her shame in hiding the broken pieces from the judgmental eyes of the malevolent Mrs. Danvers. Why, as the lady of the house, would she have to hide the accident? Because she feels guilty; she is there because Rebecca has died, and the broken pieces become the physical embodiment of that guilt, of the crime of replacement—and, worse, of inadequate replacement. The ingénue has gone from being the henpecked servant of an ill-tempered older woman to being an aristocrat with a house full of her own servants. Yet she feels more insecure than ever.

Tricked into the worst of her marital blunders by the malevolent Mrs. Danvers, Mrs. de Winter, unwittingly, ends up wearing a costume that is identical to the one Rebecca wore the year before to the costume ball. She descends the staircase, so girlishly proud of the way she looks in her off-the-shoulder tulle dress and beribboned, floppy hat—until Maxim turns and catches sight of her. Enraged, he orders her to take it off and put on anything else. For Mrs. Danvers, the young woman's gaucherie is one more way of proving to her that she should never have married Mr. de Winter and tried to replace her Rebecca.

◆

How many of Lisa's things did I have to use? Her bookshelves, of course, in what became my study. Grey bought me a new desk that he guided me in selecting from Scott Jordan, the store he approved of. But there was room for one other table, one he clearly wanted put to use: the one his late wife had built. Just as she and Grey had woven the ash-blue linen webbing of the dining room chairs that I sat in with him each evening over dinner. Did I have a choice? Could I have said to him, *No, you use Lisa's desk if you want to.* I silently agreed. I did not feel I had the power to say no.

◆

Once, while moving a piece of furniture in the bedroom, Grey finds a necklace and, barely looking at it, says, "Here. Take it." I recognize instantly it is not mine and must have been Lisa's. I say nothing and take the necklace. *Does he really pay so little attention to the things she had worn and that I wear?* It is a necklace with forty opaque amber beads strung together: the exact age Lisa was when she died. Amber. Fossilized resin. Jewelry that captures time past and preserves it. I wear the amber necklace sometimes as a symbol of my acceptance. That I have replaced, however imperfectly, someone else.

Grey never comments on my wearing of the necklace. I come to see it almost doesn't matter which wife he is married to. I am the *current wife*, as he refers to me. Why not wear the necklace?

♦

I often felt guilty that my good fortune—my moving out of a run-down apartment in Brooklyn's Carroll Gardens before it got trendy, a neighborhood I hated because of the sad memories it held (the death of my fiancé and my failed, annulled first marriage), and moving into a sprawling two-bedroom apartment on the Upper West Side—was all because of the accidental death from a plane crash of my husband's late wife. And so I submitted to almost all his conditions. He would have sole authority over the design of the apartment, over all the major and minor decisions of our life together.

Perhaps I agreed to so much because he promised to take care of me—something no one, not even my father, had done adequately before. Grey plucked me out of white-collar poverty. Despite my Ph.D. from Cornell, I was then teaching English as a Second Language at NYU and had been an adjunct assistant professor teaching introductory humanities courses at the Cooper Union for ten years and was going nowhere, doing some freelance editing on the side and writing poetry the whole time. I lacked pluck and self-confidence, and stayed in a position where I was exploited. I was barely eking out a living, though by living frugally I could save up enough money to travel during the summer. When I could finally afford to leave my ESL job, my relief was mingled with embarrassment. I wrote on the blackboard—I was too shaky to say it aloud to my students: "I AM GETTING MARRIED."

How many things did I clumsily break or ruin? I am seated on one of the blue-gray woven dining room chairs as I write this. (Since the divorce, I have exchanged the claustrophobic confines of my closet study for writing at the dining table in the spacious living room, with its two large north-facing windows.) Early on—before Grey's proposal or after it, I cannot remember—I accidentally toppled a glass of red wine on one of these chairs. Clumsy, as the young bride-to-be always is when she feels she is replacing a more sure-handed one.

Grey warned me, "If the stain doesn't come out or you do that again, you'll have to go." I knew he was not joking. I said nothing and cleaned up the stain, vowing to myself to be more careful.

Other, later mishaps I hid, just like Mrs. de Winter. There was a set of handmade ceramic plates in the house; once, while washing up, a large steel pot slipped from my grasp as I was placing it on the drying rack and it shattered them all. I wrapped them in newspaper, threw them all out and never mentioned it. I counted on my husband's absentmindedness. He never noticed they were missing.

♦

Something in the way Grey treated me, like a misbehaving child, reminds me of a traumatic experience I had in the second grade. I committed the unthinkable. My Brooklyn public school routinely imposed martial law on its students. Silence lining up in the schoolyard. Silence walking up the stairs. Hands at one's sides.

I am eight years old. I have gone to the auditorium to walk through the science fair with my class. There is a clay model of the surface of the moon. On impulse, without thinking, I reach out my hand to touch it and immediately a student guard wearing a silver badge runs over to write down my name. It could have been a scene out of Kafka. For the next week, I am shaking in my seat, the good student, the one who never gets into trouble, the straight-A student, waiting to be called up to Mrs. Meunier's office, the head of the guards, a monster in the form of a teacher with lockjaw who yells at children who break the rules. All of us consider getting "reported" the worst fate in life. She never summons me. I feel certain I would have died if she had.

♦

I was afraid of displeasing Grey. Terrified of the repercussions. I needed him to be the kind of father I never had. The grownup authority. The one who could give me sage advice and direction in my life. The one I could count on and trust.

Each time I brought into the apartment the smallest item—kitchen hand towels (were the colors too bright?) or potholders (black with raised white dots)—I worried, *Will they be acceptable?* I suffered over each decision, feeling the gray weight of his judgment upon me.

Eventually, as our marriage went into its decline, Grey would end up concurring with his mother (whose ideas he had always derided) and acting out her formula: *The secret to a good marriage is separate bedrooms.* When our son kept coming into our bed and disturbing us and I insisted that Grey, the sounder sleeper, put him back in his own bed, eventually Grey gave up and ceded the bed to me and my son, while he went off to sleep in his study, a room which increasingly became his sanctuary away from the family. There he had his meditation cushion, a shrine set up with a Buddha, the urn that had contained his dead wife's ashes, and her photograph. Then he had a Japanese cabinet made by hand to house his clothes, moving more and more of his belongings out of what increasingly became *my* bedroom.

I see now I was complicit in it all. I no longer enjoyed having sex with Grey, he snored loudly, he woke me up. I much preferred the warm, sleeping tumble of limbs of my beautiful little son. A troubling, yet perfect, Oedipal arrangement that could not last.

♦

Rebecca strikes me as a movie about memory: lived and imagined, constructed and deconstructed. As my marriage—built on the fault line of two deaths, my fiancé's and my husband's wife's—was about memory.

As I rewatch *Rebecca*, the movie more and more embodies for me the power of narrative truth as opposed to historical truth. "Narrative truth," wrote Donald Spence in *Narrative Truth and Historical Truth*, "can be defined as the criterion we use to decide when a certain experience has been captured to our satisfaction . . . [and] the fit of the pieces takes on an aesthetic finality." Narrative truth "becomes just as real as any other kind of truth." It may sound odd to call a movie a historical memory, given that most movies (including Hitch's) are oneiric, fictional narratives. And yet we can watch a movie over and over again, replay a scene to make sure we are not misremembering.

No matter how many times I replay the movie, the *lived memory*—my *narrative memory*—of it, the one that convinces, that captures it to my aesthetic and psychological satisfaction, is not the one that the ending reveals. The *historical truth* of *Rebecca* must take into account the ending: that Rebecca is actually an evil character, that Maxim did not love her, that she was cheating on him and then cheated death (Rebecca had just learned she was ill with cancer) by accidentally hitting her head while quarreling with Maxim over her infidelities. All of these revelations are somehow psychologically, even aesthetically, unsatisfying.

The *feeling history*—the narrative truth—of the movie is that Rebecca will always haunt the new young wife because of her "breeding, brains, and beauty," as Maxim himself summarizes Rebecca's allure. The new wife will always feel inadequate against the idealized memory of Rebecca Mrs. Danvers has kept alive.

♦

The young woman, the new wife, "never had a name," as Hitchcock admits to Truffaut. She is a woman whose identity is entirely subsumed by her various roles. First, she's the "paid companion" of Mrs. Van

Hopper. Then she is Maxim's rescuer, saving him from suicide. Once back at Manderley, she is the new Mrs. de Winter, the clumsy ingénue, the object of his brooding narcissism.

♦

In my marriage, my husband soon took to calling me by generic names. Quickly, I became *Girlfriend.* I was, after all, his fourth wife and I surmised that, by this expedient, he would not have to worry about any slip-ups in or out of bed. Or else he would refer to me as his *current wife.* I accepted these somewhat awkward terms of endearment, justifying his use of the label as an expression of his ability, as a Buddhist, to live and place us in the midst of the momentary. At the time, I never understood the darker implications of that nickname, the temporary status it gave me.

Who *was* I, after all, to him, but a replacement for the dead wife who would always loom larger than the living? She was the better one, the more successful one, the one he must have loved more—despite his telling me that I was easier to live with, that Lisa could be difficult in private. I never quite believed him. What I saw and registered, *my* narrative truth, was that he had preserved the apartment as a shrine to his dead love. Perhaps he only married me out of loneliness, and so that he would have someone to assist him in these efforts. I felt his love for her must have matched his efforts at maintaining the apartment-as-shrine. I knew it was impossible for me to compete with the dead.

When we purchased a new refrigerator, it *had* to be black to go along with the black stove, black floor, black marble countertops that Lisa had designed. The only one we could find was too tall for the nook into which it had to fit. In an unspoken agreement with my husband, the building's superintendent, who had known Lisa, spent two days working to cut down and preserve the cabinets above the refrigerator, making it possible for the space to accommodate the new appliance. It seemed as though everyone was in on this conspiracy of memory. At the time, I felt so touched by the gesture, the sheer effort it took to accomplish.

Now, I see it as one more macabre link in the chain that bound me to a straitened way of seeing and living.

When our marriage is failing, and I try to buy a replacement kitchen garbage can, we fight.

"You can't bring anything stainless steel in here. Don't you know that? Take it back."

"Why?"

"It has to be black. Now return that one before I throw you both out of here."

And so I do. I find an acceptable black can to match the black floor, the black stove, the black refrigerator. My blackened heart.

♦

Late in our marriage, Grey said, "If you don't stop complaining and instead show some more gratitude, you're going to have to leave." I brushed it off. *I'm the mother of his only child, our son. He can't be serious.* He had married me. He had promised me a stable, domestic home. He knew my background. Yet as it turned out, even after all these years of marriage, he was serious. Only *he* would be the one to leave—something I could never have imagined, given the symbolic status of our apartment. By then he was already making plans for a new life with a new lover, a truth my naïve trust in him would not allow me to face.

Now I have become the reluctant guardian of this neglected shrine. Grey's late wife liked pastels, he preferred dull colors. I have had the walls in the hallway painted tangerine; my bedroom is now teal; the kitchen, sunflower yellow; my bathroom, apple green. The kitchen fixtures and floor are still black. I still have to use baby oil to polish the absurdly impractical, black marble countertop she chose. I still find myself buying a new black stove because it matches.

♦

The living wife must have felt some degree of guilt toward Rebecca. Living or dead, Rebecca was being *replaced* by her. Mrs. Danvers becomes the human embodiment of that guilt. (Some have theorized a lesbian relationship between Rebecca and Mrs. Danvers, or at least an erotic attachment of Mrs. Danvers to Rebecca; perhaps this transgressive sexuality, for 1940, explains why Mrs. Danvers had to be burned alive along with the house.) Mrs. Danvers is also the stand-in for Rebecca, the reminder of all the ways this simple young woman, clearly not of an aristocratic background, could never measure up. Of course, every wife is replacing someone, even if it is usually the man's mother and not a dead wife.

♦

In discussing the movie with Truffaut, Hitch points out the flaw in the story—of the other woman's body found down the beach at the same time that Rebecca's is discovered, and the lack of an inquest to determine the identity of this second body. Truffaut confirms that narrative memory overrides the historical memory of the movie: "[T]he whole story is so completely dominated by the psychological elements that no one pays any attention to the explanations, particularly since they don't really affect the basic situation." Truffaut, as astute a reader of film as any, actually asks Hitchcock to explain the movie's ending, about what actually happened to Rebecca and "whether the husband believes himself that he is guilty." Hitchcock says no. It's almost a laughable moment but so psychologically revealing. Truffaut, like myself (and, I'd wager, many viewers), is caught under the same spell of belief about Rebecca as is the young bride. The historical truth of the movie (what actually happened at the end) wars with the narrative truth or memory.

Even Hitch himself misremembers the ending of his own movie while talking to Truffaut: "Well, the explanation is that Rebecca wasn't killed by her husband; she committed suicide because she had cancer." Or at least he forgets to add that this explanation also turns out to have been false.

I keep rewatching the movie's ending in order to remember what Maxim confesses to his young wife. He admits he went to the cottage to confront Rebecca over her affair with her cousin Favell; he admits that he struck her, after she told him she was pregnant. Then she fell and hit her head "on a heavy piece of ship's tackle," which killed her. An accidental death. Maxim covers it up at the inquest because he fears he will be accused of murder as the jealous husband. Instead, he makes her death look like a suicide by drowning in her boat. Finally, at the movie's end, the London doctor Rebecca visited on the day she died reveals that Rebecca was not pregnant after all—as she had led her husband, her lover, and even Mrs. Danvers to believe—but had inoperable cancer. The detective for the inquest, the cousin-and-lover, and even Mrs. Danvers all end up believing Rebecca committed suicide and her motive was that she was dying of cancer. Only Maxim, the new Mrs. de Winter, and the audience are privy to what really happened.

What a convoluted, messy ending—one that I, like so many viewers, can never quite hang on to. Can never quite believe. The eerie music, the mood, the gaunt, ghostlike, dread-inducing figure of Mrs. Danvers whose sudden appearances all build such a powerful narrative memory—a poetic memory—may overwhelm what actually happened, may be truer than the truth.

◆

What is the narrative truth of my marriage as opposed to the historical truth? And which is the one I am writing now?

I must have been happy, at least for the first few years, but it was always an anxious happiness. Perhaps I felt guilty that I no longer remained faithful to the memory of my dead fiancé. After eleven months of mourning, I, too, had moved on, though I continued to think and write poems about him.

I recently found an unpublished poem I wrote shortly after Grey and I began dating. I had almost forgotten that there was ever an erotic charge between us—a charge coupled with my idealization of Grey, which he thrived on. It was, I think, his apparent stability that I found so compelling.

You

Untwisted
at the core—all petal

a water lily floating
even in fall

all my life I've loved
men of such beauty

yet all, all

with the stem thrown back
so the petals fall askew

into my waiting hands

or, as in raku, crackled
through and through to seal the glaze

but you—just sitting—
a green pad that floats

the bud
        bending

that rights itself again
in my palm at night

When my idealization of Grey crumbled, as it did after we had a child—when we began to argue and I realized I was as much an expert at parenting as he, if not more so—Grey retreated, first by sleeping in a bed in his study. As a longtime practitioner of Buddhist meditation, he also chose to spend more and more time away from home at his meditation center. At the time, I failed to understand that Grey did not weather rough patches in a marriage. I don't believe he knew how to work through a marriage's inevitable difficulties. Nor did he believe in trying.

As Grey went numb in my presence and withdrew more and more, I accepted it. Partly because our relationship had always been based on accommodating myself to him, partly because subconsciously I must have experienced this altered Grey as a version of my drugged mother, who was subdued and silent most of the time. Grey liked to take naps, and when he did, he bent one elbow to cover his eyes—exactly as my mother had done. I found his emotional vacancy unsettling but oddly familiar. This is what love felt like. And my trust never wavered.

I thought this difficult time would pass. In retrospect, I see he had begun searching for my replacement—first attempting to seduce a younger version of me (who happened to have been my student, another *crazy poet*, as he labeled us both) and then, when she rebuffed him, setting his sights on an older woman, another doctor like himself. I was number four; why not move on to number five.

I had seen Grey as a bulwark of stability, which had always been part of his appeal. Now I came to see him as a volcano that periodically erupted when the woman he was with no longer idealized him. With his silent rage, he scorched her out of his way and moved on to a new, adoring woman.

As time goes on, I realize how much I lived in the shadow of Grey's marriage to Lisa. How much her ghost haunted us both.

A singular memory arises. One of the first times, if not *the* first time, Grey brought me up to what had been *their* apartment, his key broke off in the lock. "She doesn't want us to get in," he remarked, half-jokingly. It was the closest he ever came to voicing his guilt, his own feeling of being haunted by his late wife, especially since he was replacing her so soon by bringing me into the apartment that had originally been hers. Perhaps he needed to replace her quickly, as his grief over her sudden, premature death was too much for him to bear alone. I somehow sensed as much.

Now that Grey has moved on to living with what amounts to his fifth wife, I find it difficult not to view my role (no matter that our marriage lasted over a decade and we had a child together) as the transitional relationship that got him through the protracted, oblique period of mourning for his third wife Lisa.

Perhaps I have inhaled the smoky fumes of *Rebecca* a bit too deeply in reflecting upon my marriage. That has always been a danger.

In *Rebecca*, the widower Maxim is finally freed from the past when Manderley goes up in flames, a fire set by Mrs. Danvers that also consumes her. My widower-husband—I can't help but see it this way— finally freed himself from the past when he torched our marriage.

Vertigo: What Do Men and Women Want?

If I let you change me, will that do it? If I do what you tell me, will you love me?

–Judy to Scottie

I CAME DOWN with the flu for the first time in thirty years, my fever spiking up into the triple digits: 102, 103. Home alone. The lost week. Day sweats. Night extinction. Moaning. Skin painful even to the non-touch.

Returning home in a cab after an evening of sex with a man who had grown increasingly violent with me, I could feel a fever coming on. I think this was my body's best way of making certain I withdrew from an unlovely thing.

I fell ill in order to give myself time to heal from a situation I otherwise could not or would not face: I was involved with a man who needed to dominate me. His powerful, desperate desire for me, which felt like a drug when we were together, was predicated on his need to control and limit my movements and any impulse that did not coincide with his own.

At its best, sex can feel like an intimate conversation between two people through the medium of their bodies. This was not a conversation so much as a sexual harangue: his body attempting to subjugate and bludgeon mine.

◆

I met Carl on a dating site. He was tall, with glasses and a receding hairline. In his early sixties, he had a wiry body that he kept in shape by running several miles daily. We arranged to meet for a drink at Trattoria Dell'Arte across from Carnegie Hall, where I was headed afterwards.

When Carl enters the restaurant and takes his seat beside me, the attraction between us is palpable. Neither of us speaks of it. It all happens wordlessly—"with looks and smiles," as Tolstoy put it—and we both understand it is happening. I remember feeling a bit drunk—a combination of nerves and desire—though neither of us imbibes any alcohol that night.

Carl grows animated when he talks about his interests—architecture, French New Wave cinema, cemeteries—and his passion for Russian literature, which is something we share. We both happen to be reading the new translation of *Anna Karenina*, a book I have read at least three times. Carl is a retired journalist, still hoping he can manage to finish the novel he has been working on for years.

On this first date, I bring along a copy of *Poetry* magazine to give to him, which contains several of my poems along with a short interview. I do not want to overwhelm him with a whole book but I do want him to know I am a serious poet. He thanks me and puts it on the small shelf in front of him. Afterwards, while sitting at the concert, I realize with a jolt that he has left it there. I run back during intermission and find the magazine still in the same place, untouched. Carl has even forgotten that he has forgotten it.

◆

Though he never said so directly, Carl dismissed anything not in his purview. I can still see his face going blank when I brought up the name Pessoa. Not that I minded that he did not know who Fernando Pessoa was; I was happy to tell him about the Portuguese Modernist poetic master of masks and why his work intrigued me. But I saw Carl did not really care to know. He asked no questions, looked slightly bored, so I fell silent. He moved on quickly to talk about the history of Green-Wood Cemetery, something he had been researching for his novel.

How, how could I have found myself with someone—a writer and an intellectual, no less—who had no interest in my interests? Who had, alas, no interest in me? Did the power of our sexual attraction override everything else?

The indifference went so deep that I was not really there as more than a woman-cipher.

How did I allow myself to be extinguished? Why—how—is it so easy for me (is this true for other women?) to slip from being open to someone to being trespassed upon, even erased? How can I hold on to my sense of self as a woman while still remaining open to the otherness of a man?

◆

During one of those long nights in bed with the flu, in my feverish haze and with a bored antipathy to so much mediocre cinema, I found myself wanting to see something darkly complex. Hitchcock, I knew it had to be. So I chose *Vertigo* (1958) because I could not remember it well and, now that I was running a high fever and feeling vertigo, it seemed the appropriate movie to watch. Both fever and vertigo involve the dizzying feeling that we are not in control of the space we inhabit. That we might fall—into delirium, or into love, or off a rooftop.

◆

"I look up, I look down," Scottie (James Stewart) says in an early scene in *Vertigo*, while he is visiting his old girlfriend and college buddy Midge (Barbara Bel Geddes) in her North Beach apartment. He feels safe climbing up and down her yellow, step-stool chair because he has his wits about him, until he happens to glance down through her window at the street below and his vertigo returns—a vertigo brought on, initially, by a traumatic rooftop police chase in which a fellow cop fell to his death in attempting to save Scottie's life.

When Scottie first visits Midge, they are chatting away as she is busily sketching a design for a new brassiere. Midge, the blonde woman in glasses, the fashion designer who is in love with Scottie, tells him he is the only man she would marry, but for Scottie (whom Midge calls Johnny-O) she lacks any sexual allure, any mystery. With his cane he points to the pink, frilly, strapless contraption hanging from some wires beside her desk lamp. "What's this doohickey?" he asks earnestly, as though he has never seen a bra before. "It's a brassiere. You know about those things. You're a big boy now," Midge chides him. I love the way that moment reveals how little, in general, Scottie knows about women, setting him up for being hoodwinked.

Scottie falls in love with "Madeleine," who is a mere stand-in for his old friend's wife. He has lost his balance, even before he has an attack of vertigo. She is a simulacrum. Judy (Kim Novak) falls in love with Scottie, even though she is tricked out as Madeleine, the supposedly possessed, suicidal wife of Scottie's old friend. Judy wants to believe Scottie has fallen in love with *her*, not with Madeleine.

When Madeleine runs up the Mission San Juan Bautista steps to the bell tower, Scottie tries to follow, but has an attack of vertigo when he makes the mistake of looking down. Thinking he has seen Madeleine jump to her death, he suffers a mental collapse. In fact, she is acting as a cover for the murder of his friend's wife, whose already dead body is dumped from the bell tower ledge in her place while Judy, the simulacrum, hides.

A year or so later, Scottie encounters an auburn-haired shop-girl version of Madeleine on the street. The *real* woman. Or, rather, the woman who acted the part of Madeleine. But does he want her with her real name, Judy Barton, and her working-class accent? "I want to know who you are," Scottie says on their first meeting, when he follows her to the Hotel Empire where she rents a room. Does he really want to know who Judy is?

What Scottie wants is the dead woman. The fake. The gray-suited, dyed-platinum blonde in a swept-up hairdo with a rich, breathy vulnerability. Rather upper class. He is relentless until he has perfectly transformed Judy the sales clerk into Madeleine the sophisticate. Or as perfectly as he can.

When he takes her shopping, he compels her to try on suit after suit until he finds the exact one Madeleine wore. Judy puts up a weak resistance, saying she does not like the suit. It is much the same gray suit that Doris Day wore two years earlier in *The Man Who Knew Too Much* (1956). Perhaps this is Hitchcock's fetish—the blonde woman in the gray suit— as much as Scottie's.

What is it Judy wants? As Freud famously asked, *What do women want?* I keep asking myself that question throughout the entire movie. She wants—as my brief, cruel lover put it—the spectacle of his desire for her, which she hopes will eventually turn into love for her.

The power of a woman's need to be desired and to allow herself to be transformed into someone else: this finds its complement in the power of a man's need to control and make over the object of his desire.

◆

What is it I have wanted in relationship after relationship? When I think back on my own recent affair, my lover and I were painfully enmeshed in this perverse dynamic of desire: I wanted to be desired at almost any cost, he wanted to turn me into a fetishistic cipher of his own desire. Who was he to me? The man who desired me. Who was I to him? A woman he wanted to leave his mark on. Literally. He insisted on sex that was highly ritualized—the same ritual, no doubt, enacted with every lover he had. He pulled my legs straight up in the air before entering me so I was immobilized. I had no control. It felt like my whole body was being held in a vise. He wanted—needed—to dominate me.

He wanted to bite me and leave a mark, he said. I demurred. "I want to slap you so hard, it will leave a mark when you look in the mirror." I said nothing, hoping it would never come to that. Had I remained with him, I know I would have been obliterated.

What is it men want? Most heterosexual women I know, at some point in their adult lives, ask themselves this question. Is it to dominate? To love and be loved? To feel worshiped? To be mothered? To abuse or be abused?

◆

In *Vertigo*, Judy gets to feel desired by Scottie for a brief time—but only by complying with his compulsion to make her over into an exact replica of Madeleine. How can it last? Madeleine, the Madeleine he desires, is—as she well knows—a fiction.

Scottie recognizes that Judy is wearing Madeleine's pendant, at which point he realizes he has been duped. He feels compelled to confront her by bringing her back to the scene of the crime where, through her deception of Scottie, she had been an accomplice in the murder of his friend's wife. Though Judy's death is "accidental" (startled by the arrival of a nun, she falls off the same ledge as the "original" Madeleine), it feels psychologically accurate: Judy has to die because for Scottie, Judy never really existed.

♦

A few years after my divorce, while I was out walking my dog in Riverside Park, I caught sight of a man running from the tennis courts at 120th Street who returned my gaze. He was tall, with curly dark-brown hair and an intelligent, sad look in his eyes. I guessed he was in his early fifties, like me. The attraction for me was instantaneous, and I could feel it was reciprocated, as he fixed his gaze on me, slowed down, and turned around to do a double take. I put one hand on my hip and worked up a faux Mae West, "I haven't seen *you* here before." He smiled and said he had to go but hoped to see me in the park in the next few days.

The next day he went running by with his dog and, once again, I watched him turn around to look at me. I felt like Atalanta, who tossed out her golden apples and tripped up Hippomenes, slowing him down in his path.

At the end of the week, we finally met up during off-leash time, as before 9 a.m. is known to dog owners in New York City. As his black Lab scooted on ahead and my Brussels Griffon shadowed me, we talked. Neil possessed a fierce intelligence that impressed me. I talked to him about Isaiah Berlin's division of writers into two groups, the foxes and the hedgehogs: "The fox knows many things, but the hedgehog knows one big thing." Neil suspected that the line came from an ancient Greek source, Archilochus. When I went home to check, I discovered he was right.

On another early-morning walk, Neil told me he was a documentary filmmaker who made his living as a film editor. Now he was working on a project, but he would not reveal its subject. He had just seen the movie *Bright Star,* about Keats and Fanny Brawne. "Maybe I haven't mourned long enough," he said. Did he mean like Fannie, who went on to marry after Keats's death? Neil had told me he was widowed five years before, so I assumed he must have been referring to his late wife, a Japanese woman who died of breast cancer. We climbed the steps out of the park. What could I say to him? We had only just met. *Five years seems long enough.*

One night I receive a puzzling email from him in the shape of a short-lined poem that he sends using his iPhone. Almost anyone can spill down some feelings, hit the return key, and say they have written a poem. This one reads like a sad love poem, addressed to "you" and written in the past tense. But he has sent it to me, with no greeting, no explanation. Just the poem. It ends something like this: *Wasn't my love, once, / when I held you ever / enough to make you feel whole?* I read the poem over several times, especially those lines, with some confusion. We have barely kissed. Why is he be sending me this poem? Several hours later, he calls me up.

"I've just been to a memorial for my friend."

"Oh. What friend?"

"My ex-girlfriend. The one I told you about who committed suicide in July. She was a poet. Like you."

"You never told me that. You just said she dumped you."

"Oh. I thought you knew. I was sure I told you."

Another poet. So here he was sending me the poem he wished he could have sent to her. Now I understood, though I resisted understanding. Without my knowledge or assent, he had turned me into a surrogate for Lori, his wealthy East Side girlfriend. To him, we were both blonde poets.

The following week, when he visited me at my apartment, I did the worst thing I could have done (how could I have known?): I made an exception and allowed him to enter my private, tiny, book-lined study, where I keep a large poetry collection. Scanning the shelves, he shook his head. "They're the same books she had."

Neil invited me to a party in the West Village at the home of a couple who were his patrons. The two of us strolled outside. Leaning against the balcony together, alone for a few minutes, he held me, stroked my hair. That evening, it felt like we were a couple.

Back inside, one of our hosts, an older woman with silver hair twisted up into a tight bun, took me aside to show me her art collection, leading me down the hallway, gesturing at a few abstract lithographs. "Please be very careful with Neil. You know how much he's been through already." I nodded, wishing someone might say the same thing to him about me.

Why, at that moment, did I fail to understand that a person who has been through loss of a damaging kind might actually prefer it? That he might prefer the girlfriend, beautiful as she was, being cruel to him, even throwing him out the same day he lost his film-editing job? On the night of her suicide, they had planned to meet, even though they were no longer lovers. "She had a way of reeling me in," he told me. Even dead, she still had him hooked.

Had he been seeking someone disturbed, someone cruel, much as I had often ended up with someone difficult and, at times, cruel to me?

I invited Neil to a party held in a cavernous bar in Dumbo. I was wearing a black, tight faux-leather skirt and a black lace bodice with pink satin underneath. I wanted to look hot, wanted him to desire me. That is what I always want from a man. When we met in front of my building, he did not comment on my outfit.

We arrived at the party, and I could sense his mood dropping precipitously. As I spoke to other artists and friends, I watched him wander around the edges of the room. He waved off my attempts to introduce him to friends. "Oooh, you look fabulous," said Jason, a gay photographer friend. I thanked him, wishing I had heard the same from Neil. We left the party and ended up back on a train to Morningside Heights, where we both lived.

Over dinner at Toast, a local restaurant, Neil grew more and more morose, saying little. I assumed I would just be heading home afterwards. "Why don't you come over and we'll walk Arnie together," he said. We got his dog, the beautiful black Lab that always stuck his snout between my legs. This time was no different, and we stepped outside, heading over to Riverside Park. A fine rain had begun falling, so in a few minutes we came back inside.

Neil lies down on his couch with a sigh, saying, "I'm exhausted," and briefly puts his arm up over his eyes. His long body barely fits the length of the couch. He uncovers his eyes to see me still standing. I motion to him that perhaps I should sit in a chair nearby. He waves me over to sit by him on the edge of the couch. I sit down and look around the living room, at the crumbly gray-white walls. Looking up, I notice a hand-colored sepia portrait of a woman with wavy hair from the Fifties; he says it is his mother. Her photo occupies the highest place in the room and seems to dominate the gloomy space.

Neil coaxes me to lie on top of him. As he lies there, almost comatose, I can feel him aroused beneath me. But he will not actively respond when I touch him. As though he were willing himself dead. He does not touch me. When I lean over to kiss him, he keeps his mouth closed, so the kisses that fall on his lips are no more than small pecks. I remember watching myself at the time, feeling the absurdity of the situation. *Here I am, lying on top of this man in my fishnets and faux-leather skirt and lacy top, feeling him turned on but unwilling to hold me or be affectionate.* This is a new predicament for me.

"I can't," he finally says, and gestures for me to get up and move away from him. I know he means not just at the moment. I see how utterly pointless it has been because I know, in part, he cannot distinguish me from his dead girlfriend. As a poet, I remind him too much of the suicidal poet who had been so cruel to him. Being a poet has become a liability in my love life.

I hear it raining more heavily outside. I pick up the umbrella I have left leaning in a corner by the door and look over at him with hurt bafflement, shaking my head. He fills it in for me. "I know, you think I'm going to regret this. Maybe I will. In a month or two." There is no point in responding. He does not have it in him to get up and show me to the door. I walk home in the rain.

For months afterwards, I dressed up for my morning walk in Riverside Park with my dog, hoping to bump into Neil, hoping he would see me and desire me and realize how wrong he had been. Dressing up the way I imagined he would find irresistible. Wearing my black boots and a short skirt. A tight-fitting dress with the right amount of décolleté. I performed this futile exercise until I ground myself into a state of despair because I knew—though he might, now and then, give me an admiring glance, even a compliment—I could never be seen, could never be desired by him for who I was.

♦

At about an hour and a half into *Vertigo*, the point of view shifts. Up until then, the viewer has seen everything through the eyes of Scottie—especially the mysterious, seductive figure of Madeleine. His desire for her. His inability to figure out why she sits for hours before a portrait of her "ancestor" in the Palace of Fine Arts. He is puzzling her out. The mystery of Madeleine that is wrapped in—or that has him rapt with—desire. She is the mysterious object of his desire.

The switch happens when Judy the shop girl agrees to have dinner with Scottie, closes the door, and we see first the back of her auburn head, then her profile, then her agitated three-quarter view as she looks up into her memory (in a brief flashback) of the way she tricked Scottie into believing that she (as Madeleine) had plunged to her death. She decides to flee, but first writes a letter of confession to Scottie (and we hear it all in voice-over): "I'm still in love with you and I want you so to love me. If I had the nerve I'd stay and lie, hoping that I could make you love me again as I am for myself. And so forget the other, and forget the past." Then she tears it up.

I suppose *that* is what a woman wants: to be loved for herself, to have the beloved forget the Other (there has always been an Other). But who is the "I" that is "myself"? Judy seems to believe in an essential self, a true self, which has nothing to do with being an accomplice to a murder, to having played the part of Madeleine. The false self was Madeleine. How ironic that she bears the name of the small cake whose taste became for Proust the catalyst for his early childhood memories, particularly of his love for his mother.

The British psychoanalyst D. W. Winnicott introduced into common parlance the notion of a True Self, an authentic self, as opposed to a False Self, which he also labeled a "compliant False Self." Compliant: that's what Judy becomes, though not without a struggle.

Our empathy from this point on in *Vertigo* moves toward Judy. We understand her wish to be loved for herself, and her desire to tell the truth, warring with her fear that she will lose Scottie if she dares tell him.

Now Judy's desire, or her desire to be desired, is the lens through which we watch the denouement: her slow abasement, her complete surrender to being made over into a facsimile of Madeleine. In his documentary *The Pervert's Guide to Cinema*, the Slovenian cultural critic Slavoj Žižek focuses our attention on the profile shot of Judy sitting by the darkened window of her room after her first dinner with Scottie:

> Scottie: We could just see a lot of each other.
> Judy: Why? [Pause] 'Cause I remind you of her? [Pause] It's not very complimentary.

Says Žižek of this scene:

> The profile shot in *Vertigo* is perhaps the key shot of the entire film. We have there Madeleine's, or rather Judy's, identity in all its tragic tension. It provides the dark background for the fascinating other profile of Madeleine in Ernie's restaurant. Scottie is too ashamed, afraid to look at her directly. It is as if what he sees is the stuff of his dreams, more real in a way for him than the reality of the woman behind his back.

The stuff of dreams. Perhaps that is what men want.

In the famous climactic scene, Judy comes back to her hotel room, where Scottie has been anxiously awaiting her full transformation into Madeleine. She is wearing the gray suit Scottie picked out for her, having had her hair and eyebrows dyed, her make-up and fingernails done, before she submits to his final demand by retreating to the bathroom to pin up her hair. When she wordlessly steps out and walks toward him in that spectral light for the full embrace, Judy's voice is absent: the one part of her that picks her out as an individual—a working girl from Salina, Kansas, not the high-society Madeleine of Nob Hill. This is what Scottie can silence, has silenced, with his kiss.

♦

Both *Vertigo* and my own erotic history lead me to wonder: Is female desire self-extinguishing? Though we want to be loved for our True Self, why are we (or some of us) willing to put on a False Self to please a man, in order to feel his desire welling up for us?

And what do men want? What does Scottie want? Does he want to make love to a dead woman?

According to Žižek: "It is as if in order to have her, to desire her, to have sexual intercourse with her, with the woman, Scottie has to mortify her, to change her into a dead woman."

Is *that* what men want?

In desire, we love most what we fail to understand. The desire may be as much about the mystery, the inability to know the Other fully, as about our projection onto the Other of what we want. As soon as we *think* we know the Other (for many this means having sex), the mystery and the desire both vanish—or at least attenuate dramatically. Then, something else comes to the foreground: the inability to accept that the Other will always remain so. In sex, in love, we remain a mixture, a composite, of how we see ourselves and how we are seen by the Other. Tragedy occurs when they fail to coincide at all.

♦

A few years ago, I met a photographer named Lewis at an opening for his work in a small gallery in Williamsburg, Brooklyn. His photographs were of strange creatures. Or what looked like strange creatures—sticks and other bits of nature confected in the mud. I couldn't figure them out; they bordered on the macabre. Yet he intrigued me. His clothes did not entirely match. He wore a brash tie-dyed tie and a brown wool jacket. He had greased up his hair for the occasion and put on black-and-white clown shoes.

We went to his apartment after one of our first dates. He occupied a cramped, peculiar space in the East Village with his large, smooth-coated dog. I walked in and there were clothes hanging above my head at the entrance. He pointed to a space up a short flight of steps, where he had his work studio, then motioned me to his small bed wedged into a tight corner, right off the kitchen. We tousled around. "Those are sexy boots you have on. Now why not take them off." I was wearing my black leather boots that came up to the top of my calves, with silver buckles down the side. I unzipped them and pulled them off. We kissed and touched each other, but I was not ready to take off anything else.

The next night, Lewis drives uptown to my apartment. There is almost always this sense of urgency with men before they have had sex. They have to have me or they will die. I fall for it every time. He has condoms with him and we begin having sex. He knows just when to stop and when to continue, in order to prolong things for the both of us. "Wait. Stop a minute," he says, with me on top of him. And so we wait, then continue.

By the end of the evening I can feel myself opening up to him. We go to sleep and all through the night, every time he touches me, I let out a small sigh. He turns his back and continues sleeping. Is his dog there? She must have been sleeping at the end of the bed with mine.

"Gee, you made a lot of noise last night," Lewis says upon awakening. "Really? Did I snore?"

"No, you just moaned a lot. It was kind of annoying."

"Oh. Sorry." What has brought me closer to him has also removed him from me.

We spoke on the phone a few days later about Christmas Eve. Though neither of us were planning to celebrate the holiday—both of us were Jewish—I was wondering if he had plans. "Oh. I think I'll stay downtown and take my dog to a theater piece my friend is doing." Nothing more. He was not inviting me. He had a date with his dog.

We made plans to spend New Year's Eve together at my place. With his dog. I told him they could both stay over. I bought fish for the two of us, and papadum that I crisped up with a bit of oil on the stove. And a bottle of wine. He brought over some asparagus that I asked him to roast in the small electric oven. "Please make sure not to overcook them; I hate when they turn that ugly olive-green color." He agreed, and overcooked them anyway.

After dinner, we move into my living room. I choose the couch, hoping he will join me. Lewis heads for the recliner. After a minute, he gets up and starts pacing, as his dog and mine look on. The thing that struck me almost immediately about Lewis is that he will not make eye contact with me. But he looks his dog in the eye constantly and talks to her. He turns to me as he is pacing, still not looking at me.

"I don't know what it is. Why I feel like pulling away. I don't know why I feel so distant, you're perfect for me."

At first, I am quiet. "Maybe if you looked at me. You never look me in the eyes when you're talking to me."

"Yeah. That's just what my mother always tells me. 'You gotta look people in the eye if you want them to like you.'"

"So why don't you." He stops pacing and looks at me for an instant. Then looks away, bends down and begins talking to his dog, looking her right in the eyes.

We went to bed that night and he was unresponsive when I touched him. "Maybe not tonight. Maybe we should know each other better." He rolled away from me. I was furious. *What is wrong with him?*

Over breakfast, Lewis was eager to show me some of his photographs. He had been working up a series of black-and-white photos he had taken in the Eighties to make into a book. Most had a Diane Arbus eeriness to them, set in a seedy Times Square. Odd portraits of odd characters, and always taken on the sly. A transvestite in a wig looking up at a movie marquee. A couple shot from below so their faces were doubly distorted, by the lights and the vantage point.

Lewis's favorite one, the one he had to show me on his phone because he thought it was so brilliant, was set against the backdrop of an El train, probably in Brooklyn or the Bronx. I looked closely at the photograph. At least half a dozen people must have just exited from the station: a man is smoking and looking to his right; a short woman in a flowery hat is looking down; another man in profile is lost in thought, looking into the distance directly past the woman. I was puzzled. *Why does he love this particular photograph so much?* I said nothing and nodded my head as he talked on about the beauty of its composition.

After Lewis left with his dog, I continued to muse over that photograph. And then it struck me: no one was making eye contact, either with each other or with the photographer. Without realizing it, Lewis had taken his own self-portrait. No wonder he singled it out for special praise. That photograph was his best mirror. And when I looked inside it, I disappeared. His sense of self, his very being, depended on my disappearance. The best way, the safest way, he could conjure himself up was to avoid—even extinguish—my gaze and look into the eyes of his dog.

♦

The ambivalence of desire: that is what I am left with. "In Freud's vision of things we are, above all, ambivalent animals," explains Adam Phillips. "[W]herever we hate, we love; wherever we love, we hate. If someone can satisfy us, they can frustrate us; and if someone can frustrate us, we always believe they could satisfy us."

I have yet to find my way out of the conundrum of desire. But the concept of ambivalence does help me understand that my repeated attempts, no matter how futile, to seek satisfaction—even love—from men who frustrate me is stitched into the very fabric of desire. It is the reverse side of the cloth that first swaddled me as an infant, whereby the one who satisfied me—my mother—could also frustrate me.

As much as I did bond with my mother, her predictably unpredictable behavior became the norm for me as a child, so that even as an adult I may have continued to recognize love most readily as a form of frustration. I have to hope it is still possible for me to form a romantic attachment based on mutual trust. To experience love as a somewhat secure, at least intermittently, satisfying bond.

Hitchcock in Manhattan

I've decided not to be someone else after all. If I won't be myself, who will?

–Alfred Hitchcock

I DREAM I AM with my friend Chuck, a writer whom I have always admired for his daring theater pieces. He challenges me to do an odd activity he says he enjoys practicing, which entails jumping off the side of a building and just hanging off the edge of the roof from a horizontal pole that looks like a chin-up bar. He demonstrates first—hanging by his fingers, like Scottie at the beginning of *Vertigo*, only without the fear.

In the opening scene of *Vertigo*, Scottie is climbing a rooftop in hot pursuit of a criminal when he loses his step and slips off the edge. He is left hanging on for life to the roof gutter by the grip of his hands until another policeman leans over and, in an attempt to rescue him, loses his balance and plunges to his death. From this traumatic episode, Scottie has developed acrophobia (fear of heights) and vertigo.

In my dream, Chuck achieves this same pose calmly, deliberately, hanging by his hands for sport. He continues to coax me to join him. After initially hesitating, I decide to take him up on his invitation—he seems to be managing quite easily and enjoying himself—and so I leap, to land with my hands hanging on to the bar, with my friend hanging on beside me. I do not even marvel at my newfound agility and strength.

In my dream, I am also the observer watching the two of us as we eagerly choose, then maintain, this position. We could be two trapeze artists. Just hanging there nonchalantly, like buddies hanging out together. That's what we writers sometimes do.

This dream feels like my final gift from Hitchcock, after I have spent so much time watching and thinking about his movies while watching and thinking about my life.

"Beauty unbuckles pain's armoring," wrote the poet Jane Hirshfield. I have chosen to take my memories of painful experiences and transform them into something beautiful—or at least of my own making. That is what Hitchcock's movies do. That is what I have sought to do. It is an erotic project, as all creative acts must be, governed by desire, whose direction has not been entirely under my conscious control. In this way, I have sought to achieve catharsis, a purging of my emotions, through a different—not necessarily more accurate—perspective on my life.

I have always admired and dreamt of following Flaubert's advice to writers: "Be regular and orderly in your life, so that you may be violent and original in your work." Not by conscious choice, I have found myself living a life of periodic, violent upheaval and disorder, which has compelled me to be regular and orderly in my writing practice.

"Without a wound, there is no author," the Israeli writer Amos Oz once said. My mother may have given me my primal wound along with her love—even (without my conscious awareness) the desire to write. I turned to writing poems as a young teen for refuge, not to heal the wound but to do as the Japanese do with broken pottery: to suture it with gold. As I have sought to do with these memory-wounds.

"I look up, I look down," Scottie says, practicing to maintain his equilibrium. With the help of Hitchcock's lens, I have looked down the long, painful chute of memory.

Now I hang on and look up.

Notes

All quoted dialogue from Hitchcock movies is based on what I hear the actors saying, not on published screenplays.

Conversations between François Truffaut and Alfred Hitchcock are drawn from *Hitchcock*, by François Truffaut (revised edition, Simon & Schuster, 1984).

Lines from Yehuda Amichai's poem "A Man in His Life" were translated by Chana Bloch, from *The Poetry of Yehuda Amichai*, ed. Robert Alter (Farrar, Straus and Giroux, 2015).

All poems and excerpts of mine are previously unpublished.

Photo Credits

Still of Betty (Nova Pilbeam) from *The Man Who Knew Too Much* (1934): Copyright 1997, Carlton Film Distributors, Ltd., p. 10.

Still of Miss Froy (Dame May Whitty) and Iris (Margaret Lockwood) from *The Lady Vanishes* (1938): Copyright 1997, Carlton Film Distributors, Ltd., p. 28.

Still of Marion (Janet Leigh) and Sam (John Gavin) from *Psycho* (1960): Copyright 2017, Universal Studios, p. 52.

Still of Melanie (Tippie Hedren) from *The Birds* (1963): Copyright 2017, Universal Studios, p. 74.

Still of Thorwald (Raymond Burr) from *Rear Window* (1954): Copyright 2017, Universal Studios, p. 94.

Still of Miriam (Laura Elliot) from *Strangers on a Train* (1951): Copyright 2017, Warner Bros., p. 120.

Still of Francie Stevens (Grace Kelly) and John Robie (Cary Grant) from *To Catch a Thief* (1955): Copyright 2017, Paramount Pictures, p. 134.

Still of Dr. Edwardes (Gregory Peck) and Dr. Petersen (Ingrid Bergman) from *Spellbound* (1945): Copyright 2017, ABC/Disney/Buena Vista, p. 160.

Still of Mrs. de Winter (Jean Fontaine) and Mrs. Danvers (Judith Anderson) from *Rebecca* (1940): Copyright 2017, ABC/Disney/Buena Vista, p. 198.

Stills of Judy (Kim Novak) and Scottie (James Stewart) from *Vertigo* (1958): Copyright 2017, Universal Studios, pp. 228, 246.

Author photo by Alfredo Rossi.

All family photographs are from the author's personal collection.

Acknowledgments

I am grateful to the editors of the following publications, in which earlier versions of some chapters first appeared:

Brooklyn Nonfiction: "The Lady Vanishes and My Absent Mother" (Semi-Finalist, Brooklyn Nonfiction Prize)

Drunken Boat: "*Strangers on a Train* and the Stalked Woman in Glasses"

Five Points: Journal of Literature and Art: "*The Man Who Knew Too Much* and the Girl Who Knew Too Little" (listed in "Notable Essays and Literary Nonfiction" in *Best American Essays 2016*)

Witness: "*Rear Window*: The Ethics of Seeing and Telling"

Abundant gratitude to my editor and friend Evan Eisenberg, whose copious amounts of wisdom, sensitivity, and support were vital to my finishing this project, as well as to my publisher David Rothenberg at Terra Nova Press for believing in me. Thanks to Martin Pedanik for his patience and diligence with the design. Thank you to my agent William Clark for his persistence and support. Thank you to Wendy Salinger who gave me early encouragement. Thank you to Cassandra Garbus, Ellen Geist (of blessed memory), Patti Horvath, and Steve Kuusisto for reading earlier drafts and for their invaluable advice. Thank you to Mireia Estrada of Jiwar in Barcelona for granting me several artist residencies while I was working on this project as well as to The MacDowell Colony and The Virginia Center for the Creative Arts.

Special thanks to these individuals who helped to support the publication of this book: Peter Covino, Jill Pearlman, Page Starzinger, Barry Magid, Tom Gardiner, Ilene Levinson and Rem van Tijen, Marsha Howard, Sarah Key, Phillis Levin, Eve Kahn, David Kaufman, Jonathan Cohen, Jacqueline Doyle and Stephen Gutierrez, Patricia Behrens, Sofi Zezmer, Betty Medsger, Marcia Shultis, Larry Schwartz and Shelley Levine, Jill Danenberg, Kimberly Rowe and Sam Zabor.

This book has been seven years in the making. Thank you to all the friends and family who have encouraged me and seen me through to the end of this project. Thank you, in particular, to Barbara Addleman, Peter Covino, Jill Danenberg, Jackie Doyle, Jody Feld, Jeff Friedman, Steve Gutierrez, Ilene Levinson, Amy Lemmon, Phillis Levin, Alfredo Rossi, and Betsey Shevey for their love and support. My gratitude to the Romemu community, which has given me a second home as well as spiritual sustenance during both joyful and trying times.

Finally, this memoir could not have been written without the complicated love I received from both my parents and it is to their memory that I dedicate this book. Leonard Cohen sang about "the crack in everything" being the way "the light gets in." Perhaps it was my parents' imperfect love that, in part, created the crack inside of me through which these words of light could sing.

Sharon Dolin is the author of six poetry collections, most recently *Manual for Living* (2016) and *Whirlwind* (2012). Her fourth book, *Burn and Dodge* (2008), won the AWP Donald Hall Prize for Poetry. A Fulbright Scholar, Pushcart Prize Winner, and recipient of a Witter Bynner Fellowship from the Library of Congress, she has been a fellow at the Corporation of Yaddo, the MacDowell Colony, and the Virginia Center for the Creative Arts. She has taught at the New School, Hofstra University, NYU, the Cooper Union, Poets House, and the Unterberg Poetry Center of the 92nd Street Y. Sharon Dolin lives in New York City where she is Associate Editor at Barrow Street Press and directs Writing About Art in Barcelona.